IN ROOSEVELT'S BRIGHT SHADOW

The Centre for the Study of Democracy's (CSD) Library of Political Leadership

One of the first questions to ask about any leader is what are his or her priorities and do they run with or against the grain of history? An essential way of determining this is to research the public record and then compare dreams versus accomplishments. It is the public record of measured words that remains the most reliable barometer of either consistency or change in one's purpose. As Lord Acton wrote to the contributors to the Cambridge Modern History Project, "archives are meant to be explored". And because the written word is the key to describing ruling currents and interpreting sovereign forces, "we must provide a copious, accurate, and well-digested catalogue of authorities". To understand a public figure it is necessary to start with what he or she said and what they wrote. This is the second volume in the CSD's Library of Political Leadership, an occasional series of collections of the public addresses of Canadian Prime Ministers, Premiers, opposition politicians and significant foreign leaders in the Canadian context.

Thomas S. Axworthy
Chair, Centre for the Study of Democracy
Library of Political Leadership Series General Editor

Back cover photo: Bernard Thibodeau, House of Commons. All other pictures courtesy Queen's University Archives.

In Roosevelt's Bright Shadow

Presidential Addresses About Canada
from Taft to Obama in Honour of FDR's 1938
Speech at Queen's University

Edited by
Arthur Milnes
Foreword by
Tom Williams, Principal, Queen's University

Volume II in the Queen's Centre for the Study of Democracy
Library of Political Leadership Occasional Series
Thomas S. Axworthy, Series General Editor
School of Policy Studies, Queen's University
McGill-Queen's University Press
Montreal & Kingston • London • Ithaca

Copyright © 2009 School of Policy Studies, Queen's University at Kingston, Canada

SCHOOL OF
Policy Studies

Publications Unit
Policy Studies Building
138 Union Street
Kingston, ON, Canada
K7L 3N6
www.queensu.ca/sps/

All rights reserved. The use of any part of this publication for reproduction, transmission in any form or by any means (electronic, mechanical, photocopying, recording or otherwise), or storage in a retrieval system without the prior written consent of the publisher—or, in case of photocopying or other reprographic copying, a license from the Canadian Copyright Licensing Agency—is an infringement of the copyright law. Enquiries concerning reproduction should be sent to the School of Policy Studies at the address above.

Library and Archives Canada Cataloguing in Publication

    In Roosevelt's bright shadow : presidential addresses about Canada from Taft to Obama in honour of FDR's 1938 speech at Queen's University / foreword by Tom Williams ; edited by Arthur Milnes.

(Library of political leadership occasional series ; v. 2)
Published for the Centre for the Study of Democracy, School of Policy Studies,
    Queen's University.
ISBN 978-1-55339-230-9 (pbk.).--ISBN 978-1-55339-231-6 (bound)

    1. Presidents--United States--Messages. 2. Speeches, addresses, etc., American. 3. Roosevelt, Franklin D. (Franklin Delano), 1882-1945. 4. Canada--Foreign relations--United States. 5. United States--Foreign relations--Canada.
I. Milnes, Arthur, 1966- II. Queen's University (Kingston, Ont.). Centre for the Study of Democracy III. Series: Library of political leadership series ; v. 2

J81.4.I52 2009   352.23'840973   C2008-907651-6

Table of Contents

Acknowledgements — XI

Foreword — XV
Tom Williams, Principal, Queen's University

Introduction — XVIII
Thomas S. Axworthy, Chair, Centre for the Study of Democracy

PART ONE — 1
FDR and Queen's

Chapter 1 — 3
President Franklin Roosevelt's Visit to Queen's University 18 August 1938, Professor Fred Gibson

Chapter 2 — 35
A Speech for the Ages, David Mitchell

Chapter 3 — 37
The Birth of an Alliance, Jordan Press

Chapter 4 — 41
Canada and the United States need a leader like FDR, Arthur Milnes

Chapter 5 — 43
President Franklin D. Roosevel's, Convocation Address, Queen's University 18 August 1938

Chapter 6 — 47
President Franklin D. Roosevelt, Remarks upon the opening of the Thousands Islands Bridge, Clayton, New York 18 August 1938

Chapter 7   51
Eleanor Roosevelt at Queen's University 8 January 1948

PART TWO   55
Presidents Before Canada's Parliament

Chapter 8   57
President Franklin D. Roosevelt's Address to a Joint Session of Parliament 25 August 1943

Chapter 9   61
President Harry S. Truman's Address to a Joint Session of Parliament 11 June 1947

Chapter 10   67
President Dwight D. Eisenhower's Address to a Joint Session of Parliament 14 November 1953

Chapter 11   73
President Dwight D. Eisenhower's Address to a Joint Session of Parliament 9 July 1958

Chapter 12   79
President John F. Kennedy's Address to a Joint Session of Parliament 17 May 1961

Chapter 13   85
President Richard M. Nixon's Address to a Joint Session of Parliament 14 April 1972

Chapter 14   91
President Ronald W. Reagan's Address to a Joint Session of Parliament 11 March 1981

Chapter 15   97
President Ronald W. Reagan's Address to a Joint Session of Parliament 6 April 1987

Chapter 16   113
President William J. Clinton's Address to a Joint
Session of Parliament 23 February 1995

PART THREE   123
"Hear, Hear!" and Applause: Presidential
Speeches Outside Canada's Parliament

Chapter 17   127
Former President William Howard Taft's
"Fraternal Relations" The Empire Club, Toronto
20 January 1919

Chapter 18   133
President Warren G. Harding
Stanley Park, Vancouver, British Columbia 16 July 1923

Chapter 19   137
General Dwight Eisenhower
Canadian Club, Ottawa 10 January 1946

Chapter 20   143
Former President Herbert Hoover's Report on the
World Famine, CBC Broadcast, Ottawa 28 June 1946

Chapter 21   149
Senator John F. Kennedy
The University of Montreal 4 December 1953

Chapter 22   159
President Richard Nixon
Rideau Hall, Ottawa 13 April 1972

Chapter 23   163
President Jimmy Carter on the Return of Six Americans
From Iran Telephone Discussion with Prime Minister
Joe Clark 31 January 1980

Chapter 24 165
President George H.W. Bush at the Air Quality
[Acid Rain] Agreement Signing Ceremony West Block,
Parliament Hill, Ottawa 13 March 1991

Chapter 25 167
Former President George H.W. Bush on The Thrill of
Fishing in Arctic Canada *Deh Cho Drum*, Fort Simpson,
Northwest Territories, 31 August 1997

Chapter 26 169
President William J. Clinton at a Dedication Ceremony
for the New US Embassy in Canada Ottawa, Canada
8 October 1999

Chapter 27 171
President William J. Clinton to the
Forum of Federations Conference
Mont-Tremblant, Canada 8 October 1999

Chapter 28 181
President George W. Bush Halifax, Nova Scotia
1 December 2004

Chapter 29 185
President Barack Obama - Prime Minister Stephen Harper
Press Conference Parliament Hill, Ottawa 19 February 2009

PART FOUR 189
Speaking About Canada in Washington

Chapter 30 193
Governor General Vincent Massey's Address to the
US Congress Washington, D.C. 4 May 1954

Chapter 31 195
Toasts by President Lyndon B. Johnson and Prime Minister
Lestor B. Pearson, Washington, D.C. 22 January 1964

Chapter 32   197
Lyndon B. Johnson with Prime Minister Pearson at the
Columbia River Treaty International Peace Arch
Blaine, Washington 16 September 1964

Chapter 33   199
President Richard M. Nixon: Toasts of the President
and Prime Minister Pierre Trudeau
The White House 24 March 1969

Chapter 34   203
President Gerald R. Ford Announcing Plans from the
White House for an Economic Conference in Puerto Rico
Washington, D.C. 3 June 1976

Chapter 35   205
Prime Minister Pierre Elliott Trudeau's Address to the
US Congress Washington, D.C. 22 February 1977

Chapter 36   211
Future President Ronald Reagan on The Canadian Seal Hunt
Radio Address 15 May 1978

Chapter 37   213
Prime Minister Brian Mulroney's Address to the US Congress
Washington, D.C. 27 April 1988

Chapter 38   219
President Ronald Reagan's Radio Address to the Nation on the
Canadian Elections and Free Trade 26 November 1988

Chapter 39   221
President George H.W. Bush's Address on His Administration's
Goals Before a Joint Session of Congress
Washington, D.C. 9 February 1989

Chapter 40   223
President George W. Bush's Remarks Following
Discussions With Prime Minister Jean Chrétien of Canada
The White House 24 September 2001

Chapter 41   225
Former Prime Minister Brian Mulroney's Eulogy to
President Ronald Reagan Washington, D.C. 11 June 2004

Acknowledgements

This book would not have been published without the support of many people. David Mitchell, president of the Public Policy Forum and a noted political historian, played a key role in both honouring the anniversary of FDR's visit to Queen's, and in supporting this volume during his service as Vice Principal (Advancement) at Queen's. The Centre for the Study of Democracy's (CSD) Dr. Thomas S. Axworthy (Chair) and Julie Burch (Coordinator) supported the project from its conception in the spring of 2008, Valerie Ashford and Mat Johnson also made excellent contributions. Senator Hugh Segal and his wife Donna, Sally Barnes, Ray and Helen DiRinaldo and Dr. Hans Westenburg also provided support and encouragement throughout this project. Arthur Sweetman, Director of the School of Policy Studies at Queen's, has also been an enthusiastic supporter of this book.

Queen's University Archivist Paul Banfield and the entire Queen's University archive staff at Kathleen Ryan Hall deserve acknowledgement for their tireless work in the promotion and preservation of our history, both at Queen's and in the wider community. This is now the second book on which I have worked with Mark Howes and the staff of Queen's University's School of Policy Studies publishing unit; again, this unit, and Mark in particular, deserve my personal thanks and recognition for their work.

I am grateful to *Kingston Whig-Standard* Managing Editor Steve Serviss, City Editor Claude Scilley, Editorial Page Editor Paul Schliesmann, Stephanie Miller, Kerry Sammon, Rob Tripp and Jordan Press, among others. The Whig has long supported local, regional and national history, witnessed by the impressive volume of space this newspaper, unlike many others, devotes to the subject. In particular, I owe thanks to Claude Scilley, my editor and supervisor when I was a *Whig-Standard* staff writer, for his encouragement.

I thank editor and co-publisher John B. Johnson Jr. and editorial page editor John McFadden of the *Watertown Daily Times* for their support and their emphasis, in the spirit of FDR and Mackenize King, on coverage of Canadian-American relations in their paper.

Globe and Mail journalists Lawrence Martin and Jane Taber have been very supportive of this volume. I read Martin's book, *The Presidents and the Prime Ministers*, in high school, and it inspired, in part, my life-long interest in Canadian prime ministers and American presidents. *TV Ontario*'s Steve Paikin has also encouraged this work.

Nancy Roosevelt Ireland, Eleanor Roosevelt's literary executor, graciously granted us permission to include the former First Lady's *My Day* column on her visit to Queen's University in 1948. At the Franklin Roosevelt Presidential Library at Hyde Park, supervisory archivist Robert

Clark also deserves special thanks, as does Justin Cooper of the office of former president William J. Clinton.

Staff at the Jimmy Carter, Dwight Eisenhower, Gerald R. Ford, Herbert Hoover, John F. Kennedy and George H.W. Bush Presidential Libraries provided numerous resources, as did the Ronald Reagan Presidential Foundation. Canada's Parliamentary Librarian William Young and the staff of the Library were very helpful.

41st US president George H.W. Bush gave us permission to include the fishing column, which he wrote at my request for the *Deh Cho Drum* in Arctic Canada more than a decade ago. For this, I thank him, his chief of staff Jean Becker, as well as his spokesperson and speechwriter (and my close friend), Jim McGrath. President Carter took time in Plains, Georgia, to share with me his impressions of Prime Ministers Joe Clark and Pierre Trudeau, and to recount his role in the clean-up of the Canadian nuclear facility at Chalk River, Ontario in the 1950s, and I am most grateful for this opportunity. Carter's Vice President Walter Mondale also shared his views on Canada's leaders during a telephone interview last spring. President Bill Clinton, while attending an event at the New York State Fair in Syracuse, agreed to an interview with me on the subject of his relationship and joint work with former Prime Minister Jean Chrétien, and for this privilege I extend my sincere thanks. I would also like to thank President Clinton for sending to Ottawa, during his terms in office, Ambassador James Blanchard of Michigan and Ambassador Gordon Giffin of Georgia, each of whom provided great encouragement, as did their colleague David Wilkins, US Ambassador to Canada under George W. Bush. The late president of the United States, Gerald R. Ford, granted me an interview in 2001 where he recalled his friendship with Pierre Trudeau, an experience for which I will always be grateful.

I would also like to thank Margaret Gibson of Kingston and her family for giving us permission to re-publish an essay written in 1973 by her late husband, Professor Frederick Gibson of Queen's University, concerning FDR's visit. I had the pleasure of speaking to Professor Gibson about his work for Mackenzie King when I was a student.

Former Prime Minister Joe Clark graciously allowed me access to his private papers while I researched this book, and Maureen Hoogenraad of Library and Archives Canada undertook searches in the Clark papers; I would like to thank both for their assistance. Thanks to John Turner, Canada's 17th prime minister, who shared his memories of Richard Nixon and other US presidents he encountered throughout his career.

Between 2003 and 2008, while I assisted him in the research and preparation of his memoirs, the Right Honourable Brian Mulroney answered my countless questions about the American presidents that he has known: Richard Nixon, Gerald R. Ford, Jimmy Carter, Ronald Reagan, George H.W. Bush, Bill Clinton and George W. Bush. I will always be grateful for Mr. Mulroney's many hours of informal discussion on Canadian-

American relations and history, foreign affairs, the craft of politics and speech-making and much more. I thank also, for their contributions, Mila Mulroney and their children.

Kingston and the Islands MP Peter Milliken, Speaker of the House of Commons, along with his assistant Heather Bradley, made it possible (in what is now known as the 'Obama book caper') for President Barack Obama to receive a copy of this book during the President's visit to Parliament Hill earlier this year. I am very much indebted to them.

I have long admired Ontario's former premier, Bob Rae, who presented President Obama with another copy of this book on 19 February 2009. Mr. Rae also once recalled for me his childhood memories of serving, with his brother John Rae (of Queen's) as Richard Nixon's paperboy. I would like to thank both members of this illustrious Canadian family for their support.

My wife and best friend, Alison Bogle, is my partner and my guide. This volume could not have been prepared without the support of the woman who has traveled with me to Hyde Park, the FDR Memorial in Washington and Warm Springs, Georgia and I dedicate this book to her.

Arthur Milnes
Kingston and Scarborough
June 2009

Foreword

Last year was a special anniversary year in both the history of Queen's University and the wider, and very related, subject of Canadian-American relations. In August 2008, the university marked the 70th anniversary of the visit to campus by President Franklin D. Roosevelt. In doing so, Queen's was assisted by former Prime Minister Brian Mulroney, who generously donated to the Queen's University Archives a special facsimile copy of FDR's personal speaking notes from his momentous day at Queen's.

This framed copy of portions of the speech had been presented to him by President William Jefferson Clinton on 5 February, 1993. On that day Mulroney became the first foreign leader to be received by the new President of the United States at the White House at the dawn of a new administration and era in Washington. That the 42nd president and his senior officials chose to present Canada's prime minister with the FDR-Queen's notes attests to the historical significance to Canadian-American relations of FDR's visit to Queen's, 70 years ago.

It is also worth noting that Franklin Roosevelt is not the only member of the illustrious American family of Hyde Park, New York to make the trip to our campus. Last year was also the 60th anniversary of Mrs. Eleanor Roosevelt's receipt of an honourary degree from Queen's. Mrs. Roosevelt, a pioneering First Lady of the United States of America and a political and social force in her own right, spent a day at Queen's on 8 January 1948, in which she made a passionate defence of the United Nations during her convocation address to an over-flow crowd at Grant Hall.

With these unique and proud connections that Queen's University holds with the US Presidency through the Roosevelts, it should be no surprise the Queen's University Centre for the Study of Democracy, chaired by Dr. Thomas S. Axworthy, has chosen to highlight Canada-US relations. November of last year was the 20th anniversary of the most significant moment in Canada-US relations, since FDR's words at Queen's; the re-election of the Mulroney government, with a second majority, which then implemented the Free Trade Agreement (FTA) between Canada and the United States.

The CSD has also made it a priority to preserve and publish the speeches and writings of political leaders through the CSD's Library of Political Leadership (of which this is Volume II, *Politics of Purpose 40th Anniversary Edition*, a collection of former Prime Minister John Turner's speeches, including a chapter chronicling his Crusade for Canada during the 1988 election, when he stood passionately before Canadians in opposition to the FTA, being Volume I) and the Centre felt this collection had particular resonance. The aim of Library of Political Leadership is to highlight the written and spoken words of Canadian prime ministers, premiers, opposition leaders, and, as is clear from this volume, world leaders visiting Canada.

While Canada and the United States face challenges in their bilateral relationship today, and always have, our two countries, are, as this book demonstrates, a model for the world in how we cooperate, disagree and ultimately engage as neighbours and allies, particularly at the president to prime minister level. Since that historic day at Queen's 70 years ago, all the presidents and prime ministers that have followed have indeed stood in Roosevelt's bright shadow.

It is these reasons the CSD has chosen to publish this book providing the text of FDR's speech at Queen's, his address at the opening of the International Bridge linking New York State and Ontario the same day, and his speech to a joint-session of Canada's Parliament in Ottawa—the first time an American President did so—on 25 August 1943. It is also fitting that all the presidential addresses to Canada's Parliament following FDR's are included as well. A selection of speeches by future, sitting, and past presidents outside of Parliament is also included, as well as the words of two prime ministers and one governor-general before the US Congress.

As Principal of Queen's University I would like to offer my congratulations to Dr. Axworthy and his team at the CSD for working so diligently to mark this historic anniversary with this impressive volume.

Tom Williams
Principal and Vice-Chancellor
Queen's University
June 2009

Introduction

As on a Darkling Plain: Franklin Roosevelt, Barack Obama and the Politics of Hope

In this time of economic peril and foreign policy threat it is possible that too many of us are overwhelmed by doubt or immobilized by fear. Policy makers too are certainly not immune to confusion when cascading events destroy a lifetime's assumptions. Alan Greenspan, former Chairman of the Federal Reserve of the United States, in testimony to the Congress about the financial meltdown of Wall Street, for example, exclaimed, "Those of us who have looked to the self-interest of lending institutions to protect shareholder's equity, myself included, are in shocked disbelief."

But we cannot allow ourselves to become prisoners of our fears. History shows that humankind has always alternated between cycles of pessimism and cycles of optimism. Writing in 1851 about the loss of religious faith, Victorian poet Matthew Arnold gloomily concluded:

> And we are here as on a darkling plain,
> Swept with confused alarms of struggles and flight,
> Where ignorant armies clash by night.

The Victorian age, however, soon recovered its equipoise and went on with stunning confidence to build an array of enduring institutions such as public health, public education and the modern political party.

Today we are also in a "darkling plain" as we do not know how or far-reaching the North America financial crisis will be. But the recent election of Barack Obama is a shaft of light that has the potential to lift our heads from the gloom.

President Obama faces a fearsome agenda of economic distress and conflict in Afghanistan and Iraq. But his display of character during the course of his successful election campaign gives the world grounds for hope. He withstood the attacks of the Clintons during the Democratic primaries, and then triumphed over the worst of the infamous Republican attack machine. Throughout this two-year American marathon of campaigning, he was calm, self-deprecating, inspiring, and most of all, he consistently traveled the high road. When the stock market crashed in September 2008 and his more experienced opponent resorted to media gimmicks, such as canceling a scheduled debate, it was Obama who appeared presidential. I recall former Senator Alan Simpson introducing Gerald Ford to the Kennedy School when I taught at Harvard with the words: "If you have integrity in politics nothing else matters, if you don't have integrity, nothing else matters." We already know from this campaign that Obama has integrity.

Obama's actions right after his election followed the same high road as his campaign. Obama met with his former rival John McCain to discuss how they could cooperate in the future to address the crucial issues facing the United States. He reached out to strong figures, such as Hillary Clinton. At Obama's first press conference as president-elect he annouced he had consulted with all living former presidents. In short, he sought to engage all the talents to help him as he prepares to take office. Here, there are lessons for Canada.

In contrast to Obama's high road, last year's Canadian election campaign was a dirty ditch with negative advertising and personal insults reaching an all-time low. The parliament that preceded it was one of the worst in living memory. We do not use the experience and expertise of former prime ministers in promoting the national interest. Jean Chrétien, for example, knows the Clintons and a host of senior Democrats. Will his advice be sought as the Canadian government adjusts to a new administration? Will the talents and ideas of all parties in the House of Commons be encouraged, and partisanship put aside as we cope with recession or even depression? Obama's high road is a route that Canadian politicians desperately need to discover.

Seventy-years-ago, in another time of crisis, another president gave Canadians hope. On 18 August 1938, President Franklin Delano Roosevelt visited Queen's University, and gave the most important speech ever by an American president on Canadian soil. With Nazism ascendant, Roosevelt declared: "I give to you assurance that the people of the United States will not stand idly by if domination of Canadian soil is threatened by any other Empire."

That famous undertaking has remained a pillar of Canadian security policy ever since. But Roosevelt had some other things to say about the Canadian-American relationship that should endure. Roosevelt spoke about the necessity of new ideas and mutual learning. "Thought is not anchored in any land," he said. "And the profit of education redounds to the equal benefit of the whole world. That is one form of free trade to which the leaders of every opposing party can subscribe."

On the specifics of the Canadian-American relationship he proclaimed:

> We as good neighbours are true friends because we maintain our own rights with frankness, because we refuse to accept the twists of secret diplomacy, because we settle our disputes by consultation and because we discuss our common problems in the spirit of the common good.

Roosevelt's speech has not been the only important Presidential speech made on Canadian soil. Over the past 70 years, presidents have helped shape the Canada-US relationship through their oratory. President Kennedy's declaration to our Parliament, for instance, that:

> [G]eography has made us neighbours. History has made us friends. Economics has made us partners. And necessity has made us allies. Those whom nature hath so joined together, let no man put asunder

and President Clinton's parliamentary address: "We're neighbours by the grace of nature. We are allies and friends by choice," cemented ties between our two nations. President Reagan's observations of what Canada and the United States share achieved this as well: "a vast continent, with its common hardships and uncommon duties; generations of mutual respect and support; and an abiding friendship that grows ever stronger."

A youthful Senator John F. Kennedy even quoted Canada's first prime minister Sir John A. Macdonald during his first ever visit to Canada to speak in Montreal in 1953:

> It is the fashion now to enlarge on the defects of the Constitution of the United States, but I am not one of those who look upon it as a failure. I think and believe that it is one of the most skillful works that human intelligence has created; [it] is one of the most perfect organizations that ever governed a free people. To say that it has some difficulties is but to say that it is not the work of omniscience but of human intellect.

Other Presidents have spoken to the range of issues which under lie our nations' friendship, including trade, defence and foreign affairs. Others have not been afraid of using these opportunities to appeal directly to Canadians over the heads of their leaders. Whether their rhetoric was soaring, critical or even pedestrian, we listened, we responded and we were often inspired. We have come a long way from Roosevelt's first speech at Queen's and the subsequent opening of the International Bridge at the Thousand Islands, which saw a Canadian prime minister and American president open a milestone together as brothers in peace. Nevertheless, the groundswell of excitement generated by President Obama's February 2009 visit was not much different from the reception received by Roosevelt in 1938.

Standing on the shoulders of the Presidents who have come before him, President Obama has the opportunity to inspire new generations of Canadians, to reaffirm the ties that bind our two nations together, and to cast his own unique shadow on this most enduring of friendships.

In 1938, Franklin Roosevelt suggested to his Kingston audience that, to overcome the extreme crises of that era, we needed to "cultivate three qualities to keep our foothold in the shifting sands of the present—humility, humanity and humour." In that spirit he lit the "darkling plain" of the 1930s. Let us pledge to work in that same spirit today with a new American president, so that our children and grandchildren will forever enjoy the bounty of a shared North America. As with Roosevelt, Obama too offers "change we can believe in."

Thomas S. Axworthy
Chair, Centre for the Study of Democracy
Queen's University
June 2009

PART ONE

FDR and Queen's

When I was a boy, my mother and grandmother once sat talking with me nearby, and recalled how they both, in my grandparents' kitchen, had broken into tears in April of 1945 when news of the death of President Franklin D. Roosevelt came over the radio.

My grandmother had by then lost her youngest brother in the fighting in Sicily. While firm believers (my grandmother in particular), in King, Country and Empire during those dark days of war, FDR was the man who led us, on both sides of the border, as we jointly fought the Second World War.

He was as well, through his famous Fireside Chats and his fearless first Inaugural Address, the wealthy patrician from Hyde Park who brought hope into houses like my grandmother's across North America. He promised action against the Great Depression – rather than preside over a government and economy frozen at the calamity that visited Canada and the United States in the Dirty Thirties.

As I got older and began to study history in high school and university, I began to understand more about the New Deal, Canada-US relations with FDR in the Oval Office and the Canadian-American partnership during the Second Great War. By 1988, I was a student at Queen's University, and was employed part time as a student assistant at the University Archives. One of my tasks that year was to assist an archivist, George Henderson, to prepare displays to mark the 50th anniversary of FDR's visit to Queen's University campus – my university – on 18 August 1938. It was then I first heard, thanks to an audiotape in the Queen's Archives collections, the voice that had inspired my grandmother and mother so long before.

> We as good neighbours are true friends because we maintain our own rights with frankness, because we refuse to accept the twists of secret diplomacy, because we settle our disputes by consultation and because we discuss our common problems in the spirit of the common good,

FDR said about Canada and the United States that day at Queen's. "We seek to be scrupulously fair and helpful, not only in our relations with each other, but each of us at home in our relations with our own people."

I listened to the late president's address, imagining what it must have been like at a tiny campus of fewer than 2,000 students in a city with a population of just over 20,000, to host a giant of world history like Roosevelt. George showed me pictures of the event and the University Doomsday book with FDR's signature, in full – a rare thing for FDR to do. This is one of the university's true prized possessions.

That was 21 years ago. Both George and I are a little older now. That speech still rings true today as it did when I first heard it in 1988.

> The Dominion of Canada is part of the sisterhood of the British Empire," FDR said at Queen's in a phrase that has rung through history. "I give to you assurance that the people of the United States will not stand idly by if domination of Canadian soil is threatened by any other Empire.

FDR and Prime Minister William Lyon Mackenzie King, Canada's longest-serving leader, after their visit to Queen's opened the International Bridge at Ivy Lea 71 years ago. "This bridge stands as an open door. There will be no challenge at the border and no guard to ask a countersign. Where the boundary is crossed the only words must be, 'Pass, friend.'"

I pass over that bridge often, as countless thousands in our area in both New York state and Ontario do themselves each year. It is a vital link between our two nations, and a symbol of our joint custody over the St. Lawrence Seaway.

Today, with such a historic anniversary to recall, it is important that we remember FDR's visit of so long ago, and his hopes for a future built on a lasting and permanent friendship between our two nations.

Arthur Milnes

Chapter I

President Franklin Roosevelt's 18 August 1938 Visit to Queen's University

By Frederick W. Gibson

Kingston is the oldest European settlement in Ontario. In 1973, Kingstonians celebrated the first 300 years of their existence as a settled community. In 1938, the centenary of the incorporation of Kingston as a town was also celebrated. Should any future historian be interested in a comparison of the festivities which attended these two commemorative years, this historian will, I think, be able to report that they differed markedly in scale, in cost, and in the degree of popular enthusiasm which they aroused.

The Tercentenary festivities of 1973 were launched with great *éclat* on New Year's Day, with a Mayor's *Levee* which turned into a huge birthday party. There followed, within a fortnight an elaborate civic banquet and costume ball. These two events were only the beginning, however, of a seemingly endless stream of public functions and commemorative enterprises. A special song was written. We have seen the premiere production of a Canadian play in a Kingston setting. Three new books about Kingston have been published and at least four more are to come. In *Heritage Kingston* we have seen this summer a brilliant exhibition; in the Agnes Etherington Art Centre, of art and artifacts illuminating the history of Kingston; this is the first of its kind in Canada.

We have been greatly honoured by guests. The Royal Winnipeg Ballet performed for us in February; the Governor General was here in April to hold a citizenship court; the Royal Society of Canada and other learned societies, including the Ontario Historical Society all met in June. The procession of distinguished visitors ascended to a fitting climax on June 27, when Her Majesty Queen Elizabeth honoured us with her presence. Since then the festive round has continued unabated and it now may be confidently predicted that, when the events of the year finally conclude, scarcely a week will have been allowed to pass without the appearance of some exhibition or tour, some festival or jamboree, some competition or tattoo – the whole collectively designed to offer, in the words of the city's official brochure, "something for everyone no matter what the time of year."

In 1973 civic pride and civic expectation apparently know no bounds.

In 1938 matters were quite otherwise, and in fact, the centennial celebration of that year was conducted on a severely limited scale. Indeed, it appeared for a time that the whole idea of an official celebration, so enthusiastically advanced by Mayor Harry Steward in his inaugural address,[1] had foundered and would have to be abandoned for lack of funds.

This paper, however, is concerned with the Kingston of 1938 and principally with one unexpected episode which took place here in that year and which briefly lifted the community out of its prevailing mood of despondency and apprehension onto a plane of genuine thankfulness and even of hope.

The trouble was, of course, that 1938 was anything but an auspicious year for public celebrations. It was the ninth year of a world depression with sickening tenacity – a cold fog that lifted only to disclose the central and terrifying features of a more deadly storm which had been gathering in Asia and in Europe. For 1938 was also the year of Munich, the shabby autumnal climax to the prolonged Czechoslovakian crisis which had opened the previous spring and which was itself merely the latest of a series of humiliating retreats on the part of the democratic nations before the forces of fascist aggression. These terrible events made their impact everywhere, including this Canadian community at the head of the great river.

Kingston in the 1930s was a somewhat sleepy lake town of some 23,000 persons, barely supported by a cluster of faltering local industries and commercial establishments. It was not very different in outward appearance from a score of other towns and small cities dotted along the St. Lawrence River and the lower Great Lakes except, perhaps, in the high quality of some of its public and domestic architecture. Aside from its celebrated "Old Stones," Kingston's principal distinguishing features were an old, and now slowly expanding military establishment which included the Royal Military College, a handful of institutions of civil administration – some penal, others therapeutic – and a small university which was then within three years of achieving its own centenary. This complex of public and semi-public institutions loomed even larger in the Kingston of the 1930s than it does today, because it was able, by drawing in monies from outside, to bolster the local economy and thus afford a measure of shelter against the blizzard of depression. But the shelter was far from adequate. In April 1938 there were still 1,442 Kingstonians in receipt of public relief, and they eked out an existence at a level described by the Queen's professor of bacteriology as "nothing more than a slow starvation."[2] When, in the same year, the city authorities called for applications for the post of driver of a new garbage truck, there were 92 applicants for the job. It paid $21.00 a week and this was distinctly greater than the average unskilled workman could make at the prevailing rate of 30 cents an hour.[3] In 1938, Kingston's share of direct relief costs, including debt charges, totaled $125,000, an amount more than half the sum which the city was then paying for primary and secondary education in its public school system.[4] In these chilling circumstances, it is perhaps not surprising that when a request from the Mayor's Centennial Committee for $5000.00 for a civic celebration came before the Finance Committee of the City Council, it was sharply cut to $2000.00. Thereupon, the Centennial Committee resigned and it appeared that there would be no official celebration.[5]

It was not long, however, before this initial decision was reconsidered, for it aroused vigourous protest from interested citizens and organizations; 1938 had begun to show definite signs of improvement in the local economy. Building permits rose in the spring. Queen's was beginning work on a new biochemistry building; the federal government's defence estimates included funds for new Permanent Force buildings and an anti-aircraft centre at Barriefield. The reconstruction of Fort Henry, which had been proceeding rapidly with assistance from the Dominion and Ontario governments, was nearing completion, and it was announced in March that it would be ready for opening in the summer as a historic site and tourist attraction.[6]

In March, the Canadian Locomotive Company received a contract to build fifteen locomotives for the Canadian Pacific Railway, a project which was expected to employ 600 men from July to October; and in April the S. S. Lemoyne, the pride of the Canada Steamship Lines, docked at the Kingston Elevator with half a million bushels of American corn for transshipment down the St. Lawrence.[7] On the strength of these improving prospects and with assurances of private financial support, the Kingston Chamber of Commerce offered to revive and take over the management of a centennial celebration, provided only that the City would increase its appropriation to $2500.00. Thereupon the City Council fell into line, the Centennial Committee was reconstituted and it proceeded to draw up a programme of festivities for the first week of August, when it was expected that the summer flood of tourist and homecoming Kingstonians would be at its peak.[8] The programme featured the official opening of Fort Henry by the prime minister of Canada on July 31, followed in succeeding days by an elaborate historical pageant, a civic parade, and whole panoply of horse races, athletic competitions and water sports, including the Dominion Regatta of the Canadian Canoe Association. The weather held fair most of the time; the events were well attended, and by the end of the week Kingstonians could feel that their centennial had been well and truly marked.[9]

Yet, as matters turned out, the highlight of the centennial year was none of these events. The principal local event of 1938 fell on the 18th of August, when President Franklin Roosevelt came to Kingston to receive an honourary degree from Queen's University at a special convocation.

It was, in several respects, a quite unprecedented occasion. No president of the United States had hitherto paid an official visit to any part of the province of Ontario. Nor had an American president ever accepted, while in office, a degree from a Canadian University. It was the first time that Queen's university conferred a degree to the head of a foreign state and, although the university had previously held one special convocation to honour the Prince of Wales, this was the first occasion when Convocation met out of doors, in the George Richardson Memorial Stadium. The warmth of popular enthusiasm with which President Roosevelt was received had not been matched since the visit of the Prince of Wales in 1919; it was not to be exceeded until the day, nearly a year later, when Their Majesties King George VI and Queen Elizabeth visited the city during their tour of Canada. What made the presidential visit of 1938 all the more remarkable was that President Roosevelt's choice to include, in his address to convocation an important statement on American foreign policy. It was this statement, made by this visitor, which lifted the occasion above the level of a local or even a national event and made Kingston, for a brief, shining moment of its centennial year, a focus of international attention.

President Roosevelt's visit to Queen's was not planned as part of Kingston's official centennial celebrations. It was much affected, however, both in its occurrence and in its timing, by another ceremony of international significance which took place on the same day some 25 miles down the river. There, a new international bridge, soaring over the St. Lawrence from island to island in five great spans, and connecting Ivy Lea, Ontario with Collins Landing, New York, had been under construction since the spring of 1937, and was due for completion in the summer or autumn of 1938. Almost from the beginning, the officers of the Thousand Islands Bridge Authority had conceived that the bridge should be officially opened at the height of the 1938 tourist season, at an impressive dedication ceremony to be presided over by the heads of the two nations. They had formed a Canadian-American committee to plan the arrangements for the opening. The American members of the Committee believed that the prospect of persuading the president of the United States to accept an invitation would be much improved if they could secure a prior commitment from the prime minister of Canada. Accordingly, George Fulford, the Canadian Co-Chairman of the Dedication committee, and a close personal and political friend of Prime Minister King's, took up the matter with King in the autumn of 1937 and obtained a verbal commitment to attend. Armed with Mackenzie King's provisional acceptance, Grant Mitchell, the Executive Secretary of the Bridge Authority, attempted in January 1938 to approach President Roosevelt through James A. Farley of New York, then postmaster-general in the Roosevelt Administration and chairman of the National Committee of the Democratic Party. Farley, to Mitchell's dismay, gave him no encouragement, and Mitchell was driven to seek more helpful avenues to the White House. Before he could find one, word of what was afoot leaked out, reached Kingston and became public knowledge.[10]

The source of the leak, in all probability, was Mitchell himself. He was a close friend of Dr. Harry Stewart's, Kingston's Mayor, and early in 1938 he confided to Stewart his plans for the bridge-opening ceremony. During a citizen's meeting held on February 2 to discuss centennial plans, the Mayor announced that "it had been intimated" that President Roosevelt would attend the bridge-opening ceremony in the summer. The Mayor added that, if Kingstonians so desired, an effort would be made to have the president visit Kingston and take part in the civic centenary. A report of the Mayor's statement appeared in the Whig-Standard the next day. At this date the city's centennial plans were still at a highly tentative stage, and as we have noted earlier, they were soon to be thrown into complete disorder by a financial squabble which led on March 7, to the resignation of the Mayor's Centennial Committee. Before the financial obstacle was overcome and the committee reconstituted in April, the initiative, at least with respect to President Roosevelt, had been taken up by Queen's University.

Specifically, the idea rose in the mind of Dr. George Humphrey, the head of the department of Philosophy, that it would be a good stroke for Queen's to take advantage of President Roosevelt's presence in the neighbourhood to confer upon him an honourary degree.[11] Queen's was then a small and intimate university with about 1,800 intramural students, and with a faculty whose members were long accustomed to discussing their concerns directly with the principal. Accordingly, Dr. Humphrey took his idea straight to Principal Wallace.

Robert Charles Wallace was then in his third year as principal, but he already thought of Queen's in the expansive terms that Grant had long before him, as a university with a national responsibility and a national mission. Principal Wallace had been greatly pleased to have Queen's act as host to a special conference on Canadian-American relations in the previous summer; beyond this, he believed strongly that the links between the British Commonwealth and the United States should be strengthened in every possible way, both practically and symbolically. The principal had no difficulty, therefore, in perceiving the merits of Humphrey's idea, and he himself took it before the March meeting of the University Senate. "Principal Wallace pointed out," the Senate minutes record,

> that the president will be in this vicinity at the opening of the International Bridge on the first of August; therefore he would like to nominate President Roosevelt for the degree of Doctor of Laws to be given at a special convocation at that time

The nomination was referred at once to the Standing Committee on Honourary Degrees. The committee withdrew and reported later in the same meeting in favour of the proposal. The report was adopted forthwith.[12]

Queen's had decided to extend the invitation; it remained however, to obtain the president's acceptance. It was understood that, since the prospective honorary graduate was the head of a foreign government, the invitation should go forward through the Canadian diplomatic service. It was a channel which, at least in this instance, appeared to offer definite advantages, since the Under Secretary of State for External Affairs was Dr. O. D. Skelton, formerly a distinguished member of the Queen's faculty and currently a member of the Board of Trustees. Accordingly, on the day after the senate meeting, Principal Wallace wrote to Dr. Skelton, informed him of the University's decision, pointed out that the date selected for the special convocation, August 1, had been chosen so as to coincide with the President's expected visit to the International Bridge, and requested him to ascertain "whether it may be possible for President Roosevelt to accept at that time, the degree which Queen's University would honour itself in giving."[13] A few days later Dr. Skelton laid the matter before his minister.

His minister, Mackenzie King, was then in the third year of his third term as Prime Minister of Canada and Secretary of State for External Affairs, and in neither role, in 1938, were his affairs prospering. The depression had not evaporated under Liberal policies of freer trade and fiscal orthodoxy; even the moderate and uneven progress which had been achieved by 1937 was abruptly checked in the autumn of that year by the drought which devastated the prairie wheat crop and by the effects of the sharp recession in the American economy. By every economic indicator, 1938 represented for Canada a setback over the previous year.

Abroad, the whole international situation was rapidly going from bad to worse. Canada, under the leadership of Mackenzie King, was following in the wake of those policies of appeasement by which the British government of Neville Chamberlain endeavoured to compose a _distraught Europe. Europe, which in the 1920s had receded into the background of Canadian consciousness, now loomed up again in the mid-1930s with frightening menace and importance, recalling to men and women everywhere memories of the insane holocaust of the Great War and bringing to Canadians additional recollections of the bitter racial and social strife to which the conscription issue had given rise in that earlier conflagration.

Canada's autonomy had been too recently acquired for her to develop a mature or independent foreign policy, and, although there was a great deal of public controversy within the country on that subject after 1935, there was no general agreement upon how to use the national status which it had previously deemed so desirable. A deeply rooted isolationism still pervaded French Canada; some English-speaking Canadians urged a policy of complete pacifism and neutrality. But the main body of English Canada, though sharing the general abhorrence of war, still felt ties with Britain, as well as a continuing attachment to the transatlantic world.

Privately, Mackenzie King, like a majority of English-Canadians, believed that Canada should not, and could not, remain aloof from a war threatening the existence of Great Britain, but he also knew the depths of

French-Canadian suspicions of involvement in war through the British connection. On this point, Mackenzie King believed that the minority could be persuaded to march with the majority only if it were satisfied that his government had gone to great lengths to avoid war and the commitments which might draw Canadians into war. To be sure, King warned Hitler in a private interview in 1937 that the members of the Commonwealth, including Canada, would rally to Britain's side in a defensive war, but in the same interview, King completely mistook the supreme megalomaniac of the 20th century for a simple, mystical nationalist of egalitarian disposition, bent on restoring Germany's self-respect, and rectifying the Treaty of Versailles, but not likely to risk a general war for these objectives. It was, of course, a profound miscalculation, but one to which Mackenzie King clung with a desperate faith. It all but completely disqualified him for the task of educating the Canadian people about the nature of the menace confronting the western democracies.

In these circumstances, it is not surprising that Canadian foreign policy in the late 1930s was dominated almost wholly by domestic considerations. Above the restless and conflicting currents of Canadian opinion, Mackenzie King and his chief French-Canadian lieutenant, Ernest Lapointe, walked a difficult tightrope, employing as a balance-pole the famous formula "parliament will decide," and endeavouring, in King's case, to mask the underlying divisions with "the polished phrases of platitudinous peroration." What this meant in practice was a further contraction of Canadian commitments to the League of Nations including a refusal to enter into arrangements for military cooperation of neutrality. It was a cautious, inglorious policy, non-committal "to the point of timid isolation" but it possessed the single and, to Mackenzie King, the decisive merit of avoiding the precipitation of the main segments of Canadian opinion into positions of fixed and irreconcilable opposition.[14]

On three matters—and three alone—pertaining to foreign and defence policy was Mackenzie King willing, in the pre-war years, to take positive action. His government undertook a modest programme of rearmament, though with the emphasis carefully placed on the air force, the navy coastal defence, and on anything but preparations for an expeditionary force which might lay the ground for another national crisis over infantry reinforcements. Secondly, King planned and implemented an impressive demonstration of Canadian attachment to monarchical and commonwealth symbols in the form of a tour of Canada by King George VI and Queen Elizabeth in 1939. Thirdly, he set out to improve relations between Canada and the United States to draw the Republic closer to the Commonwealth. In the second and third of these enterprises, the prime minister's efforts were powerfully reinforced by Governor General Lord Tweedsmuir. Within a few weeks of his return to office in 1935, Mackenzie King had gone to Washington and successfully concluded, in direct discussion with President Roosevelt, trade negotiations which had been pending for over a year. The

Canadian-American trade agreement of 1935 not only increased the flow of commerce but cleared the air of economic tensions which had been running high between the two countries for the preceding five years. The agreement also opened a path to further negotiations between Great Britain, Canada and the United States, which came to fruition in 1938 in a new set of triangular trade treaties strengthening economic ties all round.

Mackenzie King was not prepared, however, to leave it at that. Not only was he anxious to improve Canadian-American relations over a broader front, but it was a favourite idea of his that Canada could "play a useful role as an intermediary between the United States and Great Britain."[15] King arranged, therefore, for President Roosevelt to pay a state visit to Canada in the summer of 1936, and for this purpose, he enlisted the help of Lord Tweedsmuir, the governor general, to act as official host. The governor general's cooperation was both enthusiastic and exceedingly helpful. As John Buchan, he was already widely and favourably known by Americans; as a public man he believed, quite simply, that the peace and freedom of the world depended on a close understanding between the British Commonwealth and the United States. On the subject of improved Canadian-American relations, he saw eye to eye with his prime minister.[16]

The prime minister and the governor general deliberately set out therefore, to cultivate the president. They did so in correspondence and, perhaps more usefully, in a series of reciprocal visits across the border, which not only symbolized the closer relations which were developing but which invariably provided opportunity for a frank and confidential exchange of views.[17] Quite early in the process, the discussions turned to the deteriorating international situation and to ways in which President Roosevelt might conceivably exercise a beneficial influence on the movement of events. The question was first raised during the president's visit to Quebec City in July of 1936. It was brought up again in March 1937, when first the prime minister and later, the governor general, on successive visits to the White House, encouraged the president to call a world conference on economic and social problems as a step to removing at least some of the causes of war. Mackenzie King told Franklin Roosevelt that "more than any other living man," he was

> in a position to save the world situation, and, with it, civilization [by] the bringing together of hostile nations in a round table conference... And Tweedsmuir told the president that no such conference could be a success except under your direct personal supervision.[18]

The governor general promptly conveyed the gist of these conversations to Prime Minister Stanley Baldwin and subsequently to his successor, Neville Chamberlain. Mackenzie King communicated the ideas of both Roosevelt and his Secretary of State, Cordell Hull, to the Imperial Conference of 1937. The British response, however, was lukewarm; no conference ensued, but across the Canadian-American border the high-level visits continued, and by 1938 it was plain that Mackenzie King and Franklin Roosevelt, with much assistance from Lord Tweedsmuir, were constructing the first, and thus far only, close relationship between a prime minister of Canada and a president of the United States.

As the junior member of this developing partnership, Mackenzie King sensibly left many of the initiatives to Roosevelt, but King was anxious that the momentum of their visits be sustained, and it was for this reason that he had agreed in the autumn of 1937 to attend the official opening of the Thousand Islands Bridge in the following summer, when it was hoped that the president would also be present. When, therefore, at the beginning of April, 1938, Dr. Skelton laid before him the invitation from Queen's University to President Roosevelt to accept an honourary degree on a date scheduled to coincide with the bridge-opening, Mackenzie King gave it his immediate approval and told Skelton that the Canadian Government "should expedite the invitation by all means."[19]

Accordingly, on 5 April, Skelton dispatched the invitation through the Canadian legation in Washington to the State Department, drawing attention to the coincidence of the bridge-opening and the proposed convocation, and adding that "the Canadian Government would be very greatly pleased if the president found it possible to come to Canada on that occasion."[20] The legation transmitted Skelton's message to Sumner Welles, the Undersecretary of State, and on 11 April, Welles passed the substance of it directly to President Roosevelt in a note of his own, asking what reply the President desired him to make.

Roosevelt's response was prompt and cordial but inconclusive. "That is a very gracious action on the part of Queen's University in Kingston," he replied to Welles, 'and I am deeply appreciative." The only obstacle, it appeared, was the date proposed. "My difficulty in regard to the August first date," the President's memorandum to Welles continued, "is that if I can get away for a four-week holiday, about the tenth of July, I am most anxious to do so and the holiday would be spent principally on the high seas." He was hoping, however, to make a short trip to the Great Lakes in September, and he suggested that "if the convocation could be held at that time, it would be most convenient for me," and that on the same trip he could "drive over" the new international bridge. As for a precise date, it was difficult for him to make any definite arrangement as far ahead as September, but he thought he would know better by the first of June.[21]

Sumner Welles sent the text of the president's memorandum to the Canadian Minister in Washington, adding that as soon after 1 June as possible, the president would give him a definite decision and he would pass the word on. This reply was subsequently forwarded to Queen's. Dr. Wallace replied that he was very pleased to learn that the president might find it possible to come in September and that the University would be very happy to make its arrangements to suit his personal convenience.[22]

Meanwhile, however, President Roosevelt came under pressure from a different quarter to visit the Canadian border in the summer. The Thousand Islands Bridge Authority was not only anxious to have the bridge officially open in August, but exceedingly desirous for the publicity which the president's attendance at the opening ceremonies would ensure. For this purpose the Authority's executive secretary, Grant Mitchell, succeeded in enlisting the support of Senator Robert F. Wagner of New York. Wagner was the senior Democratic Senator of the Empire State, was an old friend of Franklin Roosevelt, had been a consistent supporter of New Deal measures, and was now chairman of the powerful Banking and Commerce Committee of the Senate. Senator Wagner's intervention proved very helpful; he got the president to agree in principle and he arranged for him to receive a delegation from the Bridge Authority, at which time the invitation might formally be presented.[23] The president received the delegation on 21 April, and the date for the bridge-opening, August 18, was selected to coincide with a high point in the tourist season and to meet the requirement of the bridge contractors. It had the further advantage, from the president's standpoint, of falling after his return from his projected holiday at sea. The president told the delegation that he would very much like to accept but that he could not, as yet, definitely bind himself to a specific date. Nevertheless, the members of the Bridge Authority were sufficiently encouraged to proceed almost at once to the issuance of official invitations for the August 18 date, and, as soon as formal acceptances came in from the governor general and the prime minister of Canada, Grant Mitchell saw to it that copies were immediately sent off to the White House.[24]

Notwithstanding these confident expectations, the president continued to think of other commitments and alternative dates. In the middle of May, he wrote to the governor general saying that he had been invited to open two international bridges—the Thousand Islands Bridge and one between Sarnia and Port Huron, as well as a peace gateway between North Dakota and Manitoba, all of these early in September. He suggested to Lord Tweedsmuir that "it would be most amusing and delightful if you and I could arrange a sort of joint dedicatory tour."[25] Lord Tweedsmuir replied that he would be in the Canadian west in September, but that he had provisionally accepted an invitation to the Thousand Islands Bridge for August 18. "Would a meeting there," Tweedsmuir inquired, "suit your plans?"[26] It began to look as if it would; a few days later, at the beginning of June, Roosevelt instructed his White House staff to work out, in cooperation with the State Department, a tentative programme for a series of visits along the Canadian border, beginning with the Thousand Islands Bridge on August 18. Ten days later, this collaboration produced a preliminary schedule which included Queen's University on August 19, followed by the other items which had been mentioned in the president's letter to the governor general.[27] All these arrangements, however, were still highly tentative. In the end, both the

Thousand Islands Bridge Authority and Queen's University had to wait a further month for final word from the White House.

In all probability, the reason for the president's procrastination was that he had more important and more perplexing problems on his mind. In 1938, in fact, Franklin Roosevelt had reached the lowest point in his presidency. The early successes of the New Deal and his enormous personal popularity, which had enabled him to sweep all but two states of the Union in the presidential election of 1936, had been greatly dissipated a short year later, by his abortive attempt to "pack" the Supreme Court and by the severe recession in the American economy. Opposition to the president was mounting along the Potomac and throughout the country, and although he was now contemplating further measures to revive the economy, he knew that they would encounter heavy opposition, not only from Republicans, but from conservative elements within his own party. He was planning, therefore, a series of political forays into opposition territory, which he hoped would result in a "purge" of conservative Democrats, a scheme that was to be all but completely blasted by the results of the mid-term elections of November 1938.

The outlook abroad during Roosevelt's second term filled him with dismay and frustration. He watched, with growing concern, the rise of dictatorship in Europe and Asia. He detested fascism; he was appalled at the brutal progress of international banditry; he had deep misgivings about Chamberlain's appeasement policies; and he had no illusion that the United States could remain unaffected by a general European or world war. These were Roosevelt's private views; his efforts to make them publicly effective were, for the most part, uncertain and unsuccessful. The people of the United States who had turned their backs on Europe in 1919 were still of the same mind, and in the 1930s, the force of American isolationism reached a terrible intensity. The Neutrality Acts of 1935-37 made isolationism the law of the land, and, arrayed behind these ramparts, there stood a powerful phalanx of defenders in the Congress, reinforced by large sections of the public. Americans generally had no sympathy for fascism, but its rise and frightful progress confirmed their deepest prejudices that the European system was beyond redemption. It is tempting to say that "the worse the situation appeared in Europe, the more determined the American people became to keep out of it."[28]

President Roosevelt made two notable attempts to break out of this straitjacket, both of them unsuccessful. In his famous Quarantine speech, delivered in Chicago on 5 October 1937 at the beginning of the Sino-Japanese War, he proposed a general embargo against any aggressor nation: in other words, an extreme form of sanctions. His speech produced in the United States "a strong and country-wide protest among Democrats as among Republicans," and the president promptly backed off.[29] A few months later, in the wake of Lord Halifax's mission to Berlin, Roosevelt returned to the idea of calling a world conference, somewhat along the lines originally suggested by Mackenzie King and Tweedsmuir, but now expanded by Sumner Welles to include problems of treaty revisions and the rights and obligations of neutrals in war. On 11 January 1938, the president sent a confidential message to Prime Minister Chamberlain, outlining the plan. Chamberlain, however, without consulting any of his colleagues, turned the plan down out of hand as a project which might cut across his own direct efforts to appease Germany and Italy – an act of transatlantic rejection which Winston Churchill subsequently described as "the loss of the last frail chance to save the world from tyranny otherwise than by war."[30] Thus, hamstrung at home and rebuffed abroad, President Roosevelt fell back on the oldest American foreign policy – no entanglements with Europe – and on a diplomacy of no risks and no commitments, which one of his biographers has described as a diplomacy of "pinpricks and righteous protest."[31] In these circumstances, the United States counted for very little in the teetering balance of world politics in the late 1930s, and it is not in the least surprising that Adolph Hitler should have so heavily discounted American influence.

In one area alone, that of national and hemisphere defence, did President Roosevelt possess real freedom to manoeuvre, and in the late 1930s he made considerable use of it. With the "Good Neighbour" policy enunciated in Roosevelt's first inaugural, he and Secretary Hull put into effect in Latin America a succession of moves which marked the withdrawal of "Yankee imperialism" and its conversion into growing Pan-American solidarity. Even before this, the president proclaimed in a speech at Chatauqua, New York, on 14 August 1936, that the United States, while shunning European entanglements, could, and would if necessary, defend itself and its neighbourhood; it was plain that the neighbourhood which he had in mind included his neighbours to the north. Roosevelt had welcomed the overtures and visits of Mackenzie King and Tweedsmuir, and he reciprocated in kind. He made a state visit to Quebec City in July of 1936, delivering one public address partly in French. He broadcast a message of birthday congratulations to the Canadian people on Dominion Day, 1937. He paid a flying visit to the city of Victoria in September 1937, which initiated the first of a series of informal conversations between the military advisers of the United States and Canada.[32] The unusual frequency of these proceedings, combined with the warmth and charm with which Franklin Roosevelt invariably invested in them, imparted to Canadians the agreeable and somewhat startling impression that a president of the United States actually knew and cared something about their existence.

By Christmas 1937, the president was suggesting to Mackenzie King that, in view of the war in the Far East and "the threats of armed banditry in Europe," the time had come "for us to chat again." He invited the prime minister to visit the White House at his convenience.[33] Mackenzie King put off the invitation because of the imminence of the 1938 parliamentary session, but the beginnings of the Czechoslovakian crisis in the spring of 1938 revived their desire to meet again; the invitations from the Thousand Islands Bridge and from Queen's University clearly pointed to an opportunity in the summer. In addition, from Roosevelt's standpoint, a visit to the bridge would enable him to meet Senator Wagner's wishes, and at the same time afford an occasion to strike a blow in public in favour of the controversial St. Lawrence seaway project. The president was now thinking of this enterprise as a great project of regional redevelopment under joint, public international auspices. This was an enterprise running into heavy opposition from private power and railway interests in both countries, as well as from the premiers of Ontario and Quebec.

It was probably this combination of influences which finally decided President Roosevelt to make a brief northern trip in August. On 7 July he left Washington by train for the Pacific coast. On the following day, the State Department informed the Canadian Minister in Washington that the president would be pleased to accept an honourary degree from Queen's University on Friday August 19, either before or after the opening of the Thousand Islands Bridge on that date. This information was promptly relayed to the Department of External Affairs, but a few days later it was followed by a second message stating that the president would open the bridge on the 18th instead of the 19th. It was suggested, that the Queen's convocation be held on the morning of the 18th, at an hour which would allow sufficient time for the president to have lunch and reach the bridge for the opening ceremonies at 3 o'clock.[34] The substance of the amended message Dr. Skelton conveyed to Principal Wallace by letter, 15 July. Skelton's letter reached the University on 18 July, precisely one month before the date which had now been assigned for the President's visit, and an official announcement appeared in the press on the same day.

The news set in motion a flurry of arrangements at Queen's University, though, interestingly enough, Principal Wallace extricated himself from all the details right from the beginning. Dr. Wallace opened Skelton's final letter on the morning of the day when he had planned to leave with his family for a month's vacation in Quebec. He discussed the matter with his vice-principal, Dr. W. E. McNeill, and decided on the spot to go ahead with his holiday plans, suggesting that 11 o'clock in the morning would be a suitable time for the convocation and that the University might also give a luncheon for the president, but left the final decision on these and all other arrangements in Dr. McNeill's hands.[35] It was a swift but altogether safe delegation of responsibility.

Successively professor of English, registrar, treasurer and vice-principal, William Everett McNeill was an old Queen's hand and, as Principal Mackintosh later said of him, Queen's University had become his life. As vice-principal he was a cool and demanding administrator with a high sense of the importance of academic occasions. He now rose handsomely to this occasion and staged the entire performance.

Some problems seemed easy enough to solve. The vice-principal settled on 11 o'clock for convocation and decided to offer the president the hospitality of a luncheon immediately after the ceremony; both decisions were, however, subject to presidential confirmation. Dr. McNeill then drew up a tentative programme which held to the essential elements of the traditional Queen's laureation ceremony. The question of where convocation should meet presented greater difficulty. The customary place was Grant Hall, but the hall would not hold more than 1,600 people, and it soon become perfectly evident that this would not suffice for the numbers who were besieging the vice-principal's office for invitations. The most spacious alternative was the George Richardson Stadium, which could accommodate 7,000, but this would mean that the ceremonies would take place in the open air, and there was always the danger of rain. Still, the covered grandstand on the west side of the playing field could shield over 2,000 people from anything but a driving storm, and Dr. McNeill decided to take the risk, holding Grant Hall in reserve in the event of a "high east wind with rain." It was also decided that a small platform with a covering canopy should be built in front of the grandstand to hold the official party, and that it should be constructed at the level of the running board of a car so that the President could step on to it with the least difficulty. All the arrangements pertaining to tickets, seating and ushering were placed in the capable hands of the principal's secretary, Miss Mary Anglin.

There were, however, a number of other problems, matters of official procedure and protocol, which could not be settled by the university authorities alone and which gave rise to complex and prolonged negotiations. The guest of honour was a head of state, and Dr. McNeill soon discovered that, since Kingston would be the president's first point of landing in Canada, he would have to be received here with full honours—civil, military, and academic—and this meant that he must be greeted by a representative of the Crown and by representatives of the Dominion, provincial and city governments, together with appropriate University officers. For these purposes, governments at every level had to be consulted and detailed arrangements had to be worked out through a whole network of officialdom.

Quite early in these proceedings, it became known that the governor-general, who had previously accepted an invitation to the bridge, would be unable to attend either ceremony because of illness.[36] Thereupon, George Fulford of the Bridge Committee invited His Honour, Albert Matthews, the Lieutenant-Governor of Ontario, to represent the Crown and the province of Ontario at the Bridge opening, and it was subsequently arranged that the lieutenant-governor should also act in these capacities in Kingston.[37]

To facilitate the other complex negotiations, Dr. McNeill framed a list of 15 central questions, and sent them off hopefully along the network of officials; the rate of response tried his patience severely. At length, answers to those questions directed to Ottawa indicated that the prime minister considered the president a guest of the Government of Canada while he was on Canadian soil. The prime minister would be on hand to help welcome the president to Kingston, would accompany him throughout his visit, and would see to it that railway facilities, military guards and salutes, and an RCMP escort were provided. Some answers came back with infuriating slowness, especially those which had to go back and forth between Ottawa and Washington and thence, in some instances, on to the president, now happily cruising down the Pacific Coast on the USS Houston en route through the Panama Canal to Pensacola, Florida. Eventually, however, and by stages, Dr. McNeill was informed that the president would arrive in Kingston at 10 o'clock on the morning of the 18th; that he would be accompanied by a party of 50, including reporters, broadcasters, photographers and secret service men; that he approved of the 11 o'clock hour for Convocation; that he would wear formal dress; that he would speak for about 10 minutes; that he would probably attend a university luncheon if it could be held at an early hour and at a place easily accessible; and that he had no objections either to an outdoor convocation, or to the presence of newspapermen and photographers, or to having the proceedings broadcast by radio.[38]

Once these pieces of information were assembled, the final details were thrashed out on 5 August at a meeting in Dr. McNeill's office with a representative of External Affairs, the American Charge d'Affaires in Ottawa, members of the bridge committee and Colonel Starling, the head of the president's secret service. Colonel Starling went over every yard that the president would cover and decided that the president's convenience could best be protected if he came to Kingston by train from Buffalo, and that in Kingston, the president should detrain not at the inner station but at the outer station where there was more room. Starling also suggested that as many as seven people could be crowded into several of the official cars in the cavalcade: "Oh, we are used to it," he said, "that is the way we always do these things." Dr. McNeill received the suggestion with a frigid objection and privately decided that more cars would be more dignified and that on this occasion, "we will do things the Canadian way." He also decided that the principal and the rector of the university should be among the welcoming reception at the outer station and that the chancellor and the chairman of the board of trustees should receive the president at the stadium.[39] By 9 August, all the main problems had been resolved, the invitations had gone out, and the final arrangements were announced in the press. Barring a torrential downpour or some other act of God, Queen's University was ready to receive the president of the United States and to welcome a multitude of guests in a setting appropriate to the occasion.

In Kingston, Thursday, 18 August dawned overcast and dark. Prime Minister King, whose railway car No. 100 had been deposited at the outer station during the night, rose at 7:30, pulled aside the curtains and noted that "the day looked very threatening."[40] Nevertheless, by nine o'clock a crowd of spectators had gathered at the station, a guard of honour was drawn up and the welcoming committee stood fidgeting on the station platform.

The man for whom they were all waiting was far from unknown to them. Like everyone in North America, Kingstonians had heard his voice in dozens of "Fireside Chats" and in two sparkling election campaigns; they had seen his face in countless newsreels and front pages. They knew him as the originator of the New Deal, as the champion of the "Forgotten Man," and as a leader who had restored hope to a stricken nation. Yet few Kingstonians, it is safe to say, had ever seen him in person. They were now to have their first, and, as it turned out, only opportunity to do so. Before the day was out, a great many of them had taken the opportunity to see Roosevelt, and had made it very plain how they felt about him.

At 9:58 – two minutes ahead of schedule – the presidential train pulled into the station, and the president's railway car, the "Marco Polo," drew up at one end of a runway which had been placed between the platform of the railway car and the station platform; at the other end of the runway the president's motor car, an open, black Cadillac, stood waiting. A few minutes after 10 o'clock, Lieutenant-Governor Matthews and Prime Minister King were escorted into the "Marco Polo." "Hello Mackenzie," said the president, "you are looking much thinner." Mackenzie King remarked that the president looked not only thinner but very fit, and went on to say how glad he was to see him in Canada again and how sorry the governor-general was not to be able to be present. They talked briefly about Lord Tweedsmuir's health, and then the lieutenant-governor and the prime minister withdrew and descended to the station platform.[41]

At 10:30, the door of the "Marco Polo" opened and a radiant Franklin Roosevelt stepped forth onto the railway car platform. He paused, cocked his head, beamed at the crowd, and made his way on the arm of his military aide, Colonel Watson, down the runway to his automobile. He stood there for a few moments while the prime minister presented Principal Wallace, Norman Rogers, the Rector of Queen's, Mayor Steward, George Fulford, T. A. Kidd, the provincial Member for Kingston, General F. F. Constantine, the officer commanding Military District No. 3, General V. A. S. Williams, the head of the Ontario Provincial Police, and other dignitaries. During the introductions the photographers began taking pictures and, after the president got into his car, a New York photographer requested that the prime minister to move closer to the president so that he could get the two of them. "I'll get as close to him as I can," smiled Mackenzie King. "That works both ways," Franklin Roosevelt replied, laughing.[42]

With that, the members of the reception committee, the photographers and newspapermen were escorted to their cars. The lieutenant-governor and Principal Wallace rode in the president's car, with American service men standing on the running boards and on the rear bumper and walking along beside. The second car, following close behind, was filled with secret service men. In the third car came the prime minister, the rector of Queen's, the mayor, and Marvin McIntyre, the president's secretary. They were followed by nine other cars. The signal was given to start, and the president's car moved slowly through the station grounds, passing through a guard of honour consisting of two ranks of RCMP constables, and stopping at the station exit where a second guard of honour from the Royal Canadian Corps of Signals was drawn up. The signals guard presented arms and the band of the Prince of Wales Own Regiment played "The Star-Spangled Banner." Afterward, the president's car led the cavalcade out into Montreal Street and began to move along slowly behind motorcycle squad of twelve provincial and dominion police.

The scene that greeted them was colourful and extremely crowded. The mayor had requested that stores and other places of business close their doors between 10:00 and 1:00 p.m., and the throngs of released Kingstonians and their families were joined by thousands of visitors from the neighbouring countryside and from across the border. Virtually every inch of the three mile route from the outer station to the stadium was lined with spectators standing, at many points, three and four deep. People watched the parade from every vantage point: they leaned from windows; they crowded on rooftops; they stood on cars and trucks; and small boys of all ages waved from trees and telephone poles. The curbs were lined with hundreds of policemen. The Kingston police looked particularly impressive in their English "Bobby" hats. Everywhere there were flags: Union Jacks predominated, but hawkers did a brisk business moving among the crowds and selling the Stars and Stripes in assorted sizes. A *Globe and Mail* reporter wrote; "Everything in Kingston that could be decorated was decorated."[43]

In response to all this, Franklin Roosevelt ran true to form. Tanned and rested from his holiday cruise, he looked to be in a particularly happy and jocular mood. He turned his head from side to side, smiling broadly at the unbroken lines of spectators, and holding his black silk top hat at arms length in the air. "He did not wave it up and down," a reporter noted, "he vibrated it until the sunlight danced from its sleek crown."[44] As he passed along, the crowds clapped and cheered and waved their flags and many people tried frantically to focus their cameras. The general warmth and enthusiasm were unmistakable, and yet it was a very Canadian crowd. "The cheering and applauding were not boisterous," wrote a Whig-Standard reporter. "It was a more refined welcome." Mackenzie King, riding two cars back and hoping, no doubt, that some of the applause was intended for him, wrote later in his diary: "I felt very proud with the appearance of the city and the behaviour of the crowds. The evident good-will on all sides was a striking and memorable feature."⁴⁵ A nice thing happened on the way to the stadium. The clouds, which had hung low and menacing all morning, lifted suddenly, and the sun shone forth, bathing the entire city in brilliant light.

The cavalcade arrived at the north-east gate of the Richardson Stadium at 10:55, and the gate opened upon another vivid spectacle. The grandstand and the adjoining open stands on the west side of the playing field were packed. Members of the faculty in their academic robes occupied the front and centre sections. Surrounding them, row upon row, were summer school students, trustees of the University, graduates and alumni officers, representatives of the city, clergy and laity, and their wives and husbands. Another 500 people or more were seated in the bleachers on the east side of the field. The front of the grandstand and the speaker's platform were draped in red, white and blue bunting. High above, two large Union Jacks floated from the north and south towers; on poles extended from each end of the grand stand roof hung two "Stars and Stripes" and half-way between them, a huge "Union Jack."

President Roosevelt rode in with a broad smile and with his right arm outstretched: A wave of applause rose from the assembly. The president's car swept in a long curve half-way around the field, and stopped beside the entrance to the low platform in front of the centre section of the grand stand. Chancellor James Richardson stepped forward to welcome him, followed by J. M. MacDonnell, the chairman of the board of trustees, followed in turn by a somewhat ashen Vice-Principal McNeill who explained to the president the order of proceedings and where he was to stand. During these preliminaries, the other official cars emptied. Some of their occupants were escorted to places on the platform; newspapermen scurried to tables placed on the cinder track in front of the grandstand; secret service men and RCMP constables took up their positions around the platform and facing the crowd; movie cameramen set up their equipment; and photographers converged from every direction. The door of the leading car opened. President Roosevelt was assisted to his feet and moved slowly forward on the arm of his military aide to a position beside the study lectern, which had been built for his convenience, and which was bolted to the floor. The ceremony was about to begin.

As the president reached the front of the platform, the Rotary Club Boy's Band struck up a highly unusual rendition of the American national anthem and the audience rose to their feet. The Rev. Dr. J. R. Watts of Queen's Theological College opened convocation with scripture reading and prayers. Afterwards, the audience took their seats, but the platform party remained standing throughout the ceremony because of the difficulty which the president experienced in sitting and in rising. What followed was simple and brief, but unhurried. The principal presented Franklin Delano Roosevelt to the chancellor as a good neighbour and one whom Queen's University desired to honour as "the head of a great people with whom Canada is weaving bonds of peace not to be broken asunder with the passing of years." The chancellor pronounced the customary formula of laureation for the degree of Doctor of Laws, shook hands with the president, and presented him with his diploma. The vice-principal hooded the president and invited him to sign the university's Doomsday Book. As he took up the pen, the president remarked quietly to Dr. McNeill: "I am going to do what I very seldom do; I will write my name in full."[46] After the signing, the Chancellor presented the president to the audience and invited him to address convocation. The audience broke into applause; the president composed himself at the lectern bristling with microphones; movie cameras started grinding; and the photographers snapped pictures of the scene from every conceivable angle.

President Roosevelt's address took about 13 minutes, but in that time he managed to include the one important commitment on American foreign policy that he was willing to make in pre-war years. His theme was unity and interdependence – the unity of civilization and the interdependence of all free and civilized peoples. Civilization was not national; it was international. Ideas were not limited by national borders; they were the common inheritance of all free people. Yet this view was being challenged in some parts of the world and, for that reason, people in the Americas stood charged with maintaining that tradition. The day had passed when Canadians and Americans could be indifferent to dangers from overseas:

> We in the Americas are no longer a faraway continent, to which the eddies of controversies beyond the seas could bring no interest or no harm. Instead, we in the Americas have become a consideration to every propaganda office and to every general staff beyond the seas. The vast amount of our resources, the vigour of our commerce and the strength of our men have made us vital factors in world peace whether we choose it or not.

Fortunately, Canadians and Americans could look clear-eyed at these possibilities, resolving to leave no pathway unexplored which might contribute to world peace; but, even if these hopes were disappointed, "we can assure each other that this hemisphere at least shall remain a strong citadel wherein civilization can flourish unimpaired."

Then came the climax. "The Dominion of Canada," President Roosevelt declared, "is part of the sisterhood of the British Empire. I give to you assurance that the people of the United States will not stand idly by if domination of Canadian soil is threatened by any other Empire." It was these two sentences which brought the audience to its feet in a tumult of prolonged applause, and which echoed far beyond the confines of the Richardson Stadium.

The president followed up the assurance with a warning. Canadians and Americans were good neighbours because they maintained their rights with frankness, because they settled their disputes by consultation, and because they discussed their common problems in the spirit of the common good in an atmosphere of free thought and free speech. By contrast, there were the methods of dictatorship. Roosevelt warned dictators about how free peoples were reacting to their behaviour. "There is one process," he said,

> which we certainly cannot change and probably ought not to change. This is the feeling which ordinary men and women have about events which they can understand. We cannot prevent our people, on either side of the border, from having an opinion in regard to wanton brutality, in regard to undemocratic regimentation, in regard to misery inflicted on helpless peoples, or in regard to violations of accepted individual rights. All that any government, constituted as is yours and mine, can possibly undertake is to help make sure that the facts are known and fairly stated. No country where thought is free can prevent every fireside and every home within its borders from considering the evidence for itself and rendering its own verdict; and the sum total of these conclusions of educated men and women will, in the long run, rightly become the national verdict. That is what we mean when we say the public opinion ultimately governs policy. It is right and just that this should be the case.[47]

The President concluded with a few graceful references to "my good friend" the governor-general and to the prime minister. The crowd applauded, the Queen's yell burst from the throats of the students, and the president smiled and waved. Dr. Watts pronounced the benediction. The band played God Save the King, and convocation was over. The crowd remained standing while the president and the other members of the official party returned to their cars, and the cavalcade drove slowly around the east side of the playing field, with the president stopping briefly to talk with spectators in the bleachers. Then the procession resumed its progress, moving down University Avenue to Ban Righ Hall, where the Trustees of the University gave a luncheon in the president's honour, and where the president, seated in a stout chair inside the dining room, shook hands with the guests as they entered.

The luncheon, as promised, was brief, and included only one speech delivered by J. M. Macdonnell, chairman of the Board of Trustees. Mr. Macdonnell, after expressing the University's pride in the fact that the president was now a Queen's man and suggesting that the Queen's Gaelic yell contained possibilities as a political slogan, referred to the cooperation of the United States and the British Commonwealth as "the greatest guarantee of the preservation of all that makes our life worth living." He concluded that the president's presence and "acceptance of our degree enables us to boast that we have forged another link in the chain of common sentiments, common ideals and common interests which bind us together."

Shortly after one o'clock, the president went directly to his car, and the cavalcade made its way through gay and crowded streets down to the

LaSalle Causeway, where yet another guard of honour, this time composed of members of the Canadian Corps and the 21st Battalion, was drawn up. The pipe-band of the 21st Battalion piped President Roosevelt, with Prime Minister King now seated beside him, across the bridge as far as the gate of the Royal Military College. At that point, the visit of President Roosevelt to Kingston was concluded, and he and the prime minister began a leisurely drive down the St. Lawrence to the Thousand Islands Bridge.

They arrived at the bridge shortly before three o'clock and the presidential car drew to a stop precisely at the mid-point of the international span. There, the president and the prime minister, holding the same pair of scissors, cut the ceremonial ribbon and dedicated the bridge to peace and lasting friendship between their two nations. From this they moved to a large open amphitheatre where a crowd of 10,000 people had been gathered since 6:00 a.m. An elaborate speech-making ceremony followed. In the course of it, Mackenzie King elaborated upon the symbolism of bridge-building in international relations. He drew a parallel between the present occasion and one in which he had opened a bridge over the Thames, at Chelsea; he viewed the bridge over the St. Lawrence as a symbol of friendship and goodwill between Canada and the United States, and he reminded his audience of "that wider friendship which exists between the United States and all the nations of the British Commonwealth." Franklin Roosevelt, while echoing the symbolism in felicitous terms, devoted most of his speech to a strong plea that Canada and the United States should lose no more time in developing the St. Lawrence Seaway. After the ceremony the two leaders parted: Franklin Roosevelt for Hyde Park, and Mackenzie King for Ottawa.

It had been a full day for the president and the prime minister, and a day not to be forgotten by the citizens of Kingston, the members of Queen's University, or by all the people along the border who had gathered at the bridge. President Roosevelt's remarks at the bridge on the subject of the St. Lawrence Seaway provoked an explosion of splenetic protest from the premier of Ontario, but Premier Hepburn had conspicuously absented himself from both ceremonies, and in the aftermath of that day, this latest expression of his customary bad manners was reduced to its appropriate and diminished position. It was, in fact, entirely overshadowed by the reaction to the president's address at Queen's and especially to the foreign policy pronouncement which flashed round the world and quickly gave rise to a flurry of international comment and speculation.

What did President Roosevelt's address at Queen's mean? How were his words interpreted? What effect, if any, did the address have on the international situation? What were its consequences in North America and abroad? Some of these questions are less difficult to answer than others.

One thing is certain. Neither at Queen's University nor anywhere else did Franklin Roosevelt say anything which stopped Adolph Hitler, though this was, indeed, one of the objectives which the State Department had in mind for the speech at Queen's. A. A. Berle, Jr., and Assistant Secretary of State, who, with the help of his colleague, J. Pierrepont Moffat, prepared a preliminary draft of the speech, sent it along to the president with a covering memorandum. The memorandum outlined the larger context and purposes of the speech:

> The German Army [Berle wrote] is now partly mobilized and maneuvering in Bavaria within striking distance of the Czech frontier. We have to allow for the possibility that things may be on the way to a blow-up. I do not think so; and the Warsaw Embassy agrees, but other observers think the situation is worse than it was last May. The theory of the speech is an endeavor to create a certain amount of doubt abroad as to what our intentions may be. This, it is thought, may have a moderating effect.[48]

We know that Roosevelt also made a direct appeal to Hitler on 26 September, at the height of the Czechoslovakian crisis, and that Hitler subsequently agreed to a peaceful settlement of the Czech dispute at Munich. Most scholars are agreed, however, that the credit for this temporary reprieve from war belongs not to Franklin Roosevelt but to the frantic peregrinations of Neville Chamberlain, and even more to the intervention of Hitler's Italian lackey, Benito Mussolini, as a result of which "the German dictator," in Churchill's words, "instead of snatching his victuals from the table has been content to have them served to him course by course."[49] Judged by the test of deterring Hitler from the path of conquest, Roosevelt's address at Queen's, like the whole of Roosevelt's foreign policy, was a failure.

Was the address a success, then, from any other standpoint? The answer to this question must depend in part on how the address was interpreted in various quarters. Here we enter into a maze of conflicting interpretations which may be summarized by saying that many people placed upon it the particular construction which they most desired it to convey.

The dictators hoped it meant nothing and treated it accordingly. Hitler took no public notice of it, and semi-official commentary in Germany brushed it aside as election propaganda intended for domestic American consumption. The German press as a whole stressed that it extended the Monroe Doctrine to Canada against "imaginary dangers"; but some understood it as a policy of foreign intervention, and according to the Berlin correspondent of the *Montreal Gazette*, "the consensus of all private opinion is that this speech signs and seals American participation in any war in the near future on the side of the democracies."[50]

The Italians chose to sneer. The leading member of the Fascist party chain of newspapers referred to "the absurd pretence of teaching civilization to us, who had more than twenty centuries of history, when an Italian discovered America." "Against whom was the President proposing to defend Canada," asked another Italian paper, "polar bears?"[51]

The British and the French were naturally anxious to believe that it meant something positively helpful to their interests, and the speech received very wide publicity in the press of both countries. A broad spectrum of French newspapers took the speech as an acknowledgment by Roosevelt that the United States had come to the end of isolationism. They hailed it as evidence that the American people were taking a new interest in European affairs and could be counted on to side with the democracies when a choice had to be made. Most British newspapers made no attempt to conceal their satisfaction, but L. B. Pearson, of the Canadian High Commissioner's Office, who sent a batch of British clippings to O. D. Skelton, pointed out that "the well-informed ones are careful to remember the disillusionments of the past and surround their encomiums with a note of caution."[52] Certainly, British official reaction was cautious enough. When the subject was raised in the British House of Commons three months later, the prime minister's parliamentary secretary simply stated that "His Majesty's Government in the United Kingdom took note at the time of President Roosevelt's friendly reference on behalf of the United States of America to the Dominion which is their neighbour." When pressed to say whether the British Government heartily welcomed the president's statement, Mr. Butler had no further comment to make.[53]

Canadian reactions, as might be expected, were distinctly cordial but complex. Almost every Canadian newspaper had something to say about the speech, and, without exception, they were enthusiastic, but for significantly different reasons.[54] Leading French-Canadian papers welcomed it as an official statement of what they had always understood to be the case: that Canada was an American nation; that the Monroe Doctrine extended north as well as south; and, therefore, that the first line of Canadian defence was not the British Navy but the United States. Most English-Canadian newspapers were similarly gratified by the promise of American protection in war and by the further evidence of improving Canadian-American relations, but many of them went beyond that. Many were quick to emphasize that the president's assurance did not absolve the prologue to a new Anglo-American rapprochement. The *Winnipeg Free Press*, (20 August 1938), went the whole way:

> Without saying so directly, [Roosevelt] made it perfectly clear that there is a basic solidarity of interest between his country and Great Britain. The English-speaking democracies stand together. Herr Hitler, we hope, realized what was being said.

If this was, in fact, what was being said, it was heard very imperfectly in the department of External Affairs in Ottawa. The Under Secretary, dismissing the more euphoric comments in the British press as "wishful thinking," could not detect in the president's assurance any pledge of support for the European democracies in war. He interpreted the speech narrowly as applying to Canada – and to Canada alone. The sentence in the president's speech to which Dr. Skelton attached the greatest significance came after speaking of his country's hopes of contributing to the peace of the world, after which he said "even if those hopes are disappointed, we can assure each other that this hemisphere at least shall remain a strong citadel where civilization can flourish unimpaired."[55]

The prime minister, however, was closer to political realities, at least in Canada, than his principal adviser on foreign affairs. Speaking at Woodbridge, Ontario, two days after the Queen's Convocation, Mackenzie King instinctively reflected the dualities of Canadian opinion. He expressed warm appreciation of the president's direct assurance to Canada as "the words of a friendly people and neighbour," but he was quick to affirm that Canada had no intention of shirking her own defence responsibilities which, he suggested, had been increased rather than lessened by Roosevelt's assurance. "We, too, have our obligations as a good and friendly neighbour," King said,

> and one of them is to see that, at our own instance, our country is made as immune from attack or possible invasion as we can reasonably be expected to make it, and that, should the occasion ever arise, enemy forces should not be able to pursue their way, either by land, sea or air to the United States, across Canadian territory.

Beyond this, Canadian defence would be further secured, King added, by consultation and co-operation with other members of the British Commonwealth, the sisterhood to which the president had expressly referred.[56]

Back in the United States, where, as the president had said, public opinion in the long run determines policy, public reaction was generally favourable. Isolationists saw in it nothing more than an extension of the Monroe Doctrine to Canada, and endorsed this as a necessary step in the development of the defence system of the United States. Internationalists heralded the speech in more glowing terms as the long-awaited beginning of a policy of commitment to the side of European democracies. Politically, therefore, Roosevelt's speech, in thus straddling the principal division of American public opinion, was a domestic success.

It was a success because it was ambiguous, and, in the days that followed, the president never entirely removed that ambiguity. To reporters who met him on his return to Hyde Park, he said that he had not intended to "extend" the Monroe Doctrine to Canada, but he added that he considered no extension was necessary since he interpreted the doctrine as already including Canada. To Lord Tweedsmuir, he wrote: "What I said at Queen's University is so obvious that I cannot understand why some American president did not say it half a century ago. However, the occasion seemed to fit in with the Hitler situation and had, I hope, some small effect on Berlin."[57] The "Hitler situation" was clearly much on Roosevelt's mind, but so, too, in all probability, were the approaching mid-term elections in the United States which made it necessary to avoid inflaming isolationist opinion against his party. When, at a press conference on 9 September, the president was asked whether there was any justification for the growing impression, arising from recent statements by himself, Secretary Hall and the American Ambassador to France, that the United States was in some way allied with European democracies in a "stop-Hitler" movement involving a pledge of support in war, he is reported to have replied that, "if the interpreters would read the English language and no more in what he and the Secretary of State had had to say on the subject, they would discover that they had been a hundred percent wrong in their deductions."[58]

These disclaimers notwithstanding, a question lingers, at least in my mind, as to whether President Roosevelt intended his speech at Queen's, to do anything more than cement Canadian-American relations and to serve notice that a direct attack on Canada would be treated as an attack upon the United States. Was he also endeavoring, however cautiously, to lead his country toward a more distant horizon? This is the hardest question of all to answer with any confidence. Many of his friends and colleagues have noted that Franklin Roosevelt, "for all his apparent sociability, joviality and even frivolity, was essentially a reserved and self-sufficient figure," and that this reserve was evident in his conduct of foreign relations as well as in domestic politics. He kept himself well posted, and he consulted widely, but he did not confide freely, and he did not record his inner thoughts and purposes. It behooves any historian, therefore, to approach with extreme caution the question of what Roosevelt really intended in any important public pronouncement. Having conceded all this, I draw attention to two pieces of evidence from which one might infer that President Roosevelt, in his speech at Queen's, had a larger purpose in view.

The first piece of evidence is to be found in the words of the speech itself, and, in particular, the immediate context of the assurance so emphatically given. In the two famous sentences which Roosevelt inserted into his speech in his own hand, it is not Canada as a North American nation or Canada as a hemispheric partner, but Canada as "part of the sisterhood of the British Empire" to which the assurance of American support is given. Looking at the assurance in this context, I am disposed to agree, with B. K. Sandwell, who wrote at that time that,

> if this conjunction of statements means anything at all, it means that the British Empire is the only Old World authority with which the people of the United States feel that they can cooperate, to the extent of aiding one of its members who happens to be in the American hemisphere. "This is something more," Sandwell added, "than an extension of the Monroe Doctrine to Canada."[59]

What 'more' it may have been is suggested by a second piece of evidence. This is a conversation between Franklin Roosevelt and Mackenzie King as they drove from Kingston to the Thousand Islands Bridge on 18 August, and the developments which followed from that conversation.[79] According to King's account, the president hoped that the trade agreements between Great Britain and the United States could be concluded in September, and he invited Mackenzie King to Hyde Park for the signing of the Canadian agreement. King wondered if Prime Minister Chamberlain could come over for the signing of the Anglo-American agreement; doubt was expressed as to whether Chamberlain could get away, but Roosevelt made it clear that he would like it if Chamberlain could. Beyond this, the president left no doubt in Mackenzie King's mind that he was greatly concerned about the danger of war and about whether he could do anything to stop it. The most important thing that Mackenzie King had to tell Roosevelt was that he had just learned from Lord Tweedsmuir that King George and Queen Elizabeth would, in all probability, visit Canada in 1939. To this news Roosevelt immediately responded by saying he hoped that Their Majesties would also include the United States in their trip, suggesting Washington, the New York World's Fair and his own home at Hyde Park as three possible points of call.

The president's response was no idle, fleeting gesture. On 17 September 1938, Franklin Roosevelt initiated the first personal correspondence to be exchanged between a president of the United States and a British Sovereign: I need not assure you that it would give my wife and me the greatest pleasure to see you," he wrote to George VI, "and, frankly, I think it would be an excellent thing for Anglo-American relations if you could visit the United States..."[60]

Mackenzie King, for his part, promptly sent off to the governor general a long and enthusiastic account of the events of 18 August, and especially of his latest talk with Roosevelt, and in October, King drafted a personal message to Neville Chamberlain, urging him to come to the United States for the signing of the Anglo-American trade agreement. "The impression upon Europe of such a visit," King wrote, combined with that of their Majesties to this side, next year, would be very great indeed," and he went on to emphasize "the effect, at this time upon the world of the evident friendship between Great Britain and America. Do come.[61]

Neville Chamberlain never came, but the King and Queen did, and in the summer of 1939, the Royal pair "completely won the hearts of the whole North American continent." "In Canada, the presence of the British Sovereign, for the first time in history, was a living symbol of the reality of the British Commonwealth," and that presence, made manifest throughout the land in such a universally appealing form, greatly fortified the unity of Canadians for the trials which then lay just ahead.[62] In the United States where, as with Mackenzie King in Canada, every detail of the Royal Tour received the personal attention of Franklin Roosevelt, the first visit of reigning British Sovereigns was a fantastic success. Everywhere they went, the King and Queen were received with a degree of spontaneous warmth and enthusiasm which exceeded the highest expectations—even those of the president.[63] By the time that "radiantly magnificent interlude" was over, it was plain that some ancient American animosities had been removed and that between the United States and Great Britain, a new era of good feeling was opening.

From these pieces of evidence I draw, somewhat tentatively, certain inferences about the intent of President Roosevelt's speech at Queen's and about its significance in his mind. Specifically, I infer that, just as Mackenzie King liked to think of Canada as a link between Great Britain and the United States, Franklin Roosevelt was beginning, at least by 1938, to think of Canada, not only as a good neighbour and an essential outpost of American defence, but as a stepping-stone to the larger world of the British Commonwealth and Europe. Viewed in this light, Present Roosevelt's assurance of 18 August 1938 was not simply a step on the road to Ogdensburg – the Canadian-American defence agreement which was consummated two years later to the day; it was a step on the long and painful and much more important road back to Europe, back to a mature and responsible American foreign policy which the people of the United States had forsaken, so dramatically and so tragically in 1920.

In 1938 the road back, for the American people, was still long. Canada went to war in 1939 but the United States did not. Not until the German *Blitzkrieg* did Franklin Roosevelt find in Winston Churchill his seminal transatlantic partner; and not until Pearl Harbor was the journey finally completed. In the sequence of these momentous events, the visit of Franklin Roosevelt to Kingston in August 1938 may be assigned a small but not insignificant part; and to Queen's University, on that occasion, a place not unworthy of the ideals of its definitive principal, George Munro Grant, for the university and the country which he cherished.

Notes

I wish to express my warm appreciation to Mrs. Diana Jennings for her excellent assistance in research for this paper. I also acknowledge with grateful thanks the financial aid which I have received from the Interim Research Committee of Queen's University.

1. *Kingston Whig Standard*, 4 January 1938.
2. Ibid., 10 January 1938; 9 April 1938.
3. Ibid., 15 March 1938.
4. Ibid., 8 January 1938
5. Ibid., 12 February 1938; 7 March 1938.
6. Ibid., 8 March 1938; 12 March 1938.
7. Ibid., 4 February 1938; 2 March 1938.
8. Ibid., 15 March 1938.
9. Ibid., 30 July 1938; 2 August 1938.
10. Information in this paragraph is based upon personal interviews of the author with Messrs Grant Mitchell and George Fulford.
11. The Minutes of Queen's Senate for 6 September 1938 record that Principal Wallace, in referring to the special convocation of 18 August for President Roosevelt, stated that "the University is indebted to Professor Humphrey for having suggested that the Degree be given and to Dr. McNeill for the splendid management of the convocation."
12. Queen's University, *Senate Minutes*, 25 March 1938.
13. Public Archives of Canada. Dept. of External Affairs Central Registry File 359, Robt. C. Wallace to O.D. Skelton, 26 March 1938.
14. *Mike, The Memoirs of the Right Honourable Lester B. Pearson,* (Toronto: University of Toronto Press, 1972) I, 70.
15. Franklin D. Roosevelt Archives at Hyde Park, Franklin D. Roosevelt Papers, PSF 25, Norman Armour to William Phillips, 22 October 1935, enclosed in Phillips to F.D.R., 7 November 1935.
16. Janet Adam Smith, *John Buchan: A Biography*.(London: Rupert Hart Davis, 1965) pp/420-451.
17. The approaches from Canada were welcome, and by the spring of 1936 Roosevelt was telling Mackenzie King that "it will be a good thing for both countries if governors general, premiers and presidents can, in the days to come, 'drop in and visit' with each other without making such visits the occasion of extraordinary comment." Franklin D. Roosevelt Papers, PSF 25, Canada, F.D.R. to W.L.M.K., 16 April 1937.
18. Franklin D. Roosevelt Papers, PSF Canada, W.L.M.K. to F.D.R. 8, 9 March 1937; Lord Tweedsmuir to F.D.R., 8 April 1937.
19. PAC, External Affairs Central Registry, File 359, O.D. Skelton to R.C. Wallace, 5 April 1938.

20. *Ibid.*, O.D.S. to W.A. Riddell, 5 April 1938.
21. Franklin D. Roosevelt Papers, PPF 5448, F.D.R. to Sumner Welles, 16 April 1938.
22. PAC, External Affairs Central Registry, File 359, Sumner Welles to Sir Herbert Marler, 23 April 1938; O.D. Skelton to R.C. Wallace, 26 April 1938; R.C.W. to O.D.S., 29 April 1938; Mackenzie King Papers, O.D.S. to W.L.M.K. 26 April 1938.
23. Franklin D. Roosevelt Papers, 200-DDD, Kanmee to Stephen Early, 15 April 1938.
24. *Ibid.*, Grant Mitchell to F.D.R., 18, 31 May 1938.
25. Franklin D. Roosevelt Papers, PSF Canada, F.D.R. to Lord Tweedsmuir, 12 May 1938.
26. *Ibid.*, Lord Tweedsmuir to F.D.R., 25 May 1938.
27. Franklin D. Roosevelt papers, 200-DDD, Marvin McIntyre to George T. Summerlin, 1 June 1938; Kanmee to McIntyre, 10 June 1938, with enclosures; PSF Canada, F.D.R. to George T. Summerlin, 3 June 1938, with enclosures.
28. William L. Langer, S. Everett Gleason, *The Challenge to Isolation: The World Crisis of 1937 – 1940 and American Foreign Policy*, (New York: Harper, 1964) I, 36.
29. W.L. Mackenzie King, "Principles Underlying Peace", an address at a luncheon in honour of Cordell Hull, 22 October. 1937. Franklin D. Roosevelt Papers, PSF Canada, Lord Tweedsmuir to F.D.R., 8 October 1938; Tweedsmuir told Roosevelt that it was "the bravest and most important utterance by any public man for many a day." Langer & Gleason, *op. cit.*, p. 19.
30. *Ibid.*, pp. 19-31; Winston S. Churchill, *The Gathering Storm*, (London: Cassel, Toronto: Allen, 1948) p. 254.
31. James MacGregor Burns, *Roosevelt: The Lion and the Fox*, (New York: Harcourt, Brace, 1956) p. 385.
32. C.P. Stacey, *Arms, Men and Governments: The War Policies of Canada*, 1939-1945 (Ottawa: Queen's Printer, 1970), pp. 96-97.
33. Mackenzie King Papers, F.D.R. to W.L.M.K., 21 December 1937.
34. PAC, External Affairs Central Registry, File 359, Sir Herbert Marler to O.D. Skelton, 8 July 1938; W.A. Riddell to O.D.S., 14 July 1938.
35. *Ibid.*, W.E. McNeill to O.D. Skelton, 19 July 1938; the Richardson Archives, Winnipeg, R.C. Wallace to James A. Richardson, 20 July 1938.
36. Lord Tweedsmuir had gone to Britain early in July to be installed in the Chancellorship of Edinburgh University and to undergo a physical examination. His London physician placed him in a clinic in Wales where he had to stay until mid-September, See Janet Adam Smith, *op.cit.* pp. 449-50.
37. Mackenzie King Papers, George Fulford to W.L.M.K., 25 July 1938. Lt. Governor Matthews was understood to represent the province of

Ontario as well as the Crown because Premier Mitchell Hepburn declined to attend either ceremony.
38. Mackenzie King Papers, Notes and Memoranda, 1933-39, Hector Allard to W. E. McNeill, 2 Aug. 1938, and Laurent Beaudry to W.E.M., 4 August 1938; Queen's University Archives, R.C. Wallace papers, W.E. McNeill to Wallace, 4 August 1938.
39. PAC, External Affairs Central Registry, File 359, W.E. McNeill to Howard Measures, 11 August 1938, and O.D. Skelton to Sir Herbert Marler, 13 August 1938; Mackenzie King Papers, O.D. Skelton to W. L. M. K., 13 August 1938.
40. Mackenzie King Diary, 18 August 1938.
41. *Ibid.*
42. Kingston *Whig-Standard*, 18 August 1938.
43. Toronto *Globe and Mail*, 19 August 1938.
44. *Ibid.*
45. Mackenzie King Diary, 18 August 1938.
46. Franklin D. Roosevelt Papers, PPF 5448, R.C. Wallace to F.D.R., 11 October 1938, with enclosures.
47. The complete text of Roosevelt's address was published in the *Queen's Review*, vol. XII, no. 7 (October 1938), pp. 197-199.
48. Franklin D. Roosevelt Papers, PSF Berle, A. A. Berle, Jr., to F. D. R., memorandum of 15 Aug. 1938, with enclosure. Across the top of Berle's memorandum Roosevelt penciled "Temperature Europe vs Here." Harvard University Library, J. Pierrepont Moffat Papers, Moffat Journal, 12-15 August 1938.
49. Great Britain, House of Commons Debates, 6 October 1938, John w. Wheeler-Bennett, *King George VI: His Life and Reign*, (London: Macmillan, 1958) p. 373. f.n.a.
50. *Montreal Gazette*, 20 August 1938. Mackenzie King Papers Phillipe Roy to W.L.M.K., 19 August 1938, Despatch No. 285.
51. Bologna *Resto Del Cortino*, as cited in *Montreal Gazette*, 20 August 1938; *La Tribuna*, as cited in Phillipe Roy to W.L.M.K., Despatch 285.
52. PAC, External Affairs Central Registry, File 359, L.B. Pearson to O.D. Skelton, 2 September 1938.
53. Great Britain, *House of Commons Debates*, 16 November 1938, Col 844.
54. *Montreal La Presse*, 19 August 1938; *Le Devoir*, 19 August 1938.
55. PAC, External Affairs Central Registry, File 359, O.D. Skelton to L.B. Pearson, 21 September 1938; Mackenzie King Papers, O.D.S. to W. L.M.K., 13 September 1938.
56. *Montreal Gazette*, 22 August 1938, text of Mackenzie King's speech at Woodbridge. It was presumably a growing sense of the threefold

nature of the Canadian defence system which prompted King to make the excessively comfortable reflection in his diary, 20 August 1938: "I think at last we have got our defence programme in good shape. Good neighbour on one side; partners with the Empire on the other. Obligations to both in return for their assistance. Readiness to meet all joint emergencies." Six months later the estimates of the Canadian Department of National Defence were raised to nearly $65,000,000, a figure almost double that of the previous fiscal year. See C.P. Stacey, *op.cit.* p.4.
57. Franklin D. Roosevelt Papers, PPF 3396, F.D.R. to Lord Tweedsmuir, 31 August 1938.
58. *New York Times*, 10 September 1938; Mackenzie King Papers, Sir Herbert Marler to W.L.M.K., Despatch No. 1253, 22 September 1938. Marler stressed the fact that isolation had not lost ground among the rank and file in the US.
59. Toronto *Saturday Night*, 27 August 1938.
60. Royal Archives, George VI, Private papers, Box 3, President Roosevelt to King George VI, 17 September 1938, as cited in John W. Wheeler-Bennett *op.cit.* p. 372.
61. Mackenzie King Papers, W.L.M.K., to Lord Tweedsmuir, 25 August 1938; W.L.M.K., to Neville Chamberlain, pp. 214266-7 (undated).
62. Wheeler-Bennett, *op. cit.*, p. 379.
63. *Ibid.*, pp. 381-394. "My husband invited them to Washington," Eleanor Roosevelt wrote, "largely because, believing that we might all soon be engaged in a life and death struggle, in which Great Britain would be our first line of defence, he hoped that the visit would create a bond of friendship between the two countries. He knew that, although there was always in this country a certain amount of criticism and superficial ill-feeling toward the British, in time of danger something deeper comes to the surface, and the British and we stand firmly together, with confidence in our common heritage and ideas. The visit of the King and Queen, he hoped, would be a reminder of this deep bond. In many ways it proved even more successful than he had expected." Eleanor Roosevelt, *This I Remember*, (New York: Harper, 1949) pp. 183-4.

Chapter 2

A Speech for the Ages

DAVID MITCHELL
President, Public Policy Forum

> It is impossible not to remember that for years when Canadians and Americans have met, they have lightheartedly saluted as North American friends with little thought of dangers from overseas.

These words, spoken by an American president being honoured by a Canadian university, could have been uttered in the recent past, by President George W. Bush–or perhaps in the future by President Barack Obama. They were, however, part of an important address 70 years ago at Queen's University by arguably the greatest US president of the 20th century, Franklin Delano Roosevelt. His words seem as relevant now, during a time of heightened fears over security in a world shaken by threats and acts of terror, as then.

To place FDR's words in context, in August of 1938, war clouds were darkening in seemingly far-off Europe. Memories still lingered of the many thousands of soldiers both Canada and the United States had left behind on the killing fields of France and Belgium only a generation earlier.

The president's visit to Canada, to receive an honourary degree from Queen's and to open the International Bridge at nearby Clayton, NY, coincided with growing diplomatic and political concerns abroad and a fervently determined isolationism in North America. These conflicting pressures seemed to be on the president's mind as he delivered his address to his Canadian friends:

> Yet we are awake to the knowledge that the casual assumption of our greetings in earlier times, today must be a matter for serious thought ... We in the Americas are no longer a faraway continent, to which eddies of controversies beyond the seas could bring no interest or no harm. Instead, we in the Americas have become a consideration for every propaganda office and every general staff beyond the seas. The vast amount of our resources, the vigour of our commerce and the strength of our men have made us vital factors in world peace whether we choose it or not.

On that lovely summer morning in Kingston, FDR, in retrospect, was prescient. The infamous Munich Pact would be signed the following month. The US president appeared to be bracing both himself and his audience for what loomed on the horizon. His message included a stirring homage to the constructive relationship that existed between Canada and the US:

> We as good neighbours are true friends because we maintain our own rights with frankness, because we refuse to accept the twists of secret diplomacy, because we settle our disputes by consultation and because we discuss our common problems in the spirit of the common good.

Roosevelt was as popular among Canadians of his time as he was among his own citizens, who would re-elect him to unprecedented third and fourth terms. His brief visit in the summer of 1938 represented a major event in Canada-US relations. He concluded his remarks at Queen's by saying:

> [It has been] suggested that we cultivate three qualities to keep our foothold in the shifting sands of the present – humility, humanity and humour. I have been thinking in terms of a bridge which is to be dedicated this afternoon and so I could not help coming to the conclusion that all of these three qualities, imbedded in education, build new spans to re-establish free intercourse throughout the world and bring forth an order in which free nations can live in peace.

While the humour may not have been evident, it was a speech for the ages, on the eve of a world about to be turned upside down by a global conflagration. And perhaps it is useful to remember FDR's message from that moment of relative tranquility 70 years ago; even in our apparent security and comfort in North America, we obviously cannot pretend to be immune from the forces gripping the rest of humankind.

Chapter 3

The Birth of an Alliance

JORDAN PRESS
Kingston Whig-Standard, 16 August 2008

For Sheila Woodsworth, many things remain vivid of the August day in 1938 when an American president came to Kingston. The daughter of then Queen's University Principal Robert Charles Wallace recalls watching Franklin Delano Roosevelt being driven in an open car. She remembers how much help the frail president required just to stand.

Seventy years on, there's no forgetting the electricity of the crowd. Little did Woodsworth – or the thousands of others who jammed George Richardson Memorial Stadium that day – suspect they would hear a speech that would change the course of history. "I give to you assurance that the people of the United States will not stand idly by if domination of Canadian soil is threatened by any other Empire," Roosevelt said that day. Woodsworth remembers that, too:

> The United States *will-not-stand eyed-lee by*," she says, mimicking Roosevelt's accent with accuracy that has not faded through the years, "if domination of Canadian soil is threatened by any *ah-tha emp-eye-ah* ... We weren't used to that accent.

Prime Minister Mackenzie King reciprocated the president's pledge a few days later and an alliance was born. "It really was an important moment, not just in the context of the late 1930s, but also right down to the present," says David Haglund, an expert on Canada-US relations from Queen's University. The two statements, Haglund says, "still constitute the spine of the US-Canadian defence relationship." It was a dramatic change in US foreign policy which, until that time, had been one of isolationism. Any foreign policy interests, when it came to defence, had more to do with ensuring European countries didn't interfere with Latin America than they did with Canada. "It is one of his big speeches," says Geoff Smith, a retired Queen's history professor who specializes in American history. Looking back, the president's words appear to have worked. Canada and the US became allies. Isolationism eventually crumbled in the US and Roosevelt brought his country into a new world. "It's the kind of speech that looks better with the passage of time," Smith notes.

McRae, a student usher at the event, remembers every moment. "Every seat was full; the place was packed," she says. "I remember the special lectern they had to build with special armrests to keep [Roosevelt] standing," recalls the 90-year-old McRae.

Roosevelt's car pulled up to a special platform built in front of the centre bleachers. Roosevelt's powerful shoulders loomed from the vehicle. "He was a powerful-looking man and he conveyed confidence," recalls Margaret Gibson, who was a 14-year-old usher at the convocation. "We were all startled to see how he had to be lifted out of the car by two strong men." It was among the first public signs of Roosevelt's polio, something that had been largely hidden from public view. The president's declining strength showed in another way during the ceremony; after the opening remarks, everyone in the bleachers sat down but Roosevelt stayed standing because it was difficult for him to stand up and sit down.

Principal Wallace talked, in his speech, about how Kingston was where loyalists came after the American Revolution and how it was here that fortifications were built to thwart American attacks. "Today," he said,

> in a gesture of friendship which it is fitting for a university to make, Queen's University honours the head of a great people with whom Canada is weaving bonds of peace not to be broken asunder with the passing of the years.

Roosevelt received his degree and had a black silk hood, bordered with blue, wrapped around his shoulders. He signed the Doomsday Book, a record of the university's notable events dating to 1887, and quipped quietly to McNeill: "I am going to do what I very seldom do; I will write my name in full." Then came the moment for which everyone had waited. "A momentary hush fell over the audience," the *Whig-Standard* reported,

> ... as the president composed himself at the speaker's stand, which bristled with microphones. Crack newspapermen from all parts of the continent, seated at desks in front of the speaker's rostrum, prepared to record the president's words and interpret the significance of the event for the people of two nations. Press photographers snapped pictures of the scene from every conceivable angle.

Roosevelt's voice, with its mixture of upstate New York and Harvard University hues, slowly began to fill the stadium. He complimented Queen's and Canada, slowly enunciating every syllable of every word. "An American president, as many of you are aware," Roosevelt said,

> is precluded by our Constitution from accepting any title from a foreign prince, potentate or power. Queen's University is not a prince or a potentate, but, assuredly, it is a power. Yet, in spite of

that, I can say, without constitutional reserve, that the acceptance of the title which you confer on me today would raise no qualms in the August breast of our own Supreme Court.

Applause followed almost every thought the president uttered. With the pleasantries done, Roosevelt started into the thrust of his speech. It was a speech aimed at Hitler. "Thoughts and ideas," Roosevelt said, "are not limited by territorial borders; they are the common inheritance of all free people." And yet, Roosevelt said, that idea was being challenged in other parts of the world.

In a large sense, we in the Americas stand charged today with the maintaining of that tradition. Many of us here today know from experience that of all the devastations of war, none is more tragic than the destruction which it brings to the processes of men's minds. Truth is denied because emotion pushes it aside. Forbearance is succeeded by bitterness and, in that atmosphere, human thought cannot advance.

Up until this point, Roosevelt's voice, while powerful, had remained relatively calm. His regal tone had not become emotionally charged. That changed as he climbed to the climax of his speech.

We in the Americas are no longer a far away continent, to which the eddies of controversies beyond the seas could bring no interest or no harm.... The vast amount of our resources, the vigour of our commerce and the strength of our men have made us vital factors in world peace, whether we choose it or not. (pause) Even if those hopes [for world peace] are disappointed, we can assure each other that this hemisphere at least shall remain a strong citadel wherein civilization can flourish unimpaired.

The crowd cheered. Roosevelt cleared his throat. His voice began to rise.

The Dominion of Canada is part of the sisterhood of the British Empire. I give to you assurance that the people of the United States will not stand idly by if domination of Canadian soil is threatened by any other Empire.

Roosevelt spoke emphatically, his voice booming louder than the applause that followed. The remainder of his speech, about six minutes' worth, refocused on the theme of free thought, free speech and peace, but the two sentences he wanted the world to hear echoed as large as his voice did that morning at Richardson stadium. In Kingston, the reaction was shock and excitement at Roosevelt's declaration. "War was in the air," McRae says. "I realized the importance of it. We were dazed by it at first but excited to hear it ... to think we had that support if war broke."

The day after the speech at Queen's, Roosevelt told reporters at his home in Hyde Park, NY, that the speech wasn't an extension of the Monroe Doctrine. Today, historians side with Roosevelt about what he was trying to do with the Kingston speech. "I don't think it's an extension of the Monroe Doctrine at all. He's talking about western hemisphere security," Geoff Smith of Queen's says. "That's absolutely not neutral." Smith adds that Roosevelt knew US isolationism couldn't continue. "The president was far ahead of public opinion, some would say far too much ahead, but he believed it was right."

In 1938, it wasn't the political impact that left a lasting impression on the trio of young women in Kingston – Woodsworth, Gibson and McRae – it was Roosevelt's voice, which still resonates in their minds and memories. "It was so impressive," McRae says. "It just echoed across the stadium and there was an absolute uproar."

Editor's note:

This is an edited version of a piece that appeared in the 16 August 2008 edition of the *Kingston Whig-Standard*, part of the newspaper's impressive efforts to mark the 70th anniversary of FDR's visit to Queen's University.

Chapter 4

Canada and the United States need a leader like FDR

ARTHUR MILNES
Watertown Daily Times, 14 October 2008

Our grandparents' generation both survived a Great Depression and fought a war. In comparison, our own struggles today might seem minor. But for many in Canada and the United States, one hopes our elders will forgive our fears due to the market collapse of the last few weeks. Our pensions, Registered Retirement Savings Plans and so much more are under threat when the New York Stock Exchange drops more than $1 trillion dollars in a day, and the S&P/TSX (Toronto Stock Exchange) composite index plunges more than 800 points. The headlines are stark and the reports are only getting worse. We are on the verge of crisis.

If our neighbors in Washington don't soon put partisanship aside and work together, we could experience the sort of depression that hasn't been visited upon North Americans since those Dirty Thirties suffered by our grandparents. But more to the point is the fact that Canadians are without what our grandparents had to guide them in their time: a leader with the qualities of Franklin Roosevelt. "We are stricken by no plague of locusts," he said from the steps of the U.S. Capitol Building in his famous first Inaugural Address in March of 1933:

> Compared with the perils which our forefathers conquered because they believed and were not afraid, we have still much to be thankful for. Nature still offers her bounty and human efforts have multiplied it. Plenty is at our doorstep, but a generous use of it languishes in the very sight of the supply. Primarily this is because the rulers of the exchange of mankind's goods have failed, through their own stubbornness and their own incompetence, have admitted their failure, and abdicated. Practices of the unscrupulous money changers stand indicted in the court of public opinion, rejected by the hearts and minds of men.

Americans and Canadians gathered around their radios as the new president continued. Like him, they knew full well that the barons of Wall Street in whom they had put their faith had let them down.

"Faced by failure of credit they have proposed only the lending of more money," FDR continued:

> Stripped of the lure of profit by which to induce our people to follow their false leadership, they have resorted to exhortations, pleading tearfully for restored confidence. They know only the rules of a generation of self-seekers. They have no vision, and when there is no vision the people perish.

"The money changers have fled from their high seats in the temple of our civilization," Roosevelt's patrician voice announced that da:

> We may now restore that temple to the ancient truths. The measure of the restoration lies in the extent to which we apply social values more noble than mere monetary profit. Happiness lies not in the mere possession of money; it lies in the joy of achievement, in the thrill of creative effort. The joy and moral stimulation of work no longer must be forgotten in the mad chase of evanescent profits. These dark days will be worth all they cost us if they teach us that our true destiny is not to be ministered unto but to minister to ourselves and to our fellow men.

FDR launched the New Deal which changed his country, and ours, for what we thought was forever. Government proved indeed to be part of the solution, and so the economy, led by Roosevelt, moved forward.

Our grandparents, tested by the Great Depression and then a world war, had learned the hard way that business and the markets could never again be left to their own devices. Thus in Canada, for example, it was those who experienced the Great Depression in both Progressive Conservative, CCF (Cooperative Commonwealth Federation) and Liberal cabinets in Ottawa and provincial capitals that, memories fresh, created Medicare, pensions and regulated the "money changers" abhorred by FDR.

In our untested generation, as is painfully obvious this election season, we moved the other way. Were Roosevelt in Washington today he'd know what to do. We can only hope the new president and his counterpart in Ottawa will as well.

Chapter 5

President Franklin D. Roosevelt's Convocation Address, Queen's University
18 August 1938

My newfound Associates of Queens University, To the pleasure of being once more on Canadian soil where I have passed so many happy hours of my life, there is added today a very warm sense of gratitude for being admitted to the fellowship of this ancient and famous university. I am glad to join the brotherhood which Queen's has contributed and is contributing not only to the spiritual leadership for which the college was established, but also to the social and public leadership in the civilized life of Canada.

An American president is precluded by our Constitution from accepting any title from a foreign prince, potentate or power. Queen's University is not a prince or a potentate but, assuredly, it is a power. Yet I can say, without constitutional reserve, that the acceptance of the title which you confer on me today would raise no qualms in the August breast of our own Supreme Court.

Civilization, after all, is not national – it is international – even though that observation, trite as it is to most of us, seems to be challenged in some parts of the world today. Ideas are not limited by territorial borders; they are the common inheritance of all free people. Thought is not anchored in any land, and the profit of education redounds to the equal benefit of the whole world. That is one form of free trade to which the leaders of every opposing political party can subscribe.

In a large sense we in the Americas stand charged today with the maintaining of that tradition. When, speaking a little over a year ago in a similar vein in the Republic of Brazil, I included the Dominion of Canada in the fellowship of the Americas, our South American neighbours gave hearty acclaim. We in all the Americas know the sorrow and the wreckage which may follow if the ability of men to understand each other is rooted out from among the nations.

Many of us here today know from experience that of all the devastations of war, none is more tragic than the destruction which it brings to the processes of men's minds. Truth is denied because emotion pushes it aside. Forbearance is succeeded by bitterness. In that atmosphere, human thought cannot advance.

It is impossible not to remember that for years when Canadians and Americans have met, they have lightheartedly saluted as North American friends with little thought of dangers from overseas. Yet we are awake to the knowledge that the casual assumption of our greetings in earlier times today must become a matter for serious thought.

A few days ago a whisper, fortunately untrue, raced 'round the world that armies standing over against each other in unhappy array were about to be set in motion. In a few short hours, the effect of that whisper had been registered in Montreal and New York, in Ottawa and in Washington, in Toronto and in Chicago, in Vancouver and in San Francisco. Your business men and ours felt it alike; your farmers and ours heard it alike; your young men and ours wondered what effect this might have on their lives.

We in the Americas are no longer a far away continent, to which the eddies of controversies beyond the seas could bring no interest or no harm. Instead, we in the Americas have become a consideration to every propaganda office and to every general staff beyond the seas. The vast amount of our resources, the vigour of our commerce and the strength of our men have made us vital factors in world peace, whether we choose it or not.

Happily, you and we, in friendship and in entire understanding, can look clear-eyed at these possibilities, resolving to leave no pathway unexplored, no technique undeveloped which may, if our hopes are realized, contribute to the peace of the world. Even if those hopes are disappointed, we can assure each other that this hemisphere at least shall remain a strong citadel wherein civilization can flourish unimpaired.

The Dominion of Canada is part of the sisterhood of the British Empire. I give to you assurance that the people of the United States will not stand idly by if domination of Canadian soil is threatened by any other Empire.

We as good neighbours are true friends, because we maintain our own rights with frankness, because we refuse to accept the twists of secret diplomacy, because we settle our disputes by consultation and because we discuss our common problems in the spirit of the common good. We seek to be scrupulously fair and helpful, not only in our relations with each other, but each of us at home in our relations with our own people.

But there is one process which we certainly cannot change and probably ought not to change. This is the feeling which ordinary men and women have about events which they can understand. We cannot prevent our people on either side of the border from having an opinion in regard to wanton brutality, in regard to undemocratic regimentation, in regard to misery inflicted on helpless peoples, or in regard to violations of accepted individual rights. All that any government, constituted as is yours and mine, can possibly undertake is to help make sure that the facts are known and fairly stated. No country where thought is free can prevent every fireside and home within its borders from considering the evidence for itself and rendering its own verdict; the sum total of these conclusions of educated men and women will, in the long run, rightly become the national verdict.

That is what we mean when we say that public opinion ultimately governs policy. It is right and just that this should be the case.

Many of our ancestors, your ancestors and mine, (and, by the way, I have loyalist blood in my veins too), came to Canada and the United States because they wished to break away from systems which forbade them to think freely. Their descendants have insisted on the right to know the truth – to argue their problems to a majority decision, and, if they remained unconvinced, to disagree in peace. As a tribute to our likeness in that respect, I note that the Bill of Rights, in your country and in mine, is substantially the same.

Mr. Chancellor, you of Canada who respect the educational tradition of our democratic continent will ever maintain good neighbourship in ideas, as we in the public service hope and propose to maintain it in the field of government and of foreign relations. My good friend, the Governor General of Canada, in receiving an honourary degree in June at that university at Cambridge, Massachusetts, to which Mackenzie King and I both belong, suggested that we cultivate three qualities to keep our foothold in the shifting sands of the present – humility, humanity and humor. I have been thinking in terms of a bridge which is to be dedicated this afternoon, and so I could not help coming to the conclusion that all of these three qualities, imbedded in education, build new spans to re-establish free intercourse throughout the world and bring forth an order in which free nations can live in peace.

Chapter 6

President Franklin D. Roosevelt, Remarks upon the opening of the Thousand Islands Bridge
Clayton, New York
18 August 1938

My fellow bridge builder, Mr. Mackenzie King, and you who are here today representing millions of other bridge builders on both sides of the international line; it has always seemed to me that the best symbol of common sense was a bridge. Common sense is sometimes slow in getting into action, and perhaps that is why we took so long to build this one.

It is a particular pleasure to me to meet you here, where a boundary is a gateway and not a wall. Between these islands an international gap, never wide, has been spanned, as gaps usually are, by the exercise of ability, guided by cooperative common sense. I hope that all my countrymen will use it freely. I know that they will find, as I have done today and on many other occasions, a happy welcome on the Canadian shore, and forthright fellowship with neighbours who are also friends.

The St. Lawrence River is more than a cartographic line between our two countries. God so formed North America that the waters of an inland empire drain into the Great Lakes Basin. The rain that falls in this vast area finds outlet through this single natural funnel, close to which we now stand.

Events of history have made that river a boundary, and as a result the flow of these waters can be used only by joint agreement between our two governments. Between us, therefore, we stand as trustees for two countries of one of the richest natural assets provided anywhere in the world. The water that runs underneath this bridge spells unlimited power, permits access to raw materials both from this continent and from beyond the seas, and enhances commerce and production.

When a resource of this kind is placed at our very doors, I think the plain people of both countries agree that it is ordinary common sense to make use of it. Yet up to now the liquid wealth, which flowing water is, has run in large part unused to the sea. I really think that this situation suggests that we can agree upon some better arrangement than merely letting this water contribute a microscopic fraction to the level of the North Atlantic Ocean. The bridge which we here dedicate is a tangible proof that administration by two neighbours of a job to be done in common offers no difficulty. Obviously the same process applied on the larger scale to the resource of full sea-going navigation and of complete power development offered by the St. Lawrence River can build and maintain the necessary facilities to employ its magnificent possibilities.

I suppose it is true, as it has been true of all natural resources, that a good many people would like to have the job – and the profits – of developing it for themselves. In this case, however, the river happens to be placed in the hands of our two governments, and the responsibility for getting the results lies plainly at our doors.

At various times, both the people of Canada and the people of the United States have dreamed of the St. Lawrence and Great Lakes development. They have translated those ideas into plans which, with modern engineering skill, can easily be carried out. While there has been no difference between us as to the object itself, history compels me to say that we have not been able to arrange matters so that both peoples have had the same idea at the same time. I offer a suggestion. How would it do for a change, if, instead of each of us having the idea at alternate intervals, we should get the idea simultaneously? And I am very much inclined to believe that we are rapidly approaching that happy and desirable event.

There are many prophets of evil. There always have been, before anything was done. I am very clear that prophets of trouble are wrong when they express the fear that the St. Lawrence Waterway will handicap our railroad systems on both sides of the border. We know now that the effect of a waterway in most cases is not to take traffic away from railroad lines. Actually, it creates new possibilities, new business and new activity. Such a waterway generates more railroad traffic than it takes away.

There is today, a 14-foot channel carrying traffic from the Great Lakes through the St. Lawrence River into the Atlantic Ocean. If this channel were improved and deepened to 27 or 30 feet, every city in both nations on the Great Lakes, and on the whole course of navigation from the sea to the lakes, would become an ocean port. The banks of the St. Lawrence Valley would become one of the great gateways of the world, and would benefit accordingly. Here, all that is needed is cooperative exercise of technical skill by joint use of the imagination and the vision which we know both our countries have. Can anyone doubt that, when this is done, the interests of both countries will be greatly advanced? Do we need to delay? Do we need to deprive our peoples of the immediate employment and profit, or prevent our generation from reaping the harvest that awaits us?

Now let me make an unusual statement. I am sure that on neither side of the line will you misunderstand me. I consider that I have, myself, a particular interest in the St. Lawrence, dating back to my earliest days in the Legislature of the State of New York in 1911. I have a particular duty as president in connection with the development of the St. Lawrence, both for navigation and for power. The almost unparalleled opportunity which the river affords has not gone unnoticed by some of my friends on the American side of the border. A conception has been emerging in the United States which is not without a certain magnificence. This is no less than the conviction that if a private group could control the outlet of the Great Lakes Basin on both sides of the border, that group would have a monopoly in the development of a territory larger than many of the great empires in history.

If you were to search the records with which my government is familiar, you would discover that literally every development of electric power, save only the Ontario-Hydro, is allied to, if not controlled by, a single American group, with, of course, the usual surrounding penumbra of allies, affiliates, subsidiaries and satellites. In earlier stages of development of natural resources on this continent, this was normal and usual. In recent decades we have come to realize the implications to the public: to the individual men and women, to business men, big and little, and even to government itself, resulting from the ownership by any group of the right to dispose of wealth which was granted to us collectively by nature herself.

The development of natural resources, and the proper handling of their fruits, is a major problem of government. Naturally, no solution would be acceptable to either nation which does not leave its government entirely master in its own house.

To put it bluntly, a group of American interests is here gradually putting itself into a position where, unless caution is exercised, they may in time be able to determine the economic and the social fate of a large area, both in Canada and the United States.

Now it is axiomatic in Canadian-American relations that both of us scrupulously respect the right of each of us to determine its own affairs. For that reason, when I know that the operation of uncontrolled American economic forces is slowly producing a result on the Canadian side of the border, which I know very well must eventually give American groups a great influence over Canadian development, I consider it the part of a good neighbour to discuss the question frankly with my Canadian neighbours. The least I can do is to call attention to the situation as I see it.

Our mutual friendship suggests this course in a matter of development as great and as crucial as that of the St. Lawrence River and the basin tributary to it. Fortunately, among friendly nations today, this is increasingly being done. Frank discussion among friends and neighbours is useful and essential. It is obvious today that some economic problems are international, if only because of the sheer weight which the solutions have on the lives of people outside, as well as inside any one country. To my mind, the development of St. Lawrence navigation and power is such a problem.

I look forward to the day when a Canadian prime minister and an American president can meet to dedicate, not a bridge across this water, but the very water itself, to the lasting and productive use of their respective peoples. Until that day comes, and I hope it may be soon, this bridge stands as an open door. There will be no challenge at the border and no guard to ask a countersign. Where the boundary is crossed the only words must be, "Pass, friend."

Chapter 7

Eleanor Roosevelt at Queen's University
8 January 1948

MRS. ELEANOR ROOSEVELT HONOURED AT SPECIAL CONVOCATION
Queen's Review

If we fall down in the fight to preserve the United Nations we are not only lacking in a realization of the alternatives but also in the character and spirit which developed our nations and which brought them to a point as potential leaders of the world.

These words were part of the *Alma Mater Society Lecture* delivered by Mrs. Eleanor Roosevelt in Grant Hall on January 8, after she received an honourary Doctor of Laws degree from the hands of Principal Wallace, vice-chancellor. Her address was a plea for an effort on the part of every individual to make the United Nations a success.

Sixteen hundred students and faculty members taxed accommodation in Grant Hall for the occasion. The hundreds who could not gain admittance were able to hear the ceremony and address over public address systems set up in two lecture rooms in the New Arts Building. The ceremony was also broadcast over CFRC, Queen's own radio station. The public, faculty wives, and administration staff members were not admitted to what was the students' own event.

Colourfully gowned dignitaries of the University moved in academic procession to the platform, where Vice-Principal Mackintosh presented Mrs. Roosevelt to Dr. Wallace with the following citation: ANNA ELEANOR ROOSEVELT – "distinguished citizen of our great and good neighbour, discerning and humane woman, whose courage and vision have given heart and hope to all those, of whatever nation, race, or creed, who strive for freedom and the basic ennobling human rights for themselves or for others, and – may I add, Mr. Vice-Chancellor – whose illustrious husband as he appeared in this Convocation on August 18, 1938, and the brave, prophetic words he then spoke, we now vividly and gratefully recall."

Dean Ellis hooded Mrs. Roosevelt, and Dr. Wallace conferred the degree. Leonard Brockington, K.C., rector of Queen's, was also on the platform, as were members of the Board of Trustees, University Senate, Council, Alumni Association, and civic, church and army officials.

Kenneth Phin, president of the A.M.S., introduced Mrs. Roosevelt. Shirley Johnson, president of Levana, thanked her.

In her address, of about forty minutes' duration, the widow of the late president spoke out against pessimism with regard to the future of the United Nations. As the present United States delegate to the General Assembly of the United Nations and as a veteran of many international conferences, she said: "The United Nations is a very hopeful machinery but one which cannot be changed too quickly. In the United States we know it took a long time to write the constitution and the Bill of Rights. I think the charter of the United Nations will have to go through the same kind of change, but anyone who works in the United Nations realizes what it means to reach any agreement among peoples of totally different backgrounds, totally different economic and social situations and totally different regard for human beings; to have achieved the charter at all was a major victory.

"We must say when, not if, the nations of the world learn to get along together – for learn we have to," she asserted. "If the rest of the world goes under we will go under too, for after all, the world today is very small."

"We should approach the whole work in the United Nations with the determination that the machinery shall be made to function successfully and create an atmosphere in the world in which peace can grow and in which human beings can have the chance to hope and plan for the future without living in the shadow of fear of war and fear of want."

Mrs. Roosevelt urged a greater organized belief in the ideals held by western democracies. She pointed out that countries in Eastern Europe use the word democracy continually but in a totally different sense.

"We have to know what we mean by a democratic nation and whether we are prepared to do voluntarily what the peoples in Eastern Europe are compelled to do," she continued. "When a Russian delegate goes to a UN meeting, he is told beforehand what position he is to take and which way he is to vote. He cannot disagree."

"Sometimes I have even voted without consulting my State Department. It is true I might be told the next day my vote was wrong and asked to resign, but I would not be called on at night and mysteriously disappear."

The immense destruction caused in Europe by the war has created a critical economic situation, which must be faced. "If we face this situation which destruction has brought about we will be able to preserve our civilization and proceed without using the atom bomb."

Referring to Secretary Marshall's recent assertion that there would be no peace until the economic situation of Western Europe was stabilized, she said she would go two steps further, and include both Eastern Europe and the Far East.

One of the immediate problems in Europe was that of displaced persons. Mrs. Roosevelt warned that the longer these people had to stay in

D.P. camps, the less able they would be to take their place as good citizens in any country.

Another matter of vital concern to which she referred was the starving children in Europe. One organization of the UN, the Children's Emergency Relief, is giving aid only on the basis of need, and that is one group that should be helped. "These children will never have the chance to be students unless they are helped immediately," she told her student audience.

Mrs. Roosevelt emphasized the importance of the work being done by the Human Rights Commission, of which she is a member. She noted that this is the first body on which the Russians gave their full cooperation and then only to the extent of social and economic rights and not to the rights of free speech, freedom of assembly and the press.

"Little by little this work will spell out the rights of human beings and bring people to a level that in many countries they have never even hoped for," she predicted.

She concluded with the hope that the young people today will do better than the generations that have gone before.

"I hope for you individual success but always bear in mind that success today is valuable only when it carries a service to the world and adds to the spirit of sacrifice for which so many died in the war."

Mrs. Roosevelt traveled from New York City by train and was met at Watertown, New York, on the morning of 8 January by Principal Wallace and E. Wray VanLuven of the Kingston Rotary Club. Before leaving for Kingston the party was entertained at breakfast by the mayor and other Watertown officials; also present were Dr. J.E. McAskill, Med. '14, first vice-president of the General Alumni Association and Mrs. McAskill.

On arrival at the Principal's Residence, Mrs. Roosevelt was met by the members of the executive of the Alma Mater Society. After a short visit, the group proceeded to Grant Hall for the Convocation ceremony and the Alma Mater Society Lecture. Afterwards, Mrs. Roosevelt was the guest of Principal and Mrs. Wallace at luncheon.

My Day
by Eleanor Roosevelt

Hyde Park (Sunday) – Wednesday night (January 7) I took the train to Watertown, New York, where I was met by Mr. R.C. Wallace, principal and vice-chancellor of Queen's University, Kingston, Ontario, Canada. We drove to Kingston and I had a few minutes to prepare for the morning ceremonies, at which I was given the honourary degree of doctor of laws.

The ceremonies were simple, dignified and quite perfect in all of their arrangements. I became the guest of the student body as soon as I had been taken into the fold as one of their honourary graduates. I made an address at their convocation and had a very pleasant lunch at the vice-chancellor's house afterward. I valued greatly a telegram from Prime Minister Mackenzie King, who was unable to be present, but who recalled having been with my husband when the International Bridge was opened and my husband received an honourary degree from Queen's University.

In these troubled times, it is well to emphasize again how two nations have lived so many years side by side, with quick access into each other's territory, and still have no fear of the misuse of this ready access into each other's countries. Canada, too, has, in her own country, a lesson for the rest of the world, because Quebec has kept such a distinct flavour of her French origin and yet, in all essential things, the people remain one nation.

I took the train again back to New York City on Thursday night. While I do not pine to spend two successive nights on trains at this season – not because they are cold, but because they are so very hot – nevertheless I enjoyed the whole trip. I am very gratified not only for the honour conferred upon me, but for the cordial and friendly atmosphere which surrounded my visit.

Part Two

Presidents Before Canada's Parliament

Canadians recently witnessed the excitement generated by a presidential visit to Parliament Hill, with President Barack Obama's trip to our capital on 19 February 2009. Although the new president did not then join those of his predecessors who, since Franklin Roosevelt, have addressed our Parliament in joint session, he made clear to Peter Milliken, House of Commons Speaker, upon presentation of a special edition of this volume, that he is eager to do so in future. While standing in the Library of Parliament that day, going through this book, President Obama expressed surprise at the number of US presidents who have stood in Canada's magnificent House of Commons chamber and spoken to all Canadians. Since Roosevelt, six American presidents have done so; two of them, Presidents Dwight Eisenhower and Ronald Reagan, have twice spoken in the House of Commons. Former British Prime Minister Anthony Eden once described the experience of speaking before our Parliament. "I spoke to the Canadian Parliament, which is an impressive and at first almost a daunting ceremony for the visitor," he wrote concerning his Ottawa address of 1956, "but the warmth of welcome and the response of the audience soon changes all that."[1]

American presidents have indeed been greeted warmly during their appearances before our Parliament. In 1995, Prime Minister Jean Chrétien reminded the visiting Bill Clinton that past presidents Gerald Ford, Jimmy Carter and George H.W. Bush shared something in common—none had been re-elected to a second term and none had addressed our Parliament. Clinton joked that he had never believed in the laws of history as he did at that moment as our parliamentarians and Canadians watching on television laughed.

Some of these speeches have been contentious. In the 1950s, President Eisenhower used his address to Parliament to forcefully state his nation's case during a trade dispute; John Kennedy went over our prime minister's head and appealed directly to Canada to join the Organization of American States (OAS). President Nixon declared that the days of easy and automatic relations between our two nations were over. Nixon said bluntly, "It is time for us to recognize that we have very separate identities; that we have significant differences, and that nobody's interests are furthered when these realities are obscured." In 1987, President Reagan, after an extraordinary meeting with advisors at 24 Sussex Drive, and after discussions with Prime Minister Brian Mulroney, dismissed the advice he had been given.

He chose to use the opportunity of a presidential address to Parliament to demonstrate he had been listening to Canadian concerns. Despite the views of his advisors, Reagan re-wrote the conclusion to his speech that day and said the following:

> The Prime Minister (Brian Mulroney) and I agreed to consider the Prime Minister's proposal for a bilateral accord on acid rain, building on the tradition of agreements to control pollution of our shared waters. The Prime Minister and I also had a full discussion of the Arctic waters issue, and he and I agreed to inject new impetus to the discussions already underway. We are determined to find a solution based on mutual respect for sovereignty and our common security and other interests.

Both leaders later concluded an agreement on Arctic sovereignty that will surely be the model for a permanent solution to this difficult bilateral issue in the years ahead. Like FDR at Queen's so many decades before, Reagan proved that these addresses in and about Canada matter.

Arthur Milnes

Chapter 8

President Franklin D. Roosevelt's Address to a Joint Session of Parliament
25 August 1943

It was exactly five years ago last Wednesday that I came to Canada to receive the high honour of a degree at Queen's University. On that occasion – one year before the invasion of Poland, three years before Pearl Harbor – I said that we in the Americas are no longer a far away continent, to which the eddies of controversies beyond the seas could bring no interest or no harm. Instead, we in the Americas have become a consideration to every propaganda office and to every general staff beyond the seas. The vast amount of our resources, the vigour of our commerce and the strength of our men have made us vital factors in world peace whether we choose it or not.

We did not choose this war – and that "we" includes each and every one of the United Nations. War was violently forced upon us by criminal aggressors who measure their standards of morality by the extent of the death and the destruction that they can inflict upon their neighbours.

In this war, Canadians and Americans have fought shoulder to shoulder – as our men and our women and our children have worked together and played together in happier times of peace. Today, in devout gratitude, we are celebrating a brilliant victory won by British and Canadian and American fighting men in Sicily.

Today, we rejoice also in another event for which we need not apologize. A year ago, Japan occupied several of the Aleutian Islands on our side of the ocean, and made a great "to do" about the invasion of the continent of North America. I regret to say that some Americans and some Canadians wished our governments to withdraw from the Atlantic and the Mediterranean campaigns and divert all our vast supplies and strength to the removal of the [Japanese] from a few rocky specks in the North Pacific.

Today, our wiser councils have maintained our efforts in the Atlantic area, the Mediterranean, the China Seas, and the Southwest Pacific, with ever-growing contributions; in the Northwest Pacific a relatively small campaign has been assisted by the [Japanese] themselves in the elimination of that last [Japanese soldier] from Attu and Kiska. We have been told that the [Japanese] never surrender; their headlong retreat satisfies us just as well.

Great councils are being held here on the free and honoured soil of Canada – councils which look to the future conduct of this war and to the years of building a new progress for mankind. To these councils Canadians and Americans alike again welcome that wise and good and gallant gentleman, the prime minister of Great Britain.

Mr. King, my old friend, may I, through you, thank the people of Canada for their hospitality to all of us. Your course and mine have run so closely and affectionately during these many long years that this meeting adds another link to that chain. I have always felt at home in Canada, and you, I think, have always felt at home in the United States.

During the past few days in Quebec, the Combined Staffs have been sitting around a table – which is a good custom – talking things over, discussing ways and means, in the manner of friends, in the manner of partners, and may I even say in the manner of members of the same family. We have talked constructively of our common purposes in this war – of our determination to achieve victory in the shortest possible time, of our essential cooperation with our great and brave fighting allies.

And we have arrived, harmoniously, at certain definite conclusions. Of course, I am not at liberty to disclose just what these conclusions are. But, in due time, we shall communicate the secret information of the Quebec Conference to Germany, Italy, and Japan. We shall communicate this information to our enemies in the only language their twisted minds seem capable of understanding.

Sometimes I wish that great master of intuition, the Nazi leader, could have been present in spirit at the Quebec Conference. I am thoroughly glad that he wasn't there in person. If he and his generals had known our plans they would have realized that discretion is still the better part of valour and that surrender would pay them better now than later.

The evil characteristic that makes a Nazi a Nazi is his utter inability to understand and therefore to respect, the qualities or the rights of his fellow men. His only method of dealing with his neighbour is first to delude him with lies, then to attack him treacherously, then to beat him down and step on him, and then either to kill him or enslave him. And the same thing is true of the fanatical militarists of Japan.

Because their own instincts and impulses are essentially inhuman, our enemies simply cannot comprehend how it is that decent, sensible individual human beings manage to get along together and to live together as good neighbours.

That is why our enemies are doing their desperate best to misrepresent the purposes and the results of this Quebec Conference. They still seek to divide and conquer allies who refuse to be divided, just as cheerfully as they refuse to be conquered.

We spend our energies and our resources and the very lives of our sons and daughters because a band of gangsters in the community of Nations declines to recognize the fundamentals of decent, human conduct.

We have been forced to call out what we, in the United States, would call the sheriff's posse, to break up the gang in order that gangsterism may be eliminated in the community of Nations. We are making sure – absolutely, irrevocably sure – that this time, the lesson is driven home to them once and for all. Yes, we are going to be rid of outlaws this time.

Every one of the United Nations believes that only a real and lasting peace can justify the sacrifices we are making, and our unanimity gives us confidence in seeking that goal.

It is no secret that at Quebec, there was much talk of the postwar world. That discussion was doubtless duplicated simultaneously in dozens of Nations and hundreds of cities and among millions of people.

There is a longing in the air. It is not a longing to go back to what they call "the good old days." I have distinct reservations as to how good "the good old days" were. I would rather believe that we can achieve new and better days.

Absolute victory in this war will give greater opportunities to the world, because the winning of the war in itself is certainly proving to all of us up here that concerted action can accomplish things. Surely we can make strides toward a greater freedom from want than the world has yet enjoyed. Surely by unanimous action in driving out the outlaws and keeping them under heel forever, we can attain a freedom from fear of violence.

I am everlastingly angry only at those who assert vociferously that the four freedoms and the Atlantic Charter are nonsense because they are unattainable. If those people had lived a century and a half ago, they would have sneered and said that the Declaration of Independence was utter piffle. If they had lived nearly a thousand years ago they would have laughed uproariously at the ideals of the Magna Carta. And if they had lived several thousand years ago, they would have derided Moses when he came from the mountain with the Ten Commandments.

We concede that these great teachings are not perfectly lived up to today, but I would rather be a builder than a wrecker, hoping always that the structure of life is growing, not dying.

May the destroyers who still persist in our midst decrease. They, like some of our enemies, have a long road to travel before they accept the ethics of humanity.

Some day, in the distant future perhaps – but some day, it is certain – all of them will remember, with the Master, "Thou shalt love thy neighbour as thyself."

Chapter 9

President Harry S. Truman's Address to a Joint Session of Parliament
11 June 1947

This is my first visit to Canada as president of the United States, and I am happy that it affords me the opportunity to address this meeting of the members of both houses of the Canadian Parliament. Here is a body which exemplifies the self-government and freedom of the nations of the great British Commonwealth. The history of the Commonwealth proves that it is possible for many nations to work and live in harmony and for the common good.

I wish to acknowledge the many courtesies extended to me on this visit by the Governor General, Viscount Alexander, who paid me the honour of a visit in Washington a few months ago. His career as a soldier and as a statesman eminently qualifies him to follow his illustrious predecessors.

For the courtesy of appearing before you, as for other courtesies, I am sure I am largely indebted to my good friend, Prime Minister Mackenzie King. I was particularly happy to be present yesterday, when he was honoured in the rotunda of this Parliament building. It was a wonderful ceremony, and one which I think he richly deserved.

I also appreciate very highly the political advice which he gave me. I have come to value and cherish his friendship and statesmanship. As our two nations have worked together in solving the difficult problems of the postwar period, I have developed greater and greater respect for his wisdom.

Americans who come to know Canada informally, such as our tourists, as well as those whose approach is more academic, learn that Canada is a broad land – broad in mind, broad in spirit, and broad in physical expanse. They find that the composition of your population and the evolution of your political institutions hold a lesson for the other nations of the earth. Canada has achieved internal unity and material strength, and has grown in stature in the world community, by solving problems that might have hopelessly divided and weakened a less gifted people.

Canada's eminent position today is a tribute to the patience, tolerance, and strength of character of her people, of both French and British strains. For Canada is enriched by the heritage of France, as well as of Britain, and Quebec has imparted the vitality and spirit of France itself to Canada.

Canada's notable achievement of national unity and progress through accommodation, moderation, and forbearance can be studied with profit by her sister nations.

Much the same qualities have been employed, with like success, in your relations with the United States. Perhaps I should say "your foreign relations with the United States." But the word "foreign" seems strangely out of place. Canada and the United States have reached the point where we no longer think of each other as "foreign" countries. We think of each other as friends, as peaceful and cooperative neighbours on a spacious and fruitful continent.

We must go back a long way, nearly a century and a half, to find a time when we were not on good terms. In the War of 1812, there was fighting across our frontier. But permanent good came of that brief campaign. It shocked Canadians and Americans into a realization that continued antagonism would be costly and perilous. The first result of that realization was the *Rush-Bagot* Agreement in 1817, which embodied a spirit and an attitude that have permeated our relations to this day. This agreement originally was intended to limit and to regulate the naval vessels of both countries on the Great Lakes. It has become one of the world's most effective disarmament agreements, and it is the basis for our much-hailed unfortified frontier.

I speak of that period of history to make the point that the friendship that has characterized Canadian-American relations for many years did not develop spontaneously. The example of accord provided by our two countries did not come about merely through the happy circumstance of geography. It is compounded of one part proximity and nine parts good will and commonsense.

We have had a number of problems, but they have all been settled by adjustment, by compromise, and by negotiations inspired by a spirit of mutual respect, and a desire for justice on both sides. This is the peaceful way, the sensible way, and the fair way to settle problems, whether between two nations that are close neighbours, or among many nations widely separated.

This way is open to all. We in Canada and the United States are justifiably proud of our joint record, but we claim no monopoly on that formula. Canada and the United States will gladly share the formula, which rejects distrust and suspicion in favor of commonsense, mutual respect, and equal justice with their fellow members of the United Nations. One of the most effective contributions our two countries can make to the cause of the United Nations is the patient and diligent effort to apply, on a global scale, the principles and practices which we have tested with success on this continent.

Relations between Canada and the United States have emphasized the spirit of cooperation rather than the letter of protocol. The *Rush-Bagot*

Agreement was stated in fewer than 150 words. From time to time, it has been revised by mutual agreement to meet changing conditions. It was amended as recently as last December.

The last war brought our countries into even closer collaboration. The *Ogdensburg Agreement* of 1940 provided for the creation of the Permanent Joint Board on Defence. It was followed by the *Hyde Park Agreement* of 1941, which enabled us to coordinate our economic resources with increased efficiency. Common interests, particularly after Pearl Harbor, required the creation of several joint agencies to coordinate our efforts in special fields. When victory ended the necessity for these agencies, they were quietly disbanded with a minimum of disturbance of the national economies of the two countries. Commonsense again.

The Permanent Joint Board on Defence will continue to function. I wish to emphasize, in addition to the word "permanent," the other two parts of the title. The Board is joint, being composed of representatives of each government. Canada and the United States participate on the basis of equality, and the sovereignty of each is carefully respected. This was true during the gravest dangers of the war, and it will continue to be true, in keeping with the nature of all our joint undertakings.

The Board was created, and will continue to exist, for the sole purpose of assuring the most effective defence for North America. The Board, as you know, has no executive powers, and can only make recommendations for action. The record of the Board provides another example of the truly cooperative spirit that prevails between our two countries.

The spirit of common purpose and the impressive strength which we marshaled for action on all fronts are the surest safeguard of continental security in the future.

The people of the United States fully appreciate the magnificent contribution in men and resources that Canada made to the Allied war effort. The United States soldiers, sailors, and airmen in the heat of battle knew their Canadian comrades as valiant and daring warriors. We look back with pride on our association as staunch allies in two wars.

Today, our two nations are called upon to make great contributions to world rehabilitation. This task requires broad vision and constant effort. I am confident that we can overcome the difficulties involved, as we overcame the greater difficulties of the war. The national genius of our peoples finds its most satisfying expression in the creation of new values in peace. The record proves that in peaceful commerce, the combined efforts of our countries can produce outstanding results. Our trade with each other is far greater than that of any other two nations on earth.

Last year, the flow of trade in both directions across the border reached the record peacetime total of $2 1/4 billion. We imported from Canada more than twice the value of goods we received from the United Kingdom, France, China, and Russia combined. The United States' purchases from Canada were about six times our purchases from Great Britain, nearly ten times those from China, and 11 times those from France. We sold to Canada nearly as much as we sold to Britain and France together.

Gratifying as the volume of our trade now is, it is capable of even further expansion to our mutual benefit. Some of our greatest assets are still to be developed to the maximum. I am thinking of one particularly that holds tremendous possibilities: the magnificent St. Lawrence-Great Lakes System, which we share and which we must develop together.

The St. Lawrence project stirs the imagination long accustomed to majestic distances and epic undertakings. The proposal for taking electric power from the river and bringing ocean shipping 2,400 miles inland, to tap the fertile heart of our continent, is economically sound and strategically important.

When this program is carried out, the waterway that is part of our boundary will more than ever unite our two countries. It will stimulate our economies to new growth, and will spread the flow of trade.

There have been times when shortsighted tariff policies on both sides threatened to raise almost insurmountable barriers. But the need to exchange goods was so imperative that trade flourished despite artificial obstacles. The *Reciprocal Trade Agreements* of 1936 and 1939 made possible a sensible reduction of tariff rates, and paved the way to our present phenomenal trade.

Something more than commercial agreements, however, is required to explain why Canada and the United States exchange more than $2 billion worth of goods yearly. Ambassador Atherton has aptly given the reason as not "free trade," but "the trade of free men." The record flow of goods and the high standard of living it indicates, on both sides of the border, provide a practical demonstration of the benefits of the democratic way of life and a free economy.

The benefits of our democratic governments and free economies operating side by side have spread beyond our countries to the advantage of the whole world. Both nations expanded their productivity enormously during the war, and both escaped the physical damage that afflicted other countries. As a result, Canada and the United States emerged from the war as the only major sources of the industrial products and the food upon which much of the world depends for survival.

Canada has responded as nobly to the challenge of peace as she did to that of the war. Your wheat has fed millions who otherwise would have starved. Your loan strengthened Britain in her valiant battle for recovery.

The United States is particularly gratified to find Canada at our side in the effort to develop the International Trade Organization. We attach great importance to this undertaking, because we believe it will provide the key to the welfare and prosperity of the world in the years immediately ahead.

In sponsoring the International Trade Organization, the United States, with the cooperation of Canada and other countries, is making a determined effort to see that the inevitable adjustments in world trade as a result of the war will result in an expanding volume of business for all nations.

Our goal is a vast expansion of agriculture and industry throughout the world, with freer access to the raw materials and markets for all nations, and a wider distribution of the products of the earth's fields and factories among all peoples. Our hope is to multiply the fruitfulness of the earth and to diffuse its benefits among all mankind.

At this critical point in history, we of the United States are deeply conscious of our responsibilities to the world. We know that in this trying period, between a war that is over and a peace that is not yet secure, the destitute and the oppressed of the earth look chiefly to us for sustenance and support, until they can again face life with self-confidence and self-reliance.

We are keenly aware that much depends upon the internal strength, the economic stability and the moral stamina of the United States. We face this challenge with determination and confidence.

Free men everywhere know that the purpose of the United States is to restore the world to health and to reestablish conditions under which the common people of the earth can work out their salvation by their own efforts.

We seek a peaceful world, a prosperous world, a free world, a world of good neighbours, living on terms of equality and mutual respect, as Canada and the United States have lived for generations.

We intend to expend our energies and to invest our substance in promoting world recovery, by assisting those who are able and willing to make their maximum contribution to the same cause.

We intend to support those who are determined to govern themselves in their own way, and who honour the right of others to do likewise.

We intend to aid those who seek to live at peace with their neighbours, without coercing or being coerced, without intimidating or being intimidated.

We intend to uphold those who respect the dignity of the individual, who guarantee to him equal treatment under the law, and who allow him the widest possible liberty to work out his own destiny and achieve success to the limit of his capacity.

We intend to cooperate actively and loyally with all who honestly seek, as we do, to build a better world in which mankind can live in peace and prosperity.

We count Canada in the forefront of those who share these objectives and ideals.

With such friends we face the future unafraid.

Chapter 10

**President Dwight D. Eisenhower's Address to a Joint Session of Parliament
14 November 1953**

Mr. Prime Minister [Louis St. Laurent], for the very great generosity of the personal sentiments expressed towards me, I am humbly grateful. For the reception Mrs. Eisenhower and I experienced here throughout this city, we should like to extend to all your citizens – all your people – our very deep appreciation, especially for the honour of being received before this Body. I assure you, you have given us [a] distinction that we shall never forget.

Since World War II, I have now been privileged, three times, to visit this great country and this beautiful city. On my first visit, more than seven years ago, I came to express to the Canadian people a field commander's appreciation of their memorable contribution to the liberation of the Mediterranean and the European lands. On my second, I came to discuss with your governmental leaders your country's role in the building of Atlantic security. Both visits, in the warmth and spirit of a great people's welcome, were days that I shall remember all my life.

This day, I again salute the men and women of Canada.

As I stand before you, my thoughts go back to the days of global war. In that conflict, and then through the more recent savage and grievous Korean battles, the Canadian people have been valourous champions of freedom for mankind. Within the framework of NATO, in the construction of new patterns for international security, in the lengthy and often toilsome exploration of a regional alliance, they have been patient and wise devisers of a stout defence for the Western world. Canada, rich in natural gifts, far richer in human character and genius, has earned the gratitude and the affectionate respect of all who cherish freedom and seek peace.

I am highly honoured by the invitation of the Parliament that I address. For your invitation is rooted in the friendship – the sense of partnership – that for generations has been the hallmark of the relations between Canada and the United States. Your country, my country – each is a better and stronger and more influential nation because each can rely upon every resource of the other in days of crisis. Beyond this, each can work and grow and prosper with the other through years of quiet peace.

We, of our country, have long respected and admired Canada as a bulwark of the British Commonwealth, and as a leader among nations. As no Soviet wile or lure can divide the Commonwealth, nothing will corrupt the Canadian-American partnership.

We have a dramatic symbol of that partnership in the favored topic of every speaker addressing an audience made up of both our peoples - our unfortified frontier. But though this subject has become shopworn and well-nigh exhausted as a feature of after dinner oratory, it is still a fact that our common frontier grows stronger every year, defended only by friendship. Its strength wells from indestructible and enduring sources: identical ideals of family and school and church, and traditions which come to us from the common past. Out of this partnership has evolved a progressive prosperity and a general well-being, mutually beneficial, that is without parallel on earth. In the years ahead, the pace of our mutual growth will surely be no less.

To strive, even dimly, to foresee the wonders of Canada's next generation, is to summon the utmost powers of the imagination. This land is a mighty reservoir of resources. Across it, at this moment, there moves an extraordinary drama of enterprise and endeavour – Canadians, rapidly building basic industries, converting waters into hydro-electric energy, scrutinizing your soil for new wealth, pushing into the barrens of the North for minerals and for oil. You, of Canada, are building a magnificent record of achievement. My country rejoices in it.

More than friendship and partnership is signified in the relations between our countries. These relations that today enrich our peoples justify the faith of our fathers that men, given self-government, can dwell at peace among themselves, progressive in the development of their material wealth, quick to join in the defence of their spiritual community, ready to arbitrate differences that may rise to divide them. This Parliament is an illustrious symbol of a human craving, a human search, a human right to self-government.

All the free legislatures of the world speak for the free peoples of the world. In their deliberations and enactments, they mirror the ideas, the traditions, the fundamental philosophies of their respective nations.

On the other hand, every free nation, secure in its own economic and political stability, reflects the responsible leadership and the wise comprehension which its legislature has brought to the management of public affairs.

Now, this continent uniquely has been a laboratory of self-government, in which free legislatures have been an indispensable force. What is the result? It is a mighty unity built of values essentially spiritual. This continent, of course, is a single physical and geographical entity. But physical unity, however, broken by territorial lines, fortress chains, and trade barriers, is a characteristic of every continent. Here, however, independent and sovereign peoples have built a stage on which all the world can see: first, each country's patriotic dedication to its own enlightened self-interest, but free from vicious nationalistic exploitation of grudge or ancient wrong; second, a joined recognition that neighbours, among nations as among individuals, prosper best in neighbourly cooperation, factually exemplified in daily life; third, an international will to cast out the bomb and the gun as arbiters and to exalt the joint search for truth and justice.

Here, on this continent, we present an example that other nations some day surely will recognize and apply in their relationships among themselves. My friends, may that day be close, because the only alternative – the bankruptcy of armament races and the suicide of nuclear war – cannot for long, must not for long, be tolerated by the human race.

Great has been our mutual progress. It foreshadows what we together can accomplish for our mutual good. Before us of Canada and the United States lies an immense panorama of opportunity in every field of human endeavour. A host of jobs to be done together confronts us. Many of them cry for immediate attention. As we examine them together in the work days ahead, we must never allow the practical difficulties that impede progress to blind our eyes to the objectives established by principle and by logic.

With respect to some aspects of our future development, I hope I may, without presumption, make three observations.

The first is: the free world must come to recognize that trade barriers, although intended to protect a country's economy, often in fact shackle its prosperity. In the United States, there is a growing recognition that free nations cannot expand their productivity and economic strength without a high level of international trade. Now, in our case – yours and ours – our two economies are enmeshed intricately with the world economy. We cannot risk sudden dislocation in industry and agriculture and widespread unemployment and distress, by hasty decisions to accomplish suddenly what inevitably will come in an orderly economic evolution. "Make haste slowly" is a homely maxim with international validity.

Moreover, every common undertaking, however worthwhile it may be, must be understood in its origins, its application, its effects by the peoples of our two countries. Without this understanding, it will have negligible chance of success. Canadians and citizens of the United States do not accept government by edict or decree. Informed and intelligent cooperation is, for us, the only source of enduring accomplishment.

To study further the whole subject of United States foreign economic policy, we have, at home, appointed a special commission with wide representation, including members of the Congress as well as spokesmen for the general public. From the commission's studies will come, we hope, a policy which can command the support of the American people, and which will be in the best interest of the United States and the free world.

Toward the strengthening of commercial ties between Canada and the United States, officials of our two governments have, for some months, been considering the establishment of a Joint Economic and Trade Committee. This committee, now approved, will consist of cabinet officers of both countries. They will meet periodically to discuss in broad terms economic and trade problems and the means for their equitable solution. I confidently believe that out of this process, the best interests of both our countries will be more easily harmonized and advanced.

The second observation is this: joint development and use of the St. Lawrence-Great Lakes Waterway is inevitable. It is sure and certain. With you, I consider this measure a vital addition to our economic and national security. Of course, no proposal yet made is entirely free from faults of some sort. But every one of them can be corrected – given patience and cooperation.

In the United States, my principal security advisers, comprising the National Security Council, favor the undertaking for national defence reasons. The cabinet favors it on both security and economic grounds. A committee of the United States Senate has approved a measure authorizing it. This measure provides for the United States' participation in a joint development by both countries. The proposal now awaits action by the United States Senate which, I am confident, will act favorably on it or some similar measure. The ways and means for assuring American cooperation in this great project will, I hope, be authorized and approved during the coming session of the Congress.

I have noted with satisfaction the New York Power Authority's acceptance of the Federal Power Commission's license. With this act, the stage is set for a start on the St. Lawrence Power Project which will add materially to the economic strength of both countries.

My third observation is this: you of Canada and we of the United States can and will devise ways to protect our North America from any surprise attack by air. And we shall achieve the defence of our continent without whittling our pledges to Western Europe or forgetting our friends in the Pacific.

The basic threat of Communist purpose still exists. Indeed, the latest Soviet communication to the Western world is truculent, if not arrogant, in tone. In any event, our security plans must now take into account Soviet ability to employ atomic attack on North America, as well as on countries, friendly to us, lying closer to the borders of the USSR. Their atomic stockpile will, of course, increase in size, and means of delivery will increase as time goes on.

Now, each of our two nations seeks a secure home for realization of its destiny. Defence of our soil presents a challenge to both our peoples. It is a common task. Defensively, as well as geographically, we are joined beyond any possibility of separation. This element in our security problem is an accepted guide of the service leaders, government officials and legislatures on both sides of the border. In our approach to the problem, we both realize that purest patriotism demands and promotes effective partnership. Thus we evolve joint agreements on all those measures we must jointly undertake to improve the effectiveness of our defences, but every arrangement rests squarely on the sovereign nature of each of our two peoples.

Canada and the United States are equal partners, and neither dares to waste time. There is a time to be alert and a time to rest. These days demand ceaseless vigilance. We must be ready and prepared. The threat is present. The measures of defence have been thoroughly studied by official bodies of both countries. The Permanent Joint Board on Defence has worked assiduously and effectively on mutual problems. Now is the time for action on all agreed measures.

Steps to defend our continent are, of course, but one part of the world-wide security program. The North Atlantic Treaty Organization, for example, is an essential defence of Ottawa, and of Washington, and of our neighbours to the South, as well as of communities thousands of miles to the east. Implicit in the consultations and detailed studies which must continue, and in the defences which we have already mounted, is the need for world wide vigilance and strength. But the purpose is defence. We have no other aim.

In common with others of the free world, the United States does not rely on military strength alone to win the peace. Our primary reliance is a unity among us forged of common adherence to moral principles. This reliance binds together in fellowship all those who believe in the spiritual nature of man, as the child of God.

Moreover, our country assuredly claims no monopoly on wisdom. We are willing – nay, anxious – to discuss with friends and with any others all possible paths to peace. We will use every means – from the normal diplomatic exchange to the forum of the United Nations – to further this search. We welcome ideas, expressions of honest difference, new proposals and new interpretations of old ones – anything and everything honestly offered for the advancement of man's oldest aspiration.

There are no insoluble problems. Differences can be resolved; tensions can be relieved. The free world, I deeply believe, holds firmly to this faith, striving earnestly towards what is just and equitable.

My friends, allow me to interpolate here merely an expression of my own personal faith. I call upon all of those who are in responsible position, either in civil government or in the military world. In the dark days of 1940 and 1941 and 1942, there seemed no place from which to start to conquer the enemy that bid fair to enslave us all. Already he had put most of Europe under his heel. When I stop to think of the bewilderment of our people – the fears of our people in those days, and then how in a few short years we were coming home to celebrate that great victory that we thought could at last mark the end of all wars, we see how fast human affairs, human outlooks can change, from one of despondency - almost of despair, in many quarters – to one of exultation.

Now today, as we fail to understand the intransigence that we feel marks others, as we try to colour every proposal we make with what we believe to be reason, understanding – even sympathy, as we are nonplussed as to why these offers are never taken up, let us never despair that faith will not win through.

The world that God has given us is, of course, material in its values, intellectual and spiritual. We have got to hand on to those who come after us this balance – this balance of values, and particularly the certainty that they can enjoy the same kind of opportunity in this spiritual, intellectual and material world that we, who will then be their ancestors, enjoyed before them.

That, it seems to me, is the real problem that Canada and the United States today have to meet. And it is the one reason I get such a thrill every time I come to this country, because here I sense in the very atmosphere your determination to work in that direction, not acknowledging defeat, certain that we can win because there are values that man treasures above all things else in the world that are now at stake.

The free world believes that practical problems can be solved practically; that they should be solved by orderly procedure, step by step, so that the foundation for peace, which we are building in concert with other nations, will be solid and unshakable. I deem it a high privilege to salute, through this their parliament, the Canadian people for the strength they have added to this faith – and for the contribution they are making toward its realization.

Beyond the shadow of the atomic cloud, the horizon is bright with promise. No shadow can halt our advance together. For we, Canada and the United States, shall use carefully and wisely the God-given graces of faith and reason as we march together toward it – toward the horizon of a world where each man, each family, each nation lives at peace in a climate of freedom.

Chapter 11

President Dwight D. Eisenhower's Address to a Joint Session of Parliament
9 July 1958

Mr. Prime Minister [John Diefenbaker], I want you to know of my deep personal appreciation of the warmth of the welcome you have extended to me, and of the generosity of the remarks that you have just delivered concerning me. Along that same line, I should like to express my very great appreciation of the warmth of the welcome that Mrs. Eisenhower and I have experienced throughout the city, along its streets and in every meeting in which we have had a part. We are truly grateful. This is my fourth visit to your beautiful capital.

I recall well when your gracious Queen came to Washington from Ottawa; we spoke together of the beauty of this city and of the greatness of Canada. It is good to return – to see old friends and to make new ones.

I came here first in 1946 to congratulate the Canadian people on the brilliant role played by the Canadian forces that you placed under my command in the World War which had then recently ended in victory.

My next visit was made as Commander of NATO forces in Europe. In 1953, I returned as president and talked in this House of some aspects of the relationship between our two countries. I then spoke of the St. Lawrence Seaway in prospective terms. Today it is near completion, and next year it will be open. This is truly a great joint accomplishment. It will open up important regions of both Canada and the United States to ocean traffic. It will ever stand as a monument to what can be achieved by the common effort of two sovereign nations.

On that same occasion I spoke of the need to devise ways to protect our North America from any surprise attack. Since then, we have made great strides. The Distant Early Warning (DEW) Line has been built and placed in operation. In the process of its construction, I am sure much has been learned which will contribute to the more rapid development of the northern reaches of Canada and of our new state, Alaska.

Last month, an agreement was concluded between our two governments to establish a combined air defence headquarters for this continent. We have also – both of us – striven, as we will continue to strive, for the Soviet Union's agreement to a system of inspection to protect against surprise attack through the Arctic. Recent Soviet communications have strengthened the hope that they will come to see that by such a system, any basis for their professed fears of an attack across the Pole will be removed. For Canada and for the United States, such a system in operation would add measurably to our security against a sudden attack. Possibly, it might also pave the way for still further measures of arms control, and permit some reduction of the burden and danger of modern armaments.

Both of these developments, the Seaway – a broadened, deepened road for peaceful commerce – and the strengthening of our common defence of this continent strikingly illustrate two things. The first is that change is the law of life and of relations between nations. When two great peoples such as ours, energetic and optimistic, live side by side in all the diversity that freedom offers, change is rapid and brings in its wake problems, sometimes frictions.

The second lesson that I see in these common achievements in diverse fields is that by mutual respect, understanding and with good will we can find acceptable solutions to any problems which exist or may arise between us. It is important to remember this. Such differences as are from time to time expressed never affect the similarity of purpose which binds our two countries together.

Of course, each of us possesses a distinctive national character and history. You won your independence by evolution, the United States by revolution. Our forms of government – though both cast in the democratic pattern – are greatly different. Indeed, sometimes it appears that many of our misunderstandings spring from an imperfect knowledge on the part of both of us of the dissimilarities in our forms of government.

And yet, despite these dissimilarities in form, our two governments are developing, and are increasingly using effective ways to consult and act together. This we do to meet the problems that confront us in our relations with each other, and in the relations of both with all other nations of the world.

We share the basic belief that only under free institutions, with government the servant and not the master, can the individual secure his life, his liberty, and the pursuit of happiness. We are both determined to frame and follow policies which safeguard the lives and homes of our people, their peace of mind, their material well being and, above all things, their ideals. True to these ideals, both of our countries, for example, are determined that the great decisions of peace and war will remain always under civilian control.

Moreover, we both recognize a design of aggressive Communist imperialism which threatens every free nation. Both of us face a military threat and political attack. Our system of free enterprise is challenged throughout the world by a state-directed, state-controlled economic system. Indeed, my friends, this could well be the area in which the competition will be most bitter and most decisive between the free world and Communist imperialism. We must never allow ourselves to become so preoccupied with any differences between our two nations that we lose sight of the transcendent importance of free world cooperation in the winning of the global struggle.

Now, acting in accordance with our common dedication, the two of us, with others, have drawn together in collective security arrangements. The most notable of these is the North Atlantic Treaty Organization, in which both Canada and the United States are equal partners. We are both determined to maintain what George Washington described as "a respectable military posture." We are equally determined to maintain our institutions in good repair, and to insure that our own economies function well.

Thus we seek not only to meet the expanding needs of our people but also to set an example of free men's accomplishments, which will encourage and attract those less fortunate. And finally, we are agreed that we shall never cease striving for a just and lasting peace to be achieved by negotiation with those who challenge us. We overlook no opportunity to settle the issues which divide the world, and, under safeguarded conditions, to reduce the burden of armaments.

Now, against this background of similarity in basic factors and policy, let me point to some of the matters which, it seems to me, are troublesome between us. Among some examples are the surplus wheat disposal policies of the United States, the imbalance in our mutual trade, certain aspects of United States private investment in Canada, and Canadian fears of a trend in the United States away from forward-looking policies in the field of trade.

I am sure you agree that we should talk frankly to each other. Frankness, in good spirit, is a measure of friendship. It should be the practice, I believe, on both sides so to speak, when either feels that important interests are adversely affected by actions contemplated or taken by the other. Happily, these instances are rare. Now, in mentioning today specific problems on which we do not see eye to eye, I am doing so as an American, expressing an American viewpoint. I can assure you that your prime minister, in discussing these problems with my associates and me, most loyally and eloquently, I might add, expresses the viewpoint of Canada.

It is my conviction, in which I believe he fully concurs, that for all our present problems and all our future ones, we will find acceptable solutions. It will take understanding, common sense and a willingness to give and take on both our parts. These qualities we have always found in our dealings with Canada. I hope that you have not found them lacking in us.

First then, in some detail, I would like to comment briefly on our surplus wheat disposal policies. I think that no one can quarrel with our purpose, though some of our methods may seem unorthodox by traditional standards. Simply stated, our wheat disposal program has three aspects. In times of local famine or disaster, we give wheat away. We have also bartered it for strategic materials. Finally, we sell wheat for local currency to countries which cannot afford to purchase it commercially. In these cases, our policy is to lend back to the Government in question most of the proceeds for local economic development. Our intent is not to damage normal commercial markets, and in this, I think we have been generally successful.

I know that in the past there was criticism of certain aspects of these programs, and particularly of our barter arrangements. I believe that the basis of these objections has been largely removed. Increasingly close consultation between officials of our two governments has ironed out many misunderstandings respecting our surplus disposals. Your government knows in detail what we plan. I assure you that it is our desire and intention to keep the doors of consultation always and fully open. There must never be a final word between friends.

In several respects, despite inconvenience and even occasional damage in the past, Canada stands to benefit from our moving some surplus agricultural commodities into consumption overseas. First and most evident of all, many hungry people around the world have had food which they otherwise would not have had. Secondly, had these products remained in dead storage, they would have had a depressing influence on the world market and on world prices. Finally, the funds which we have been enabled to make available to recipient countries should, in the long run, help to raise standards of living, which in turn will create enlarged markets for all of us.

I come next to the question of the imbalance of trade between our two countries. You buy more from the United States than you sell to us. This fact is of concern to many thoughtful Canadians. There are a few basic points which should be noted in this connection. First of all, the United States and Canada are not state traders. All the products of industry manufactured in the United States and sold to customers abroad are sold through the enterprise of the private seller. These articles come to you here in Canada only because of the desire of the individual Canadian consumer to buy a particular piece of merchandise. The United States Government does not place goods in Canada as part of a state-directed program. This aspect of our trade with each other is the natural consequence of two private enterprise economies working side by side and trading with each other.

Then, we should also remember that the free world represents a multilateral trading community. To try to balance our books once a month, or once a year, with every nation with which we trade would stifle rather than expand trade. I assume that Canada is as interested as we are in the expansion of world trade, rather than in its artificial redirection. Both our peoples want to buy and sell in a climate of economic vigour and expansion. An imbalance in trade with one country, in such a climate, is usually balanced or largely offset by the state of the accounts with other trading nations. This is the case with Canadian trade. Your export deficit to the United States is offset by export surpluses to other countries, and by the flow of investments to Canada. The promotion of healthy multilateral trade, as opposed to artificial bilateral balancing, is an important objective of the International Monetary Fund and the General Agreement on Tariffs and Trade, to which both Canada and the United States belong.

For a moment, I want to address myself as well to the other side of the trade equation, namely your exports to the United States. Here you can rightly say that, through quotas and tariffs, our governmental policies can either expand or restrict your opportunities to sell to us. The same is of course true of actions taken by your government, which can affect the volume of our exports to Canada. Neither of our countries is a "free trader" in the classical economic sense. Each of us feels a responsibility to provide some protection to particular sectors of our economies which may be in distress or are for other reasons deserving of governmental assistance. We have taken some actions of this sort. So has Canada.

Oil imports into our country contribute a case in point. We believe that to ensure adequate supplies of oil in an emergency, it is necessary that exploration to develop oil reserves be carried forward with vigour. This means a healthy oil industry to the continent. A healthy, domestic oil-producing industry is vital to our national security, and we recognize that our security and yours are inseparable. We have been keenly sensitive to that fact in considering the nature of the voluntary restrictions on oil imports that have been put into effect by oil companies in the United States, and have minimized their impact on your economy. Our restrictive action with respect to oil is not in any sense reflective of a change in the fundamental trade policy of the United States. Such actions must be viewed in perspective. For example, since the so-called "escape clause" was incorporated in our trade agreements legislation in 1951, there have come, from industry in the United States, a number of requests for the imposition of quotas or higher tariffs. In about a dozen cases, presidential approval for some relief has been granted. In only one of these cases was Canada directly affected as an exporter. We have always conscientiously sought to take account of your interests as well as our own in seeking the best remedy to these intricate problems. I believe that a study of the record will bear out the truth of this statement.

Next, the flow of investment funds from the United States into Canada has led to expressions of concern on your part. These funds have been attracted to your country by the business opportunities Canada has offered. Though they may raise questions in specific cases respecting control of an industry by American citizens, these industries are, of course, subject to Canadian law. Moreover, these investments have helped you to develop your resources and to expand your industrial plant at a far faster rate than could have been possible had you relied wholly on your own savings. They have thereby helped to provide employment, tax revenues and other direct benefits. These funds have also helped Canada to finance with ease its recent surplus of imports from the United States, a fact that is testified to by the premium of the Canadian dollar over the United States dollar. I am confident that if there are some defects in this investment process, ways will be found to correct them, because this is the interest of both our countries.

One final word on the foreign trade policy of the United States; in 1934, the United States took a historic decision to embark on a positive policy of fostering trade with the launching of the Reciprocal Trade Agreements program. This policy we continue to support and to practice. The Government of the United States, after a public searching of soul at times of renewal of the Trade Agreements Act, has consistently reaffirmed this policy. Have no fear that the United States will abandon a policy so well-established. The problems I have been discussing concern our economic lives. Our points of economic contact are varied and numerous, as they of necessity must be, under our chosen system of private enterprise. Our governments have a responsibility to help compose difficulties, but we must not forget that thousands of individual citizens of Canada and the United States must, themselves, find in their diversified activities the answers to many of these problems.

Finally, there is no cause to be surprised or disturbed to discover that occasionally, differences arise between us. The distinguishing character of the peoples of the free world lies in the fact that differences between them can develop, can be expressed and then amicably resolved.

We in the United States have no more desire than you have to seek in our relations with others, the silent, sullen unity that elsewhere has been purchased or imposed. The hallmark of freedom is the right to differ as well as the right to agree.

I have spoken to you in the knowledge that through you, I address a nation strong in the tradition of freedom and vigilant in its defence. You and we are alike convinced by our history, by our religious faith and our common heritage of freedom, that economic well-being and political liberty both depend upon the efforts of individuals and on their willingness to accept the responsibilities of freedom. Today, I assure you once more of the pride and of the gratification that we of the United States feel in our long and friendly association with you, our sturdy Northern neighbour.

We stand together at a pivotal point in history. All that we Canadians and Americans, and those who went before us, have built, all that we believe in, is challenged as it has never been challenged before. The new horizons of competition range from the polar areas, and extend to the infinity of outer space.

It is for us – all of us – to bring to the challenge a response worthy of ourselves and our two nations. As we do, we shall know the satisfaction of having built, in friendship, a safer and ampler home here on the earth for this generation and those who shall come after us. I thank you for your kind attention.

Chapter 12

President John F. Kennedy's Address to a Joint Session of Parliament
17 May 1961

It is a deeply felt honour to address this distinguished legislative body. And yet may I say that I feel very much at home with you here today. For one-third of my life was spent in the Parliament of my own country – the United States Congress.

There are some differences between this body and my own. The most noticeable to me is the lofty appearance of statesmanship which is on the faces of the Members of the Senate – senators who realize that they will never have to place their cause before the people again! I feel at home also here because I number in my own State of Massachusetts many friends and former constituents who are of Canadian descent. Among the voters of Massachusetts who were born outside the United States, the largest group by far was born in Canada. Their vote is enough to determine the outcome of an election, even a presidential election. You can understand that having been elected president of the United States by less than 140 thousand votes out of 60 million, I am very conscious of these statistics!

The warmth of your hospitality symbolizes more than merely the courtesy which may be accorded to an individual visitor. It symbolizes the enduring qualities of amity and honour, which have characterized our countries' relations for so many decades.

Nearly forty years ago, a distinguished prime minister of this country took the part of the United States at a disarmament conference. He said, "They may not be angels, but they are at least our friends."

I must say that I do not think that we probably demonstrated in that forty years that we are angels yet, but I hope we have demonstrated that we are at least friends. And I must say that I think in these days where hazard is our constant companion, that friends are a very good thing to have.

The prime minister of Canada was the first of the leaders from other lands who was invited to call upon me shortly after I entered the White House; this is my first trip – the first trip for my wife and myself – outside of our country's borders. It is just and fitting, and appropriate and traditional, that I should come here to Canada – across a border that knows neither guns nor guerrillas.

But we share more than a common border. We share a common heritage, traced back to those early settlers who traveled from the beachheads of the Maritime Provinces and New England to the far reaches of the Pacific Coast. Henry Thoreau spoke a common sentiment for them all: "Eastward I go only by force, Westward I go free. I must walk towards Oregon and not towards Europe." We share common values from the past, a common defence line at present, and common aspirations for the future – our future, and indeed the future of all mankind.

Geography has made us neighbours. History has made us friends. Economics has made us partners. And necessity has made us allies. Those whom nature hath so joined together, let no man put asunder.

What unites us is far greater than what divides us. The issues and irritants that inevitably affect all neighbours are small deed in comparison with the issues that we face together – above all, the somber threat now posed to the whole neighbourhood of this continent – in fact, to the whole community of nations. But our alliance is born not of fear, but of hope. It is an alliance that advances what we are for, as well as opposes what we are against.

And so it is that when we speak of our common attitudes and relationships, Canada and the United States speak in 1961 in terms of unity. We do not seek the unanimity that comes to those who water down all issues to the lowest common denominator – or to those who conceal their differences behind fixed smiles – or to those who measure unity by standards of popularity and affection, instead of trust and respect.

We are allies. This is a partnership, not an empire. We are bound to have differences and disappointments – and we are equally bound to bring them out into the open, to settle them where they can be settled, and to respect each other's views when they cannot be settled.

Thus ours is the unity of equal and independent nations, co-tenants of the same continent, heirs of the same legacy, and fully sovereign associates in the same historic endeavour: to preserve freedom for ourselves and all who wish it. To that endeavour we must bring great material and human resources, the result of separate cultures and independent economies. And above all, that endeavour requires a free and full exchange of new and different ideas on all issues and all undertakings.

For it is clear that no free nation can stand alone to meet the threat of those who make themselves our adversaries – that no free nation can retain any illusions about the nature of the threat – and that no free nation can remain indifferent to the steady erosion of freedom around the globe.

It is equally clear that no Western nation on its own can help those less developed lands to fulfill their hopes for steady progress.

And finally, it is clear that in an age where new forces are asserting their strength around the globe – when the political shape of the hemispheres is changing rapidly – nothing is more vital than the unity of the United States and of Canada.

And, so my friends of Canada, whatever problems may exist or arise between us, I can assure you that my associates and I will be ever ready to discuss them with you, and to take whatever steps we can to remove them. And whatever those problems may be, I can also assure you that they shrink in comparison with the great and awesome tasks that await us as free and peace-loving nations.

So let us fix our attention not on those matters that vex us as neighbours, but on the issues that face us as leaders. Let us look southward as part of the hemisphere with whose fate we are both inextricably bound. Let us look eastward as part of the North Atlantic Community upon whose strength and will so many depend. Let us look westward to Japan, to the newly emerging lands of Asia and Africa and the Middle East, where lie the people upon whose fate and choice the struggle for freedom may ultimately depend. And let us look at the world in which we live and hope to go on living – and at the way of life for which Canadians – and I was reminded again of this this morning, on my visit to your War Memorial – and Americans alike have always been willing to give up their lives in nearly every generation, if necessary, to defend and preserve freedom.

First, if you will, consider our mutual hopes for this hemisphere. Stretching virtually from Pole to Pole, the nations of the Western hemisphere are bound together by the laws of economics as well as geography, by a common dedication to freedom as well as a common history of fighting for it. To make this entire area more secure against aggression of all kinds – to defend it against the encroachment of international communism in this hemisphere – and to see our sister states fulfill their hopes and needs for economic and social reform and development – are surely all challenges confronting your nation, and deserving of your talents and resources, as well as ours.

To be sure, it would mean an added responsibility; but yours is not a nation that shrinks from responsibility. The hemisphere is a family into which we were born – and we cannot turn our backs on it in time of trouble. Nor can we stand aside from its great adventure of development. I believe that all of the free members of the Organization of American States would be heartened and strengthened by any increase in your hemispheric role. Your skills, your resources, your judicious perception at the council table – even when it differs from our own view – are all needed throughout the inter-American community. Your country and mine are partners in North American affairs – can we not now become partners in inter-American affairs?

Secondly, let us consider our mutual hopes for the North Atlantic Community.

Our NATO alliance is still, as it was when it was founded, the world's greatest bulwark of freedom. But the military balance of power has been changing. Enemy tactics and weaponry have been changing. We can stand still only at our peril.

NATO force structures were originally devised to meet the threat of a massive conventional attack, in a period of Western nuclear monopoly.

Now, if we are to meet the defence requirements of the 1960s, the NATO countries must push forward simultaneously along two lines.

First, we must strengthen the conventional capability of our Alliance as a matter of the highest priority.

To this end, we in the United States are taking steps to increase the strength and mobility of our forces and to modernize their equipment. To the same end, we will maintain our forces now on the European Continent and will increase their conventional capabilities. We look to our NATO Allies to assign an equally high priority to this same essential task.

Second, we must make certain that nuclear weapons will continue to be available for the defence of the entire Treaty area, and that these weapons are at all times under close and flexible political control that meets the needs of all the NATO countries. We are prepared to join our allies in working out suitable arrangements for this purpose. To make clear our own intentions and commitments to the defence of Western Europe, the United States will commit, to the NATO command, five – and subsequently still more – Polaris atomic-missile submarines, which are defensive weapons, subject to any agreed NATO guidelines on their control and use, and responsive to the needs of all members but still credible in an emergency. Beyond this, we look to the possibility of eventually establishing a NATO seaborne force, which would be truly multi-lateral in ownership and control, if this should be desired and found feasible by our allies, once NATO's non-nuclear goals have been achieved.

Both of these measures – improved conventional forces and increased nuclear forces – are put forward in recognition of the fact that the defence of Europe and the assurances that can be given to the people of Europe and the defence of North America are indivisible – in the hope that no aggressor will mistake our desire for peace with our determination to respond instantly to any attack with whatever force is appropriate – and in the conviction that the time has come for all members of the NATO community to further increase and integrate their respective forces in the NATO command area, coordinating and sharing in research, development, production, storage, defence, command and training at all levels of armaments. So let us begin. Our opponents are watching to see if we in the West are divided. They take courage when we are. We must not let them be deceived or in doubt about our willingness to maintain our own freedom.

Third, let us turn to the less-developed nations in the southern half of the globe – those who struggle to escape the bonds of mass misery – which appeals to our hearts as well as to our hopes. Both your nation and mine have recognized our responsibilities to these new nations. Our people have given generously, if not always effectively. We could not do less. And now we must do more.

For our historic task in this embattled age is not merely to defend freedom. It is to extend its writ and strengthen its covenant to peoples of different cultures and creeds and colours, whose policy or economic system may differ from ours, but whose desire to be free is no less fervent than our own. Through the Organization for Economic Cooperation and Development and the Development Assistance Group, we can pool our vast resources and skills, and make available the kind of long-term capital, planning and know-how without which these nations will never achieve independent and viable economies, and without which our efforts will be tragically wasted. I propose further that the OECD establish a Development Center, where citizens, officials, students, and professional men of the Atlantic area and the less-developed world can meet to study in common the problems of economic development.

If we in the Atlantic Community can more closely coordinate our own economic policies – and certainly the OECD provides the framework if we but use it, and I hope that you will join as we are seeking to join to use it – then surely our potential economic resources are adequate to meet our responsibility. Consider, for example, the unsurpassed productivity of our farms. Less than eight percent of the American working force is on our farms; less than eleven percent of the Canadian working force is on yours. Fewer men on fewer acres than any nation on earth – but free men on free acres can produce here in North America all the food that a hungry world could use – while all the collective farms and forced labor of the communist system produce one shortage after another. This is a day-to-day miracle of our free societies, easy to forget at a time when our minds are caught up in the glamour of beginning the exploration of space.

As the new nations emerge into independence, they face a choice: shall they develop by the method of consent, or by turning their freedom over to the system of totalitarian control? In making that decision, they should look long and hard at the tragedy now being played out in the villages of Communist China.

If we can work closely together to make our food surpluses a blessing instead of a curse, no man, woman or child need go hungry. And if each of the more fortunate nations can bear its fair share of the effort to help the less-fortunate – not merely those with whom we have traditional ties, but all who are willing and able to achieve meaningful growth and dignity

– then this decade will surely be a turning-point in the history of the human family.

Finally, let me say just a few words about the world in which we live. We should not misjudge the force of the challenge that we face – a force that is powerful as well as insidious, that inspires dedication as well as fear, that uses means we cannot adopt to achieve ends we cannot permit. Nor can we mistake the nature of the struggle. It is not for concessions or territory. It is not simply between different systems. It is an age-old battle for the survival of liberty itself. And our great advantage – and we must never forget it – is that the irresistible tide that began five hundred years before the birth of Christ in ancient Greece is for freedom and against tyranny. That is the wave of the future, and the iron hand of totalitarianism can ultimately neither seize it nor turn it back. In the words of Macaulay: "A single breaker may recede, but the tide is coming in."

So we in the Free World are not without hope. We are not without friends. And we are not without resources to defend ourselves and those who are associated with us. Believing in the peaceful settlement of disputes in the defence of human rights, we are working throughout the United Nations, and through regional and other associations, to lessen the risks, the tensions and the means and opportunity for aggression that have been mounting so rapidly throughout the world. In these councils of peace – in the UN Emergency Force in the Middle East, in the Congo, in the International Control Commission in South East Asia, in the Ten Nations Commission on Disarmament – Canada has played a leading, important, and constructive role.

If we can contain the powerful struggle of ideologies, and reduce it to manageable proportions, we can proceed with the transcendent task of disciplining the nuclear weapons which shadow our lives, and of finding a widened range of common enterprises between ourselves and those who live under Communist rule. For, in the end, we live on one planet and we are part of one human family; whatever the struggles that confront us, we must lose no chance to move forward towards a world of law and a world of disarmament.

At the conference table and in the minds of men, the Free World's cause is strengthened because it is just. But it is strengthened even more by the dedicated efforts of free men and free nations. As the great parliamentarian Edmund Burke said, "The only thing necessary for the triumph of evil is for good men to do nothing." And that, in essence, is why I am here today. This trip is more than a consultation – more than a good-will visit. It is an act of faith – faith in your country, in your leaders – faith in the capacity of two great neighbours to meet their common problems – and faith in the cause of freedom, in which we are so intimately associated.

Chapter 13

President Richard M. Nixon's Address to a Joint Session of Parliament
14 April 1972

I am grateful for this chance to return to Canada, for the opportunity of signing here a historic agreement to restore and protect forever the quality of the Great Lakes we share together. That agreement testifies to the continuing vitality of our unique relationship, which has been described so eloquently by the prime minister. I wish to discuss that relationship today in a way that has not always been customary when leaders of our two countries have met.

Through the years, our speeches on such occasions have often centered on the decades of unbroken friendship that we have enjoyed, and on our 4,000 miles of unfortified boundary. In focusing on our peaceful borders and our peaceful history, they have tended to gloss over the fact that there are real problems between us. They have tended to create the false impression that our countries are essentially alike.

It is time for Canadians and Americans to move beyond the sentimental rhetoric of the past. It is time for us to recognize that we have very separate identities; that we have significant differences; and that nobody's interests are furthered when these realities are obscured.

Our peaceful borders and our peaceful history are important symbols, to be sure. What they symbolize, however, is the spirit of respect and restraint which allows us to cooperate, despite our differences, in ways which help us both.

American policy toward Canada is rooted in that spirit. Our policy toward Canada reflects the new approach we are taking in all of our foreign relations – an approach which has been called the Nixon Doctrine. That doctrine rests on the premise that mature partners must have autonomous, independent policies. Each nation must define the nature of its own interests. Each nation must decide the requirements of its own security. Each nation must determine the path of its own progress.

What we seek is a policy which enables us to share international responsibilities in a spirit of international partnership. We believe that the spirit of partnership is strongest when partners are self-reliant. For among nations – as within nations – the soundest unity is that which respects diversity, and the strongest cohesion is that which rejects coercion.

Over the years, the people of Canada have come to understand these concepts particularly well. Within your own borders, you have been working to bring a wide variety of peoples and provinces and points of view into a great national union – a union which honours the integrity of its constituent elements. It was Prime Minister Laurier who said of Canada's differing components: "I want the marble to remain the marble; I want the granite to remain the granite; I want the oak to remain the oak." This has been the Canadian way. As a result, Canadians have helped to teach the world, as Governor-General Massey once said, that the "toleration of differences is the measure of civilization."

Today, more than ever before, we need to apply that understanding to the whole range of world affairs. And to begin with, we must apply it to our dealings with one another. We must realize that we are friends, not because there have been no problems between us, but because we have trusted one another enough to be candid about our problems – and because our candor has nourished our cooperation.

Last December, your prime minister and I met in Washington, and he asked me if I thought that the United States would always want a surplus trade balance with Canada so that we could always export capital here. My answer then, and my answer now, is "no." As I said to him at that time, we in the United States saw this same problem from the other side before World War I. We then depended on European capital for our development, and we wanted to free ourselves from that dependence. And so we fully understand that Canada is in that same position today.

Canada is the largest trading partner of the United States. It is very important that that be noted in Japan, too. [Laughter] Our economies have become highly interdependent. But the fact of our mutual interdependence and our mutual desire for independence need not be inconsistent traits. No self-respecting nation can or should accept the proposition that it should always be economically dependent upon any other nation. And so, let us recognize, once and for all, that the only basis for a sound and healthy relationship between our two proud peoples is to find a pattern of economic interaction which is beneficial to both our countries – and which respects Canada's right to chart its own economic course. We must also build a new spirit of partnership within the Western Hemisphere that we share together.

It has been said that Canada is bounded "on the north by gold, on the west by the East, on the east by history, and on the south by friends." We hope that will always be the case and we hope it will be the case not only with respect to the United States, your immediate neighbour to the south, but with respect to all your southern neighbours – and ours – who are bound by the great forces of geography and history which are distinctive to the New World.

But geography and history alone do not make a community. A true community must be a living entity in which the individuality of each member is a source of pride to all members, in which the unity of all is a source of strength to each. The great community of the Americas cannot be complete without the participation of Canada. That is why we have been encouraged by the recent decisions of Canada to upgrade its participation as an observer in the Organization of American States to ambassadorial status, and to apply for membership in the Inter-American Development Bank, for both of these institutions make the abstract concept of community within the Americas a living reality.

A sound concept of community is also important in another international arena that we share, the Atlantic Alliance. Just one month after my inauguration as President of the United States, I observed that a new spirit of cooperation within that Alliance was essential, as we began a new search for cooperation between East and West. The recent agreements concerning Berlin – the fact, for example, that thousands of families were reunited this Easter for the first time in many years – these are among the first fruits of a new era of East-West negotiation.

But as we seek better relations with our adversaries, it becomes all the more important to strengthen the alliances with our friends. We must never forget that the strength and the unity of the West has been an indispensable element in helping to bring about the new era of negotiation with the East. And that is why we began our round of summit talks last December by meeting with the Prime Minister of Canada, and then with the leaders of other close allies. That is why our East-West conversations will always be accompanied by full and genuine consultation within the Atlantic Alliance. That Alliance began as a way of pooling military resources. Today, it is a way of pooling our intellectual and our diplomatic resources as well. Like our Federal approaches to nationhood, like our Canadian-American brotherhood, like our inter-American neighbourhood, the Atlantic Alliance has achieved a creative unity in which the individuality of its members is respected and advanced.

Let us turn now to the world as a whole – for this is where the challenge of building a true community will be most difficult – and most important. We in Canada and the United States have always been proud to live in what is called the New World. Today, there is a new world coming for everyone who lives on this globe. It is our responsibility to make this new world a better world than the world we have known.

Canadians and Americans have fought and died together in two World Wars in this century. We live now in what has been called the post-war era. But mankind has known a long succession of post-war eras. And each one of them has turned out to be a pre-war era as well. The challenge we face today is to build a permanent post-war era – an era of lasting peace.

My visit to Ottawa comes midway between visits to Peking and to Moscow. In many respects, these journeys are very different. In the People's Republic of China, we opened a new dialogue after 22 years of virtually no communication. In the Soviet Union, there is an opportunity to bring a continuing dialogue to productive conclusions.

But in their central aim, these journeys to Peking and Moscow are alike. Neither visit is directed against anyone – adversary or ally. Both are for the betterment of everyone – for the peace of all mankind. However, we must not allow the fact of summit meetings to create any unrealistic euphoria.

The responsibility for building peace rests with special weight upon the great powers. Whether the great powers fulfill that responsibility depends not on the atmospherics of their diplomacy, but on the realities of their behavior. Great powers must not treat a period of *détente* as an interlude between periods of tension. Better relations among all nations require restraint by great nations, both in dealing with each other and in dealing with the rest of the world.

We can agree to limit arms. We can declare our peaceful purposes. But neither the limitation of arms nor the declaration of peaceful purposes will bring peace if, directly or indirectly, the aggressive use of existing weapons is encouraged. And great powers cannot avoid responsibility for the aggressive actions of those to whom they give the means for embarking on such actions. The great powers must use their influence to halt aggression – and not to encourage it. The structure of world peace cannot be built unless the great powers join together to build it, and its strength will grow only as all nations – of all political and social systems – come to accept its validity and sustain its vitality. This does not mean that the great powers must always agree.

We expect to continue to have profound philosophical and significant diplomatic differences with the Soviet Union and with the People's Republic of China in a number of areas. But, through opening new lines of communication, we hope to increase the chance that, in the future, we shall talk about our differences and not fight about them.

As we have prepared for both of these journeys, the experience of Canada has been most helpful. I am grateful to both the prime minister and to the Opposition Leader, Mr. [Robert L.] Stanfield, for sharing their insights with us as we embark on these endeavors.

As we continue toward our common quest for a better world order, let us apply the lessons we have learned so well on this continent:

- that we can walk our own road in our own way without moving further apart, that we can grow closer together without growing more alike;

– that peaceful competition can produce winners without producing losers, that success for some need not mean setbacks for others;

– that a rising tide will lift all our boats, that to go forward at all is to go forward together;

– that the enemy of peace is not independence but isolation, and that the way to peace is an open world.

And let us remember, too, these truths that we have found together:

– that variety can mean vitality;

– that diversity can be a force for progress; and

– that our ultimate destiny is indivisible.

When I spoke at the St. Lawrence Seaway ceremonies in 1969, I borrowed some words from the monument there which I had joined Queen Elizabeth in dedicating just ten years before. That monument, as its inscription puts it, "bears witness to the common purpose of two nations whose frontiers are the frontiers of friendship, whose ways are the ways of freedom, whose works are the works of peace." The truth to which that inscription testifies is of profound importance to people everywhere in this world.

For the ability of our two nations, Canada and the United States, to preserve the frontiers of friendship, to walk in the ways of freedom, and to pursue the works of peace provides example and encouragement to all who seek those same objectives, wherever they may live.

There is nothing more exciting than a time of new beginnings. A member of this body caught that spirit when he spoke in parliament about the beginnings of Canadian nationhood 100 years ago. Listen to him: "Blood pulsed in our veins, new hopes fired our hearts, new horizons lifted and widened, new visions came to us in the night watches."

May that same sense of excitement inspire our two nations as we help lead the world to new beginnings today.

Chapter 14

President Ronald W. Reagan's Address to a Joint Session of Parliament
11 March 1981

I came to this great capital of this great nation by crossing a border not which divides us, but a border which joins us. For those of my own party who accompanied me, I have said we've often shaken hands across this border, and we're doing it once again today.

Nancy and I have arrived for this, the first state visit of my presidency, in the spirit expressed so well by a Calgary writer and publisher some 60 years ago. He said, "The difference between a friend and an acquaintance is that a friend helps where an acquaintance merely advises." [Laughter] Well, we come here not to advise, not to lecture; we are here to listen and to work with you. We're here as friends, not as acquaintances.

Some years ago, Nancy and I both belonged to a very honourable profession in California. And as I prepared for these remarks today, I learned that among those in the motion picture industry in Hollywood, it has been estimated that perhaps as many as one out of five are of Canadian origin. Now, many of those whom I counted as close professional colleagues and, indeed, close personal friends did not come from America's heartland, as I did, but from the heart of Canada, as did most of you in this historic chamber. Art Linkletter, Glenn Ford, Raymond Massey, Walter Pidgeon, Raymond Burr are but a few of your countrymen who are celebrated in our entertainment industry.

I believe I know the very special relationship between Canada and the United States, but with all respect to those few that I have mentioned, I can do better than that. A young lady once came to Hollywood from Toronto, and before long, little Gladys Smith was embraced by our entire nation. Gladys Smith of Toronto became Mary Pickford. And I know that you'll forgive us for adopting her so thoroughly that she became known the world over as "America's sweetheart." [Laughter] But "America's sweetheart" was Canadian. [Laughter]

Affinity, heritage, common borders, mutual interests – these have all built the foundation for our strong bilateral relationship. This relationship has grown to include some of the strongest economic links among the nations of this Earth. Some 16 percent of America's total world trade is done with Canada. Our joint trade amounts to about 90 billion Canadian dollars annually. This is greater than the gross national product of some

150 countries. It's estimated that three-quarters of a million United States workers are employed in exports to Canada and, in turn, Canadian exports to the United States account for one-sixth of your gross national product. Not only is the vast bulk of this trade conducted between private traders in two free economic systems, but more than half crosses our borders duty-free. Our seaways, highways, airways, and rails are the arteries of a massive, interconnecting trade network, which has been critically important to both of us.

Thus, while America counts many friends across the globe, surely we have no better friend than Canada. And though we share bilateral interests with countries throughout the world, none exceeds the economic, cultural, and security interests that we share with you. These strong and significant mutual interests are among the reasons for my visit here. Already, I have shared with Prime Minister Trudeau very helpful discussions across a range of issues – to listen and to ensure that these important ties shall not loosen.

I'm happy to say that in the recent past we've made progress on matters of great mutual importance. Our governments have already discussed one of the largest joint private projects ever undertaken by two nations – the pipeline to bring Alaskan gas to the continental United States. We strongly favor prompt completion of this project based on private funds. We have agreed to a historic liberalization of our trade in the Tokyo Round of the multilateral trade negotiations. We've continued our efforts, begun with the *Great Lakes Water Quality Agreement* of 1972, to protect our joint heritage in the Great Lakes. We want to continue to work cooperatively to understand and control the air and water pollution that respects no borders. During my visit here, I've had the pleasure of participating in the conclusion of two other important agreements.

We are renewing the North American Aerospace Defence Command Agreement for five more years. For more than two decades now, NORAD has bound us together in our common defence, with an integrated command structure symbolizing our interdependence. This agreement represents continued progress in our relations and mutual security. And second, we have concluded an agreement regarding social security benefits between those of our citizens who combine work in both nations. And with this new agreement, these people who are employed in both countries can then be eligible for the combined benefits. And the workers will be eligible for those benefits in whichever country they choose to live.

Our deep and longtime bilateral economic interests lead me to depart from the norm today, and to give to you a report on America's progress toward economic recovery.

Five weeks ago, I reported to the American people that the US economy faced the worst economic mess since the great worldwide depression. We're a proud people, but we're also realists. The time has come for us to face up to what I described as a potential economic calamity. I raise this issue today because America holds a genuine belief in its obligation to consult with its friends and neighbours. The economic actions that we take affect not just us alone, but the relationships across our borders as well.

As we examined America's economic illness, we isolated a number of contributing factors. Our Federal Government has grown explosively in a very short period of time. We found that there had grown up a maze of stifling regulations, that has began to crush initiative and deaden the dynamic industrial innovation which brought us to where we are. We saw unbelievable deficits – this year alone reaching up to nearly $80 billion, including off-budget items. And we found that these deficits got in no one's way, because the government found it easy to fuel inflation by printing more money, just to make up the difference.

The American taxing structure, the purpose of which was to serve the people, began instead to serve the insatiable appetite of government. If you will forgive me, you know someone has once likened government to a baby. It is an alimentary canal with an appetite at one end and no sense of responsibility at the other. [Laughter] But our citizens were being thrown into higher tax brackets for simply trying to keep pace with inflation. In just the last five years, Federal personal taxes for the average American household have increased 58 percent. The results: crippling inflation, interest rates which went above 20 percent, a national debt approaching a trillion dollars, nearly eight million people out of work, and a steady three-year decline in productivity.

We decided not just to complain, but to act. In a series of messages and actions, we have begun the slow process of stopping the assault on the American economy and returning to the strong and steady prosperity that we once enjoyed. It's very important for us to have our friends and partners know and understand what we're doing. Let me be blunt and honest. The United States in the last few years has not been as solid and stable an ally and trading partner as it should be. How can we expect certain things of our friends if we don't have our own house in order?

Americans are uniting now, as they always have, in times of adversity. I have found there is a wellspring of spirit and faith in my country which will drive us forward to gain control of our lives and restore strength and vitality to our economic system. But we act not just for ourselves but to enhance our relationships with those we respect.

First, we're taking near-revolutionary steps to cut back the growth in Federal spending in the United States. We're proposing that instead of having our national budget grow at the unacceptable rate of 14 percent per year, it should rise at a more sensible six percent. This enables us to maintain the kind of growth we need to protect those in our society who are truly dependent on government services. Just yesterday, I submitted our proposed budget for the coming year – and then immediately crossed the border. [Laughter] With extraordinary effort, we've isolated some 83 items for major savings and hundreds more for smaller savings, which together amount to $48.6 billion in the coming fiscal year.

Our second proposal is a ten percent cut, across the board every year for three years, in the tax rates for all individual income tax payers, making a total cut in tax rates of 30 percent. This will leave our taxpayers with $500 billion more in their pockets over the next five years and will create dramatic new incentives to boost productivity and fight inflation. When these personal cuts are combined with tax cuts to provide our business and industry with new capital for innovation and growth, we will be creating millions of new jobs, many of them ultimately on your side of the border.

Our third proposal is to eliminate those unproductive and unnecessary regulations which have slowed down our growth and added to our inflationary burdens. We shall do this with care, while still safeguarding the health and safety of the American people and, I might add, while mindful of our responsibility to have equal regard for the health and safety of our neighbours.

Finally, we'll be working closely with our Federal Reserve System to achieve stable and moderate growth patterns in our money supply.

As I said, America's program for economic recovery is designed not merely to solve an internal problem; it is viewed by my administration as part of an essential effort to restore the confidence of our friends and allies in what we're doing. When we gain control of our inflation, we can once again contribute more helpfully to the health of the world economy. We believe that confidence will rise, interest rates will decline, and investment will increase. As our inflation is reduced, your citizens and other world citizens will have to import less inflation from us.

As we begin to expand our economy once again, and as our people begin to keep more control of their own money, we'll be better trading partners. Our growth will help fuel the steady prosperity of our friends. The control we regain over our tax and regulatory structures will have the effect of restoring steady growth in US productivity. Our goods will go into markets, not laden down with the drag of regulatory baggage or punitive levies, but with a competitive edge that helps us and those who trade with us.

Now, such new, sustained prosperity in an era of reduced inflation will also serve worldwide to help all of us resist protectionist impulses. We want open markets. We want to promote lower costs globally. We want to increase living standards throughout the world. And that's why we're working so hard to bring about this economic renewal.

There are, of course, other very important reasons for us to restore our economic vitality. Beyond our shores and across this troubled globe, the good word of the United States and its ability to remain stable and dependable rely in good part on our having a stable and dependable economy. Projecting solid internal strengths is essential to the West's ability to maintain peace and security in the world. Thus, our national interests, our bilateral interests, and our hemispheric interests are profoundly involved in truly international questions. That's why we must act now, why we can no longer be complacent about the consequences of economic deterioration. We've entered an era that commands the Alliance to restore its leadership in the world. And before we can be strong in the world, we must be once again strong at home.

Our friend, our ally, our partner, and our neighbour Canada, and the United States have always worked together to build a world with peace and stability, a world of freedom and dignity for all people. Now, with our other friends, we must embark with great spirit and commitment on the path toward unity and strength. On this side of the Atlantic, we must stand together for the integrity of our hemisphere, for the inviolability of its nations, for its defence against imported terrorism, and for the rights of all our citizens to be free from the provocations triggered from outside our sphere for malevolent purposes. Across the oceans, we stand together against the unacceptable Soviet invasion into Afghanistan and against continued Soviet adventurism across the Earth. And toward the oppressed and dispirited people of all nations, we stand together as friends ready to extend a helping hand.

I say to you, our Canadian friends, and to all nations who will stand with us for the cause of freedom: Our mission is more than simply making do in an untidy world. Our mission is what it has always been – to lift the world's dreams beyond the short limits of our sights and to the far edges of our best hopes.

This will not be an era of losing liberty; it shall be one of gaining it. This will not be an era of economic pessimism, of restraint and retrenchment; it will be one of restoration, growth, and expanding opportunities for all men and women. And we will not be here merely to survive; we will be here, in William Faulkner's words, to "prevail," to regain our destiny and our mutual honour.

Sometimes it seems that because of our comfortable relationship, we dwell perhaps a bit too much on our differences. Now, I too have referred to the fact that we do not agree on all issues. We share so many things with each other; yet, for good reasons, we insist on being different to retain our separate identities. This captured the imagination of Ernest Hemingway, when he worked as a writer for the *Toronto Star Weekly* in 1922. Hemingway was traveling in Switzerland, and he noted that the Swiss made no distinction between Canadians and citizens of the United States. And he wondered about this. He asked a hotel keeper if he didn't notice any difference between the people from the two countries. "Monsieur," he said to Hemingway, "Canadians speak English and always stay two days longer at any place than Americans do." [Laughter] Well, as you know, I shall be returning to Ottawa in July, and if you don't mind, I'll plan to stay as long as everyone else. [Applause]

I'm not here today to dwell on our differences. When President Eisenhower spoke from this spot in 1953, he noted his gratitude as Allied Commander in World War II for the Canadian contribution to the liberation of the Mediterranean. This touched my curiosity, and even though I'd participated in that war myself, I did a little research. In the Second World War, there was something called the 1st Special Service Force, a unique international undertaking at the time. This force was composed of Canadians and Americans, distributed equally throughout its ranks, carrying the flags of both nations. They served under a joint command, were taught a hybrid close order drill, and trained together as paratroopers, demolition experts, ski troops, and then as an amphibious unit.

The 1st Special Service Force became famous for its high morale, its rugged abilities, and tough fighting in situations where such reputations were hard-earned. Alerted to their availability, General Eisenhower requested them for special reconnaissance and raiding operations during the winter advance up the Italian peninsula. They were involved in the Anzio beachhead campaign in Italy, and were at the spearhead of the forces that captured Rome. The 1st Special Service Force made no distinctions when it went into battle. Its men had the common cause of freedom at their side and the common denominator of courage in their hearts. They were neither Canadian nor American. They were, in General Eisenhower's term, liberators.

So, let's speak no more of differences today. Certainly your Ambassador, Ken Taylor didn't, when he first sheltered and then spirited six Americans out of the center of Tehran, and brought them to their freedom. Their daring escape worked not because of our differences, but because of our shared likenesses.

A final word to the people of Canada: We're happy to be your neighbour. We want to remain your friend. We're determined to be your partner, and we're intent on working closely with you in a spirit of cooperation. We are much more than an acquaintance.

Merci. Thank you.

Chapter 15

President Ronald Reagan's Address to a Joint Session of Parliament
6 April 1987

It's a great honour to speak to you today. As you know, this is my third official visit to Canada. My last two were the first foreign trips I'd taken after each election, but our constitutional prohibitions being what they are, I thought it wasn't wise to wait for another election before visiting you again. [Laughter] I also wanted to time this trip after March, so people wouldn't think that these state visits were just an excuse for Prime Minister Mulroney and me to celebrate St. Patrick's Day together. [Laughter] On each of these occasions, I have been struck by how much our two nations have in common. Despite our many important differences, you see the similarities of our national characters in, among other things, the sports we share: hockey, baseball, football – with some modifications – [laughter] – and that fourth sport, which seems to be as popular on both sides of the 49th parallel, giving a hard time to political leaders of Irish descent. [Laughter]

It's truly an honour to have a second opportunity to address this August body, this great democratic legislature that has been witness to and shaper of so much of the history of freedom. I remember those days not so very long after the attack on Pearl Harbor had once again united our two nations in a world conflict, when Winston Churchill stood where I am standing today. Wake Island had fallen just a week before. On Christmas Day, after an heroic defence by Canadian troops, Hong Kong was captured by the Axis. Manila was soon to be swallowed up as well. But those who might have been expecting a picture of democracy in retreat got something very different from that indomitable spirit. "We have not journeyed all this way across the centuries," he said, "across the oceans, across the mountains, across the prairies, because we're made of sugar candy." Churchill was speaking of the members of the British Commonwealth, most specifically of the people of Canada – but I confess we Americans have always flattered ourselves that, though the thought was unspoken, he had us in mind, too. [Laughter]

As two proud and independent peoples, there is much that distinguishes us one from the other, but there is also much that we share: a vast continent, with its common hardships and uncommon duties; generations of mutual respect and support; and an abiding friendship that grows ever stronger. We are two nations, each built by immigrant refugees from tyranny and want, pioneers of a new land of liberty. The first settlers of this New World, alone before the majesty of nature, alone before God, must have been thrown back on first principles, must have realized that it was only in their most basic values that they would find the wisdom to endure and the strength to triumph. And so, a dedication was formed, as hard as the granite of the Rockies, a dedication to freedom, a commitment to those unalienable human rights and their only possible guarantee: the institutions of democratic government.

A shared history, yes, but more than that, a shared purpose. It must have seemed to Churchill, besieged and isolated as he was in the one corner of Europe still clinging to freedom, that this American Continent and his two great friends and one-time colonies had been placed here by a wise and prescient God, protected between two vast oceans, to keep freedom safe. In the crisis of the moment, Churchill said it was not then time to "speak of the hopes of the future, or the broader world which lies beyond our struggles and our victory." "We must first," he said, "win that world for our children." In a very real sense, that is still our imperative today: to win the world for our children, to win it for freedom. Today, our task is not merely the survival of liberty but to keep the peace while we extend liberty to a world desperately in need. Today, we still contend against war, against a foreign expansionism, and I will speak to that in a moment.

But I wish first to talk about a second struggle, one that must occupy an equal place in our attentions: the struggle against the plagues of poverty and underdevelopment that still ravage so much of mankind. Our two nations have committed many resources to that struggle, but we have it within our power at this moment to take a historic step toward a growing world economy, and an expanding cycle of prosperity that reaches beyond the industrialized powers even to the developing nations. We can lead, first, by our powerful example, specifically by the example of Prime Minister Mulroney's farsighted proposal to establish a free trade agreement that would eliminate most remaining trade barriers between Canada and the United States.

After the allied victory over the Axis powers, America and Canada combined their efforts to help restore Europe to economic health. Those were golden years of international economic cooperation that saw the creation of GATT, which knocked down the tariff barriers that had so damaged the world economy; the International Monetary Fund; and, 30 years ago last month, the creation of the Common Market. The theme that ran through it all was free and fair trade. Free and fair trade was the lifeblood of a reinvigourated Europe, a revitalized free world that saw a generation of growth unparalleled in history.

We must keep these principles fixed in our minds as we move forward on Prime Minister Mulroney's free trade proposal, a proposal that I'm convinced will prove no less historic. Already, our two nations generate the world's largest volume of trade. The United States trades more with the province of Ontario alone than with Japan. United States citizens are by far the principal foreign investors in Canada, and Canadians on a per capita basis are even greater investors in our country. This two-way traffic in trade and investment has helped to create new jobs by the millions, to expand opportunity for both our peoples, and to augment the prosperity of both our nations.

Prime Minister Mulroney's proposal would establish the largest free trade area in the world, benefiting not only our two countries, but setting an example of cooperation to all nations that now wrestle against the siren temptation of protectionism. To those who would hunker down behind barriers to fight a destructive and self-defeating round of trade battles, Canada and the United States will show the positive way. We will overcome the impulse of economic isolationism with a brotherly embrace – an embrace, it is not too much to hope – that may someday extend throughout the Americas and ultimately encompass all free nations. We can look forward to the day when the free flow of trade, from the southern reaches of Tierra del Fuego to the northern outposts of the Arctic Circle, unites the people of the Western Hemisphere in a bond of mutually beneficial exchange, when all borders become what the US – Canadian border so long has been: a meeting place, rather than a dividing line.

We recognize that the issues facing us are many and difficult. And, just as this proud parliament is watching our negotiations, so, too, is the United States Congress. A comprehensive, balanced agreement that provides open trade and investment on a comprehensive basis, an agreement in which both sides are winners – that is our goal. Augmenting the spirit of the Uruguay trade negotiations, prelude to our economic summit in Venice this June, our free trade discussions here will be a model of cooperation to the world. Mr. Prime Minister, this will be a pioneering agreement worthy of a pioneering people, a visionary strategy worthy of the elected head of one of the world's greatest democracies. Mr. Prime Minister, we salute you, and I pledge to you now that, for our part, we shall commit ourselves and the resources of our administration to good-faith negotiations that will make this visionary proposal a reality. And on this, the Canadian people and the Members of Parliament have my word.

Freedom works. The democratic freedoms that secure the God-given rights of man, and the economic freedoms that open the door to prosperity – they are the hope and, we trust, the destiny of mankind. If free trade is the lifeblood, free enterprise is the heart of prosperity. Jobs, rising incomes, opportunity – they must be created, day to day, through the enterprise of free men and women. We've had to learn and relearn this lesson in this century. In my own country, we have witnessed an expansion and strengthening of many of our civil liberties, but too often we have seen our economic liberties neglected, even abused. We have protected the freedom of expression of the author, as we should; but what of the freedom of expression of the entrepreneur, whose pen and paper are capital and whose profits and whose literature is the heroic epic of free enterprise, a tale of creativity and invention that not only delights the mind but has improved the condition of man, feeding the poor with new grains, bringing hope to the ailing with new cures, vanquishing ignorance with wondrous new information technologies.

In the United States, we have found a new consensus among members of both parties in a reformed tax structure that lowers tax rates and frees the spirit of enterprise of our people. Today, that consensus is broadening as your great free-market nation seeks to back the first principles of economic growth through rate-reducing tax reform. We've seen movements in Germany and Japan, as well, to cut tax rates. But this must be only the beginning, for what is simply beneficial to us is a matter of the most dire necessity to the nations and peoples of the developing world. And this is the second great example that, together, we offer to the nations of the world in desperate economic need. For the poorer, the more desperate their condition, the more urgently they need the growth that only economic freedom can bring.

We have seen time and again the healing, invigourating effects of economic freedom. Tax rate cuts lifted both Germany and Japan out of postwar stagnation and into the forefront of the world economy. Low tax rates catapulted the nations of the Pacific Basin out of the Third World, making them major economic partners today. A recent study prepared for our government found a direct relationship between the high tax rates and other statist policies of many underdeveloped countries and a cycle of deepening poverty and despair. On the other hand, the study found that countries with low tax rates and free market policies are among the fastest growing in the world, providing improved living standards and increased opportunity for all their people.

We apply the principles of economic freedom at home; we should not export central planning and statist economics abroad. When the Holy Father came to this country, he spoke of the moral obligation of the wealthier nations to share with those less fortunate. Well, it's time to take up that challenge. Both our countries have been generous donors of foreign aid, and that's important. But our own experience, the experience of this century, has shown that the only effective way to share prosperity is to share the conditions that generate prosperity. History has proven beyond a shadow of a doubt that statism spreads poverty; it is only freedom that begets wealth. And free markets, low tax rates, free trade – this is the most valuable foreign aid we can give to the developing nations of the Third World. These are the weapons of peace we must deploy in the struggle to win a future of liberty for mankind. So many have come to Canada and the United States in hope; let us now give that hope to the world.

Throughout our history, our two nations have keenly felt our international responsibilities. Instrumental in founding and maintaining the NATO alliance, through cooperative efforts in NORAD [North American Aerospace Defence Command], Canada has taken a leading role in defence of the free world. And meanwhile, we have cooperated in extending every effort to lessen the dangers of a nuclear-armed world. Over the past six years, the United States, working closely with Canada and our other allies, has sought to achieve deep reductions in Soviet and American nuclear arms. Thanks to the firmness shown by the alliance, we are moving toward a breakthrough agreement that would dramatically reduce an entire class of weapons: American and Soviet longer range, intermediate-range, INF missiles in Europe and Asia.

We've traveled far to get here, from past treaties that only codified the nuclear buildup, to the point where we may soon see the dismantling of thousands of these agents of annihilation. We're hopeful, we're expectant, but we face many difficulties still. As our negotiators continue to work toward a sound agreement, we are not going to abandon our basic principles or our allies' interests for the sake of a quick fix, an inadequate accord. We will work for truly verifiable reductions that strengthen the security of our friends and allies in both Europe and Asia, and that cannot be circumvented by any imbalance in shorter range INF systems. In short, America will stand where she has always stood: with her allies in defence of freedom and the cause of peace.

We must continue to keep in mind, as well, that a major impetus in our reduction talks has been the growing reality of our Strategic Defence Initiative. SDI supports and advances the objectives of arms control – [Audience member: "No way!"] – offering a more stable and secure environment as we pursue our goal of deep reductions in nuclear weapons. We must move away from a situation of mutual assured destruction – so aptly called MAD, the MAD policy. We need defensive systems that threaten no one, that would save human lives instead of targeting them. We must remember that the Soviet Union has spent 15 times as much on strategic defences as we have, over the last ten years, while their record of compliance with existing arms treaties continues to be a cause for concern. Most people do not understand that mutual assured destruction has left our populations absolutely defenceless. This is an intolerable situation. The truly moral course is to move forward quickly with a new strategy of peace, based not on the ability to threaten lives, but on our own confidence that we can save them. Let us choose a defence that truly defends.

As we've pursued better relations with the Soviet Union, we have laboured to deal realistically with the basic issues that divide that nation from the free world. Our insistence that the Soviet Union adhere to its Helsinki human rights agreement is not just a moral imperative; we know that no nation can truly be at peace with its neighbours if it is not at peace with its own people. In recent months we have heard hopeful talk of change in Moscow, of a new openness. Some political prisoners have been released. The BBC [British Broadcasting Corporation] is no longer jammed. We welcome these positive signs, and hope that they're only the first steps toward a true liberalization of Soviet society.

To the extent that the Soviet Union truly opens its society, its economy and the life of its people will improve. To that extent, we may hope its aggression will diminish. Disappointingly, however, there so far has been little movement on the Soviet side toward the peaceful settlement of regional conflicts that today are flaring across the globe. Despite announcements of cease-fires and talk of national reconciliation, the Soviets' terrible war against Afghanistan remains unabated, and Soviet attacks on neighbouring Pakistan have escalated dangerously. In Cambodia, Ethiopia, and Angola, the Soviet Union continues to support brutal wars of Communist governments against their own people. In Nicaragua, we see such a campaign on our own shores – [At this point, the president was interrupted by a heckler in the audience.] – threatening – is there an echo in here? [Laughter and applause] Thank you. Such a campaign on our own shores, threatening destabilization throughout Central America – this is not just a question of self-protection; the higher principle is that the people of Nicaragua have the right to decide their own future.

The surest sign that the Soviet Union truly wants better relations, that it truly wants peace, would be to end its global strategy to impose one party dictatorships, to allow the people of this world to determine their own futures in liberty and in peace. We have known that when people are given the opportunity to choose, they choose freedom. Truly, the future belongs to the free. In our own hemisphere we've seen a freedom tide sweep over South and Central America. Six years ago only 30 percent of the people of Latin America lived in democracies; today over 90 percent do. Around the world, resistance movements are rising up to throw off the totalitarian yoke. Even in China, they debate the pace of reform, but acknowledge its necessity.

On the border between Canada and the United States stands a plaque commemorating over a century and a half of friendship. It calls the border "a lesson of peace to all nations." And that's what it is: a concrete, living lesson that the path to peace is freedom, that the relations of free peoples – no matter how different, no matter how distinct their national characters – those relations will be marked by admiration, not hostility. Go stand along the border at the beginning of July. You'll see the Maple Leaf and the Stars and Stripes mixed in a swirling cloud of visitors and celebrants. As a Canadian writer once put it: "What's the difference between Dominion Day and July Fourth? About 48 hours." [Laughter] Yes, we have differences, disputes, as any two sovereign nations will; but we're always able to work them out, *entre amis* [between friends].

One area of particular concern to all Canadians, I know, is the problem of acid rain. When the prime minister and I met in Quebec two years ago, we appointed two distinguished envoys, Bill Davis and Drew Lewis, to examine the problem. They issued a joint report, which we have endorsed, and we're actively implementing many of their recommendations. The first phase of our clean coal technology program is underway, the beginning of a $6 billion commitment through 1992, and I have asked Congress for the full share of government spending recommended by the envoys, $2 1/2 billion, for the demonstration of innovative pollution control technologies over the next five years. Literally thousands of firms and millions of jobs will be affected by whatever steps we take on this problem, so there are no quick and easy answers. But working together, we have made an important start, and I am convinced that, as in the past, our disputes will bring us closer as we find a mutual accord. Our differences will become only another occasion for cooperation. Let me assure you that your concerns are my concerns.

I was struck recently by the words of a Canadian – a Hungarian-Canadian you might call him – who came to this country, as so many before him, to escape oppression. "I wanted to stretch," he said. "I needed a place where I could move mountains or carry larger stones than Sisyphus, and here was the place for it. Nobody telling me what I'm supposed to believe, as a Canadian, gave me a kind of freedom for my mind and my spirit and my creative energies that I had never experienced before in life. And I found that for me anyhow, anything could be possible here." This is your Canada, and our continent. This is the chosen place in history our two nations occupy: a land where the mind and heart of man is free, a land of peace, a land where indeed anything is possible.

Let me add a word, if I can, about our discussions today on two issues of critical interest to our two countries. The prime minister and I agreed to consider the prime minister's proposal for a bilateral accord on acid rain, building on the tradition of agreements to control pollution of our shared international waters. The prime minister and I also had a full discussion of the Arctic waters issue, and he and I agreed to inject new impetus to the discussions already underway. We are determined to find a solution based on mutual respect for sovereignty and our common security and other interests.

Thank you all very much, and God bless you all.

The President's car passed by two separate guards of honour leaving Kingston's train station on the way to Queen's University.

Prime Minister William Lyon Mackenzie King and Ontario Lieutenant-Governor Albert Matthews were all smiles greeting the 32nd President of the United States.

"I felt proud with the appearence of the city and the behaviour of the crowds. The evident goodwill on all sides was a striking and memorable feature," Prime Minister King wrote in his diary.

ADMISSION TICKET

You are requested to be at the Stadium (or in case of very bad weather at Kingston Hall) at 10.00 a.m. to join the academic procession.

This ticket admits you at entrance B on the West side of the Stadium to rooms where the procession will be organized. If Grant Hall is used this ticket admits you by the South Door of Kingston Hall.

Daylight Saving Time.

If requested before Wednesday, August 10th, the Convocation Committee will supply a ticket of admission for a member of your family. This ticket will admit to a special seat in the Stadium or to Grant Hall in case of very bad weather. Additional tickets for your family for the Stadium only may also be had.

The Chancellor
the Principal and the Trustees of Queen's University
invite you to be present at a
Special Convocation
when the honorary degree of Doctor of Laws
will be conferred on
Franklin Delano Roosevelt
President of the United States of America
in the George Taylor Richardson Memorial Stadium
at eleven o'clock, Thursday morning, August the eighteenth
nineteen hundred and thirty-eight
(Daylight Saving Time)

R. S. V. P.—Convocation Committee before August 10th.

Queen's University
invites you to be present at a Luncheon
in honour of
President Roosevelt
to be given in Ban Righ Hall
at a quarter to twelve
on Thursday, August the eighteenth

Morning dress

THIS CARD MUST BE PRESENTED FOR ADMISSION

Vice-Principal William Everett McNeill in conversation with FDR at George Richardson Stadium.

FDR listens as Chancellor James Richardson (far right) pronounces the formula of laureation for the degree of Doctor of Laws.

"I am going to do what I very seldom do; I will write my name in full," FDR said as he signed the university's Doomsday Book.

"Queen's University is not a Prince or a potentate but, assuredly, it is a power."

"The Dominion of Canada is part of the sisterhood of the British Empire. I give to you assurance that the people of the United States will not stand idly by if domination of Canadian soil is threatened by any other Empire."

The Presidental limousine leaves George Richardson Stadium.

FDR tips his hat to the crowds.

FDR and the Prime Minister dedicate the Thousand Islands international bridge that still links the province of Ontario and the state of New York to this day.

Front row: Principal Robert C. Wallace, AMS President Ken Phin, Eleanor Roosevelt, Levana Society President Shirley Johnson, Queen's Rector Leonard W. Brockington. Back Row: Dean of Medicine G. Spencer Melvin, Professor, University College Hull (first Dunning Trust Lecturer) T. E. Jessop, Theological College Principal Harold Kent, Dean of Applied Science Douglas Stewart Ellis, University Treasurer Gordon Jenkin Smith, Registrar Jean Royce, Vice-Principal William Alexander Mackintosh, Dean of Women Allie Vibert Douglas.

Eleanor Roosevelt, Honourary Doctor of Law,
8 January 1948, Queen's University

Chapter 16

President William J. Clinton's Address to a Joint Session of Parliament
23 February 1995

I thank the Prime Minister [Jean Chrétien] and all of you for welcoming me to this magnificent capital city. The prime minister first came to this Chamber to represent the people of Canada when President Kennedy was in the White House. I resent that, because when President Kennedy was in the White House, I was in junior high school – [laughter] – and now the prime minister has less gray hair than I do. [Laughter] And he does in spite of the fact that, since that time, he has occupied nearly every seat in his nation's Cabinet. The first time I met him, I wondered why this guy couldn't hold down a job. [Laughter] I can tell you this: We in the United States know that his service to this nation over so many years has earned him the gratitude and the respect of the Canadian people. It has also earned him the gratitude and the respect of the people of the United States.

I know it is traditional for American presidents, when they address this body, to speak of their affection for their ties to the Canadian people. On behalf of the United States, let me stay with that tradition, and say, *l'amitie solide*. But let me say to you that it is a big part of our life. I remember so well more than a decade ago, when Hillary and I, with our then very young daughter came to Canada to celebrate the new year. We started in Montreal, and we drove to Chateau Montebello. And along the way, we drove around Ottawa, and we watched all those wonderful people skating along the canal. I came from a Southern State. I couldn't imagine that anybody could ever get on skates and stand in any body of water for very long. [Laughter]

And I could see that Hillary had in the back of her mind all this time how much she would like to be skating along this canal. I think tomorrow Mrs. Chrétien is going to give her her wish, and we are looking forward to that. My wife has visited Toronto, and we had a wonderful, wonderful family vacation in Western Canada in Victoria and Vancouver back in 1990, one of the best times that all of us have ever had together anywhere. We are deeply indebted to your culture. Our daughter's name was inspired by Canadian songwriter Joni Mitchell's wonderful song, "Chelsea Morning."

All of you know that in the spring of 1993, the first time I left the United States as president, I came to Vancouver for the summit with President Yeltsin. Both of us at this time were under some significant amount of stress, as we tried to reaffirm our relationship and to solidify democracy in Russia. And I can say without any equivocation, the reception we received from the people of Canada, as well as from the government and the Prime Minister (Brian Mulroney), made it very, very easy for us to have a successful meeting. And for that we are very grateful.

I come here today to reaffirm the ties that bind the United States and Canada, in a new age of great promise and challenge, a time of rapid change, when both opportunity and uncertainty live side by side in my country and in yours, a time when people are being lifted up by new possibilities and held down by old demons all across the world. I came here because I believe our nations together must seize the opportunities and meet the challenges of this new age. And we must – I say again – do this together. From the oil from Alberta that fires factories in the United States to the silicon chips from California that power your computers, we are living proof of the value of partnerships and cooperation. Technologies produced in your nation save lives in our hospitals, while food from our farms line your supermarkets.

Our horizons have broadened because we have listened, in the United States, to the CBC. And our culture is much richer because of the contributions of writers like Robertson Davies, whom Hillary had the pleasure of meeting last week after reading him for years, and Margaret Atwood and because of the wonderful photography of Josef Karsh whose famous picture of Churchill I just saw. He took some pictures of Hillary and me that aren't so distinguished, but I love them anyway. [Laughter] And as a musician, I have to thank you especially for Oscar Peterson, a man I consider to be the greatest jazz pianist of our time.

"Ours is the world's most remarkable relationship" – the prime minister said, "whether we like it or not." I can tell you that on most days I like it very, very much. We have to strengthen that relationship. We have to strengthen it for our own benefit through trade and commerce and travel. And we have to strengthen it because it is our job to help to spread the benefits of democracy and freedom and prosperity and peace beyond our shores. We're neighbours by the grace of nature. We are allies and friends by choice.

There are those in both our nations who say we can no longer afford to, and perhaps we no longer even need to, exercise our leadership in the world. And when so many of our people are having their own problems, it is easy to listen to that assertion. But it is wrong.

We are two nations blessed with great resources and great histories. And we have great responsibilities. We were built, after all, by men and women who fled the tyranny and intolerance of the Old World for the new. We are the nations of pioneers, people who were armed with the confidence they needed to strike out on their own, and to have the talents that God gave them shape their dreams in a new and different land. Culture and tradition, to be sure, distinguish us from one another in many ways that all of us are still learning about every day. But we share core values, and that is more important: a devotion to hard work; an ardent belief in democracy; a commitment to giving each and every citizen the right to live up to his or her God-given potential; and an understanding of what we owe to the world for the gifts we have been given.

These common values have nourished a partnership that has become a model for new democracies all around this world. They can look at us and see just how much stronger the bonds between nations can be when their governments answer the citizens' desires for freedom and democracy and enterprise, and when they work together to build each other up instead of working overtime to tear each other down.

Of course, we have our differences. And some of them are complex enough to tear your hair out over. But we have approached them directly and in good faith, as true friends must. And we in the United States come more and more every day to respect and to understand that we can learn from what is different about your nation and its many peoples.

Canada has shown the world how to balance freedom with compassion, and tradition with innovation, in your efforts to provide health care to all your citizens, to treat your senior citizens with the dignity and respect they deserve, to take on tough issues like the move afoot to outlaw automatic weapons designed for killing and not hunting. [Applause] And I might say, since you applauded so, you are doing it in a nation of people who respect the right to hunt and understand the difference between law and order and sportsmanship.

Those of us who have traveled here appreciate especially the reverence you have shown for the bounty of God's nature, from the Laurentians to the Rockies. In a world darkened by ethnic conflicts that literally tear nations apart, Canada has stood for all of us as a model of how people of different cultures can live and work together in peace, prosperity, and respect.

The United States, as many of my predecessors have said, has enjoyed its excellent relationship with a strong and united Canada, but we recognize, just as the prime minister said with regard to your relationships to us a moment ago, that your political future is, of course, entirely for you to decide. That's what a democracy is all about.

You know, now – [laughter] – now, I will tell you something about our political system. [Laughter] You want to know why my State of the Union Address took so long? [laughter] It's because I evenly divided the things that would make the Democrats clap and the Republicans clap. [Laughter] And we doubled the length of the speech in common enthusiasm. [Laughter]

I ask you, all of you, to remember that we do look to you, and to remember what our great president of the postwar era, Harry Truman, said when he came here in 1947. "Canada's eminent position today," he said, "is a tribute to the patience, tolerance, and strength of character of her people.

Canada's notable achievement of national unity and progress through accommodation, moderation, and forbearance can be studied with profit by sister nations." Those words ring every bit as true today as they did then. For generations now, our countries have joined together in efforts to make the world more secure and more prosperous. We have reached out together to defend our values and our interests, in World War I, on the beaches of Normandy and Korea. Together, we helped to summon the United Nations into existence. Together, we stood fast against Communist tyranny and prevailed in the cold war. Together, we stood shoulder to shoulder against aggression in the Gulf war.

Now, our nations have stepped forward to help Haiti emerge from repression and restore its democracy. I thank the prime minister for what he said about that. When it was not popular anywhere in the world to worry about poor, beleaguered, abandoned Haiti, Canada was truly a friend of Haiti's.

In one international forum after another, we stand side by side to shape a safer and a better world. Whether it is at the World Population Conference, pushing together for an indefinite extension of NPT, in any number of ways, we are working together.

Now, we know that for Canada, this history of action is a matter of deep tradition and personal conviction. The tradition runs from Lester Pearson to Jean Chretien. It says we must be engaged in the affairs of the world. You have always shown the wisdom of reaching out instead of retreating, of rising to new responsibilities instead of retrenching. Your tradition of engagement continues to this day, and believe you me, it earns respect all around the world from people of all races and ethnic groups and political systems.

In places like Cyprus and the Sinai, Canadian troops have played an invaluable role in preventing more violence in those critical hot spots. Today, your 2,000 peacekeepers in the former Yugoslavia are courageously fulfilling their mission in the midst of one of the most intractable, difficult problems in our lifetime.

For a half century, the United States has shared your philosophy of action and consistent exercise of leadership abroad. And I am determined, notwithstanding all the cross currents in our country, that we shall preserve that commitment. These times may be turbulent, but we have a historic opportunity to increase security and prosperity for our own people and for people all around the world. And I want you to know that I intend to do everything in my power to keep our country constructively involved in the problems that we must face if we're going to guarantee that our children will live in a peaceful, sane, and free world.

Imagine what the Persian Gulf would look like today if we had not risen to the challenge of Iraqi aggression. Imagine what tariffs and barriers would plague the world trading system if we hadn't worked so hard together over such a long period of time from the end of World War II, to the events the prime minister described, to NAFTA, to GATT, to the Asian-Pacific Cooperation, to the Summit of Americas that was held in Miami in December. Imagine how different it would have been. Imagine how much worse the horrible tragedy in Rwanda would have been if we had not been there to try to provide essential help in those refugee camps to keep people alive.

We cannot let anyone or anything break this great tradition of our nations. In our partnership, we will find the key to protecting our people and increasing their prosperity and the power to reach beyond our shores in the name of democracy and freedom, not only because it is right, because it is in our interest to do so.

Just before we came down here, the prime minister and I agreed again that if we were going to meet these new challenges in the 21st century, we must adapt the institutions that helped us to win the cold war so that they can serve us as well in the 21st century. We have to do that. Some have evolved with the changing world. Some have, clearly, already discarded their old missions and assumed new roles. But we have also seen that the end of the East-West conflict, the advent of 24-hour financial markets, sudden environmental disasters, the rise of international terrorism, the resurgence of ancient ethnic hatreds, all these things have placed new demands on these institutions that the statesmen of 50 years ago simply did not imagine. The 21st century will leave behind those who sit back and think that automatically these problems will be solved. We simply have to face these challenges, and ask ourselves what do we have to change and how are we going to do it.

For example, to meet the security needs of the future, we must work together to see that NATO, the most successful military alliance in all of history, adapts to this new era. That means that we must make certain that the inevitable process of NATO expansion proceeds smoothly, gradually, and openly. There should be no surprises to anyone about what we are about. And we will work so that the conditions, the timing, the military implications of NATO expansion will be widely known and clearly understood in advance.

To parallel the enlargement of NATO, we have to develop close and strong ties with Russia. I have worked hard for that, and so has the prime minister. We must continue working together at the United Nations, where our nations have together taken the lead in efforts to reform our peacekeeping operations, to control costs, to improve information gathering, to make sure we have the right kind of command and control system before the young people who put on our uniforms are put in harm's way.

We have to continue also to work at reforming the international economic institutions. We've already made some great strides in reshaping the new global economy with the passage of GATT, which is the most comprehensive trade agreement in history. But the work is only beginning. At the upcoming G-7 summit in Halifax, which we're very much looking forward to, we will be working to ensure that our international trading institutions advance the cause of trade liberalization in ways that produce tangible gains for the people of the countries involved.

We also have to reexamine the institutions that were created at the time of Bretton Woods – the IMF, the World Bank – to make sure that they're going to be able to master the new and increasingly complex generation of transnational problems that face us; problems like explosive population growth and environmental degradation; problems like those that we have been facing together in Mexico and throughout Latin America in the recent financial crisis.

Real progress on all these areas will depend not only on our willingness to be involved but our on willingness to lead, as partners. Together, Canada and the United States are striving to seize all the advantages the new global economy has to offer. Trade produces high-wage jobs – we know that – the kind of jobs that give our people the opportunity to care for their families and educate their children and to leave the next generation better off than they were, a dream that has been called into question in many advanced economies in the last few years.

The success of NAFTA, which is generating new jobs and creating new markets from Monterey to Medicine Hat is the proof. And now, as the prime minister has said so well, we in NAFTA are on our way to becoming the Four Amigos. That phrase will go down in history. I wish I'd thought of it. We'll soon start our consultations with Chile for accession in NAFTA, and Chile will be a very good partner. The addition of that thriving economy will only continue to increase the benefits for all of us.

I want to take another moment here to thank Canada for its recent support and help in the financial crisis in Mexico. You understood what we had on the line; that more than Mexico was involved, that jobs and trade and future and our support for democracy and stability throughout Latin America was at issue. You understood it, and we are grateful. Because we stood shoulder to shoulder, we have a chance to preserve this remarkable explosion of democracy that we saw at the Summit of the Americas, and we should continue to do that.

I want to say a word, if I might, about the environment. As we expand trade we have to remember: we must defend that which we have inherited and enhance it if we can. The natural riches of this continent we share are staggering. We have cooperated to such great effect on our continent in the past: our air quality agreement is solving the acid rain problem; the Great Lakes are on the road to recovery; the eagles have returned to Lake Erie. Now we have to build on those accomplishments. With the NAFTA environmental commission located in Montreal, your country will play a key role in ensuring that we protect the extraordinary bounty that has been given to us for our children and our grandchildren. NAFTA is only one of the several fronts on which we can work together to both increase our prosperity and protect our environment. But we must do both.

Our nations are building on the progress of last years Summit of the Americas, as well, which will create a free trade area embracing the entire hemisphere. Across the Pacific, as the prime minister said, we paved the way for new markets and for free trade among the dynamic economies in the Asia-Pacific area. That was a very important thing for us to do because they are growing very fast, and we did not want this world to break up into geographical trading blocks in ways that would shrink the potential of the people of Canada and the United States for decades to come.

All these efforts will only enhance what is now the greatest trading relationship: yours and ours. Every day, people, ideas, and goods stream across our border. Bilateral trade now is more than a billion Canadian dollars every day – I learned to say that – [laughter] – and about 270 billion United States dollars last year, by far the world's largest bilateral relationship. Our trade with each other has become an essential pillar in the architecture of both our economies. Today, four and a half million Americans have jobs that involve trade between our two countries. Those are the concrete benefits of our partnership. Between 1988 and 1994, trade between our nations rose about 60 percent. Last year alone, it increased by 15 percent.

But the statistics don't give the human reality behind the flourishing exchange of goods and ideas. Our trade is creating real jobs for real people. In Boscawen, New Hampshire, just for example, a small company called Secure Care Products produces monitoring systems for patients in nursing homes. Recently, Secure Care began exporting its products to Canada. Sales there are already growing fast, that the company expects them to triple this year. And so Secure Care is hiring people like Susan Southwick, the granddaughter of Quebeckers, the mother of two, and now the company's 26th employee. Giving Susan and her husband a shot at the dream which Canadians and Americans share: that's what this partnership is all about.

Much further away from you in Greensboro, North Carolina, another small company called Createc Forestry Systems is showing how our trade helps people turn their hopes into realities. It was founded by a man named Albert Jenks in his family's kitchen. Createc makes hand-held computers that track lumber mill inventories. Those computers help managers assess their needs better, so fewer trees are cut unnecessarily. A few years ago, Createc began to export to Canada, and now those sales accounts have risen to nearly 20 percent of their total business. That means a more secure future for the company, for Mr. Jenks, for his son, Patrick, who works with his father in the family business. That shows how our trade can increase our prosperity and protect the environment as well.

Your companies are thriving in our markets, bringing tangible benefits to Canadians. Whether it's repairing the engines of some of the US Air Force's largest planes, or manufacturing software to manage our natural resources, or building some of the Olympic Village for Atlanta's 1996 games. Canadian firms are a strong presence in the United States. Their successes there help your people to turn their hopes into facts, and their dreams into reality.

The example of our biggest industry shows another side of this remarkable story. Working together, US and Canadian companies have integrated North America's auto industry and staged one of the most remarkable comebacks in all the history of the industrial revolution. We have drawn on each other's strengths, and today, our companies work so closely that we do not speak any longer of US or Canadian content in these vehicles, but of North American content, whether it's a Chrysler minivan made in Windsor or a Chrysler Jeep made in Detroit. I think that was the Ambassador from Michigan – I mean, from the United States, clapping down there.

Productivity and employment have risen to such a point that when I visited Detroit last fall, the biggest complaint I heard in a State that was given up as lost economically a decade ago – the biggest complaint I heard from the autoworkers was that they were working too much overtime. [Laughter] Now, where I come from, that is known as a high-class problem. [Laughter]

The auto industry now provides more than one million jobs in our countries. To reinforce our commitment to NAFTA, and to dramatically expand an important market, tomorrow our nations will sign an agreement to open the skies between our two nations. This agreement, which allows for a dramatic expansion of US and Canadian service to each other's nations, will create thousands of new jobs and billions of dollars in economic activity in our cities, yours and mine. We've reached a fair solution that will make life easier for travelers on both sides of the border, that will profit both Canadian and US airline carriers, that will increase the mutual travel and interconnections of our people. That we have done so amicably provides yet another model of how neighbouring nations can settle their differences.

Friendship, engagement: Canada and the United States have shown the best there is in partnerships between nations, all the great potential that awaits all the free peoples of this Earth if they can join in common cause. We are, as the monument at the St. Lawrence Seaway declares, "two nations whose frontiers are the frontiers of friendship, whose ways are the ways of freedom, whose works are the works of peace."

Every day, we see the enormous benefits this partnership gives us in jobs, in prosperity, in the great creative energy that our interchanges bring. But we have only seen the beginning. For the Susan Southwicks who want a chance to build better lives, and the companies like Createc that are trying to build solid businesses that will last, this partnership of ours holds a great promise with horizons as vast as our great continent.

Together, we've turned our energies toward improving the world around us for now nearly a century. Today, more than ever, let us reaffirm and renew that great tradition. Let us engage and confront the great challenges of the end of this century and the beginning of the next. We must sustain our efforts. We must enhance our efforts. We must maintain our partnership. We must make it stronger. This is our task and our mission. Together, we will be equal to it. The border separates our peoples, but there are no boundaries to our common dreams.

Thank you, and God bless you all.

PART THREE

"Hear, Hear!" and Applause: Presidential Speeches Outside Canada's Parliament

William Howard Taft of Ohio was the US President who knew Canada and Canadians best; Taft's administration partnered with Sir Wilfrid Laurier's government in 1911, and proposed a reciprocity agreement between the two countries. Beyond politics, Taft's love for Canada was demonstrated in countless ways. He had a summer home in Quebec, and, as described in journalist Lawrence Martin's seminal volume *The Presidents and the Prime Ministers*, he was a beloved figure to the residents of what was then known as Murray Bay. "Taft's birthday on September 15 was the closing event of every summer season," Martin wrote.

> The Quebecers would fill his cottage and celebrate through the night. When he was gone in the winters, they would stage skits with the largest, most jovial villager honoured to play le petit judge. But no disrespect was shown. Taft was their hero. Later, when Teddy Roosevelt split the Republican ranks, thereby ruining Taft's re-election bid, they spat in disgust at how their friend had been betrayed. When Taft died in 1930, sadness swept Murray Bay. The townspeople lit candles in his honour.[2]

Taft needed little prodding to return to Canada on numerous occasions. He was a frequent visitor to a hotel north of Kingston on the Rideau Canal system, and even gave addresses in tiny communities such as Eganville and Pembroke in Ontario's Upper Ottawa Valley. His love of our land was perhaps best expressed in remarks delivered before a raucous, cheering crowd at Toronto's Empire Club in January of 1919; this event was his second appearance before the group in five years. That second address, included in this volume, shows Taft at his best. His knowledge of Canada's history and development, and most importantly, his acknowledgment of Canada's growing status in the world community were interrupted over fifty times by shouts of approval and applause (noted as "hear, hear" and 'applause' by the transcriber at the time.) He said, on this occasion "I am not going to talk about the League of Nations in detail, because I have not the time and you could not stay." The transcript notes an audience response "Oh yes, we could!"

There is perhaps a wariness among Canadians to perceived slights from American political leaders, but many US Presidents have, in fact, taken time and care, as this section demonstrates, to understand their nation's northern neighbor. Many have expressed this will to understand Canada and Canadians through their speeches and writings. Readers will find a youthful US Senator named John F. Kennedy speaking with great eloquence (and quoting our first Prime Minister, Sir John A. Macdonald) at the University of Montreal in 1953, his first ever visit to Canada.

A few years earlier, in 1946, the greatest American general of the 20th century, Dwight Eisenhower, addressed the members of the Canadian Club in Ottawa. This address, little noted today, makes grateful reference to the infamous raid on Dieppe, in 1942, and will surely be of interest to present and future military historians:

That summer they [Canadian forces] carried out the memorable Dieppe operation, in which one of those freak chances of war resulted in a casualty list of saddening proportions. Yet let no one tell you that the Dieppe affair was devoid of valuable results. I know of no other single incident that did so much to confirm convictions that the coastal fortifications in France could be successfully breached on a large scale. Moreover, out of that operation many battle leaders derived valuable lessons that were applied later to the amphibious operations in the Mediterranean, and still later, when we lunged across the Channel for the final invasion.

In this same year, 1946, former President Herbert Hoover chose Ottawa as the site of an address in which he reported on his historic (and successful) efforts to organize famine relief after the Second World War. Millions of people worldwide owed their lives to Hoover's determined endeavors to thwart pervasive post-war hunger. Hoover, a former mining engineer from Iowa, courageously answered President Harry Truman's call to serve mankind in this way. In more modern times, even President Nixon, during his toast at a dinner in his honour at Rideau Hill in 1972, showed a relaxed quality of character rarely revealed to his own countrymen. He recalled a trip to Picton, Ontario, while Vice President, where he became the subject of a wager between a waiter and bartender who were uncertain whether or not their patron in this small local pub was indeed Richard M. Nixon:

After we had finished—he was a very polite waiter—after we had finished and were ready to leave, the waiter came up and said, "Sir, if you don't mind, I have a bet with the bartender, and you can help me win it or I might lose it." I said, "What is the bet?" He said, "I bet him five dollars that you are Vice President Nixon." I said, "Well, call him over and we will confirm it." So the bartender came over and said, "Is it true?" I said, "Yes." He said, "I would never have believed it." He gave him the five dollars, and as we started to move on, I heard him mumble to the waiter, "You know, he doesn't look near as bad in person as he does in his pictures."

Many in Newfoundland and Labrador, Quebec and the North will be pleased to be reminded that it was a Californian, future President Ronald Reagan, who took to the airwaves in a radio address in which he defended Canada's seal hunt in the late 1970s; this was indeed "one from the Gipper" for some of Canada's most economically challenged peoples.

This volume includes, as well, the transcript of a grateful President Jimmy Carter's call to Canada's Prime Minister Joe Clark, in January 1980. Here, they discuss the work of Ken Taylor, Canada's ambassador to Iran, who, with his staff, hid and then smuggled American hostages out of revolutionary Iran.

George H.W. Bush, the President who signed the Acid Rain Accord with Canada, took time after a post-White House fishing trip to Canada's Arctic in 1997 to personally pen a fishing column about his experience. Readers will see, in this volume, Bush's fondness for Canada, which he expressed upon a request to submit an account of his trip from a tiny weekly newspaper in Fort Simpson, NWT, the *Deh Cho Drum*, which has a circulation of 1,000 or so.

President William J. Clinton showed his personal commitment to strong Canada-US relations in the text of his 1999 address in Canada; this is a brilliant discussion of federalism, made on the very day he became the first sitting American President to open one of his nation's embassies (in Ottawa) in person. Today, Canadians are among the strongest backers of the Clinton Foundation's efforts to combat climate change and to bring affordable drugs to fight AIDs in Africa.

Throughout the years 2003 to 2006, former Prime Minister Paul Martin's government wrestled with plans by President George W. Bush's administration to pursue a ballistic missile defence (BMD) program. During one visit to Canada, Bush, according to Martin's recently published memoirs, agreed to publicly temper any hope of seeing Canada participate in a BMD program. Regardless, during his Halifax speech, the 43rd President "[t]urned up the pressure, publicly urging us to get on board," Martin wrote. "This was a clear violation of the agreement worked out between our officials, and it infuriated me."[3] Fortunately, breaches of this sort are altogether rare in Presidential addresses.

Canadians have had the privilege of hearing from American Presidents before, during and after their terms of office more than the citizens of any other nation. While we have very occasionally been angered, more often we have accorded these Americans the respect accorded to high office. Their words have indeed become part of our own history, and, as such, serve to illustrate the remarkable trajectory of these two new world nations. Warren Harding, the first US President to officially visit Canada said, on a summer's day in 1923 at Vancouver's Stanley Park, that Canadians and Americans "live in the power and glory of youth ... we have relatively only our present to regard, and that, with eager eyes fixed chiefly and confidently upon our future." Canada's greatest Presidential friend, William Howard Taft, shares an important connection with Harding. It was Harding who provided Taft with the means for the greatest Presidential comeback in American history, appointing le petit judge Chief Justice of the US Supreme Court, making Taft the only American to have held both posts. On that occasion, the bonfires of tribute to Taft, lit in Canada's Murray Bay, no doubt burned very high, and with considerable pride.

Arthur Milnes

Chapter 17

Former President William Howard Taft's
"Fraternal Relations"
The Empire Club, Toronto
20 January 1919

Now, I did not come here to talk about the United States, or what she has done in this war, although of course, we as Americans are proud of the demonstration of our ability to raise a great army, ["Hear, hear!"] and of what part of that army was able to do on the plains of France and Flanders [applause]. I feel that we may well be modest in outlining what we have done in this war, in the presence of an audience like this, of citizens of the city of Toronto and of the Province of Ontario, in view of what they have done for four long years in this war [applause]. The agonies and the suffering through which you have had to go in your contribution of half your able-bodied men to your armies, and in the large percentage of loss that you had to endure, at a time when the issue was very doubtful, and when you and your associates of England and Scotland and France had your backs to the wall—that is the time that tries men's souls, and that is the time when your souls stood the test. It was characteristic of the English people and the British generals that Haig should stick it out, because he knew his people. He knew they could stand true, and that instead of discouraging them and taking away their morale, it made them tighten their belts again and go into it [applause]. You could not do that with every people. One great satisfaction, the moral satisfaction of this war, is to note how a bad, immoral cause demonstrates its vicious character in the yellow streak that the fellows of Germany showed when we had them down [loud applause]. Now, you have suffered personal loss, all of you. I venture to say there is hardly a person present who, either in his immediate kin or in his close friendship, has not lost friends in this controversy. It is hard for you to contemplate, you so recently bereaved, the advantages that are to be derived by Canada from this war, hard as it has been. You are under a mountain of debt; you had better get well acquainted with those income taxes and other taxes you have been paying, because you will have to be friends with them for a long time [laughter].

And now, your boys are coming back, and the strain on those who are able to return is telling in the difficulties you have, perhaps, in finding employment, and in the difficulties presented by their psychological condition, in the reaction from the tremendous strain of the four years through which they have gone. It was to be expected. They were carried on by that spirit of patriotism and that determination to win, and so they accepted every burden and every discomfort and every suffering without a murmur. And now that the thing is over, they kick at a good many things that do not appear to be very burdensome in any way. That you have got to understand; that you have got to be sympathetic with, because it is human nature. You never knew a convalescent that was just the most agreeable person to live with [laughter].

After all those sacrifices that you had to make, think of the great future that awaits Canada. I don't mean to minimize in any degree your great prospects before the war, as if that war had not occurred. I do not mean in any way to say that there was not here a great independent dominion that was bound to occupy a great future. But you will indulge me in saying that this war has given you a quick opportunity to demonstrate to the world your character as a national dominion that you could not have had in any other way. You have put yourselves, if I may use a colloquial expression, indelibly on the map of the world ["Hear, hear!" and applause] as a factor to be considered in world matters; and you, as have Australia and New Zealand and South Africa, have brought yourselves to illustrate the utter blindness of the German mind. You responded to this war from no selfish motive. You were influenced merely by the filial affection to Mother England, who had protected you in your infancy, and made you independent in government, with an encouraging protection that you have always enjoyed [applause]. The affection was filial, due to the relation, doubtless, of most of you, to those in the Mother Country, but also, there was a national, personal feeling that you felt towards her ["Hear, hear!"]. Germany, in the grossly material view that she took of everything, and in that godless philosophy that she adopted—that might makes right, and only gain promotes connection—had assumed that neither you nor Australia nor the other daughters of England would respond and send forces to aid your mother when she was in an exigency; the impatience with which the German commentators viewed your activities and your energies as something not according to the plan of the general staff [laughter] was most enjoyable [renewed laughter].

You have had great losses in the sense that you have had to contribute much to the war, and you have had a heavy duty as well, but you have established yourselves in the British Empire as you were; not in the Empire when I had the honour to address you before ["Hear, hear!" and applause]. You said you were, and in a way, of course, you were; but now it is real ["Hear, hear!"]. It is not confined to post-prandial addresses of English statesmen ["Hear, hear!"] You have now a representative in the congress of the nations, and you are there before the world as a constituent member of the British Empire, and entitled to be heard ["Hear, hear!" and applause]. Great Britain is manifesting the proper gratitude to you for the demonstration of your filial loyalty and its importance and weight, on the one hand, and she is exercising that wise lightening of any legal bond of control in the stronger bond of affection that this war has increased in every way between you and her [applause].

Your future is a great one. What the future of England will be, or Scotland, or Ireland, what the future of France will be, what the future of Italy will be, is more involved, in the fact that they are old countries and that they have strained themselves and the productive qualities of their countries to the utmost. How they are to take care of their enormous debts is a problem that it is difficult to solve. Let us hope that the inspiration of the war will strengthen them to meet it. But in Canada there is no such doubt ["Hear, hear!"]. Your people are young, with a resiliency that shows itself in every move you make, with a physical and mental strength that comes from your environment in this great Empire of yours, and from the confidence in your own moral courage, which you have tested, in this war, yourselves [applause].

I am not advocating war, and I want to do everything I can to avoid war ["Hear, hear!" and applause] but there are some things that we must recognize in war. War gives us an opportunity to follow the old Greek injunction of knowing ourselves, and of finding that, when we are called upon to meet a great issue and to discharge a great debt, we have the innate qualities to do both. Now, that is what you have done, and with that confidence that comes from knowing yourselves and your capacity, there is going to be a springing forward in business, in enterprises, in reforms and improvements, in governmental and business methods, that you will be surprised at yourselves.

We had a war within our own borders that almost destroyed half of the country, and things looked very discouraging, and yet that spirit enabled us soon to put ourselves on our feet and to go ahead with an outburst of courageous, far-seeing energy and enterprise that made the growth of that country in the thirty years after the war a wonder of the world ["Hear, hear!" and applause]. So it is with you, my friends. You have a great domain here. It is only scratched, in many ways. You have built railroads, and you have issued bonds for them [laughter] and you have run them in a great many directions that perhaps you would not follow now if they were not in the ground [laughter] but you will catch up with that, and you will go on to build other railroads, and we will offer you, as best we can, that competition that stimulates the growth of both countries [applause]. Something was said about reciprocity, in an indefinite way [laughter] but I am content to wait [laughter and applause]. I don't have to be vindicated all at once [laughter].

Now, I further felicitate you, first, on the noble past you have made your own, that neither the world, nor you, nor your neighbours on the south will ever forget; second, on the great future that you have before you. We have got enough to attend to at home, [laughter] and you cannot grow too fast or too prosperous or too happy for us [applause]. This war has made the feeling between the United States and Canada much closer [applause]. What your [club] President has said with reference to my feeling towards Canada is true; I have always felt the deepest affection, because I think I know you, so it is more of a compliment [laughter]; and the strength of what is to come hereafter in the union of nations to prevent the recurrence of such another human disaster is to find one of its chief factors in the affection and mutual respect of the English-speaking communion [loud applause].

There is nothing invidious in that relation, in its attitude towards our respective relations to other countries, but it is natural that we who speak the same language, we who have a common history, we who look to the British people for the hammering out of the principles of civil liberty that we now enjoy, we who look to the common law as the source of those instrumentalities for guaranteeing civil liberty, should have a common feeling, and should understand the importance of a union to preserve those memories, and through that union to bring together all the nations of the world in a communion like that ["Hear, hear!" and loud applause]. We are an example to the world, you and we, of what can be done in the matter of the maintenance of peace. This example of two nations like yours and ours living together now for more than a hundred years with a border-land nearly four thousand miles in extent, and no breach of any kind in that century, without fortifications or means of war between us, is something that the world ought to cherish as a possible ideal that they can reach if they will only be reasonable and drop those jealousies and unfounded suspicions that so often unnecessarily lead to a breach [loud applause].

Now, I am not going to talk about the League of Nations in detail, because I have not the time and you could not stay ["Oh yes, we could!"], but I could not get through a speech now under any conditions, whether it was a commercial club, or a court, or elsewhere, unless I lugged in the League of Nations [laughter]. Three or four years ago it was an academic question; three or four years ago we would meet in convention, we college professors and publicists who write what you people read [laughter], and we would "resolute" and "resolute," and speak and speak, and beg money enough to print what we said [laughter]. Then we sent around the engrossed copies to catch the dust for those who received them [laughter]. It seemed remote; the war was then on, and to us in the United States, even the war seemed remote. To you the war was close, and therefore anything that involved the discussion of peace at all was regarded as irrelevant, and even ungracious to suggest.

Why, in England they got up a League of Nations having the same purpose as our League to Enforce Peace, and they would not put the word "Peace" in it [laughter], and they objected to our expression, "The League to Enforce Peace," because they said it gave rise to a misconstruction as to what our purpose was. While we were shouting in the wilderness then, we are right up on deck now [laughter]. The issue is acute, and the congress at Paris has put the League of Nations down as the first subject for consideration [applause]. Now, there are those in our country who are objecting to that, and saying that it ought to be postponed. One distinguished gentleman, Mr. James M. Beck, said that the founders of the constitution had waited five years after we got independence before they adopted the Constitution of the United States, and it seems to me that he said that we might just as well be patient as those wise ancestors of ours. Well, all I have to say about that is that if our fathers had begun earlier on that constitution they would have saved four or five years of very great discomfort [applause].

Read the descriptions by Madison and Hamilton of the conditions that prevailed under the old Articles of Confederation before we had adopted the constitution, and I am sure you will agree with me. It may have been necessary, in order to have the matter "borne in" on our ancestors—as our Methodist brethren would say—to have that period of discomfort in order to demonstrate that we needed a real nation, but do we need any demonstration of the necessity of peace in the future? If Mr. Beck wants any greater demonstration than we have had, I must regard him as an unreasonable member of the Bar [laughter].

It seems to me—and of course this is an unofficial opinion; it could not be otherwise—that the reason why they have put forward the League of Nations idea to receive the first discussion in the Congress is that, as Premier Clemenceau said, they have a League of Nations now. They have had it during the war, the League of Nations that won this war, the five great powers; and if you are going to carry out the ambitious program that the nations have subscribed to in the making of this peace, unless you do have the league of the nations of the five great powers your treaty will be nothing but a scrap of paper ["Hear, hear!" and applause]. We are going to do so much for the benefit of the world which we have promised to the world, and the world is in such a mess in Russia and in other parts of central and eastern Europe, that we are vested with the responsibility of continuing that league and providing the machinery for its operation after peace is signed. That we cannot escape. We cannot run away from it [applause].

After we have provided for the machinery that will make that League work for the great purposes of enforcing that peace, and for the enlargement of the league on the basis of that foundation, [and] if that league demonstrates its usefulness and efforts, as it undoubtedly will, for the protection of all the other nations ... those nations [will] come in and accept membership. All the advantage in that, my dear friends, is that we can get up the charter of the club before we let 'em in [laughter and great applause].

The great problem and difficulty in organizing the world League of Nations is the difficulty of inducing the lesser nations to agree on anything in which they are not going to have as full a voice as the nations who will have to carry the burden of enforcing the obligations of the league; I know about that, because in the administration now forgotten [great laughter], we attempted to get up a world court, and everybody was in favour of a world court, but it failed. And why? Because every nation wanted a permanent member or two members in that court, and instead of a court we would have a town meeting [laughter], which made it utterly impracticable. Now we have to arrange the structure of that league to secure the protection of the minor nations, because that is one of the great objects of a world league. But we have to make it practical so that it will work, and put into it machinery that shall not make it a laughingstock so that it shall thus lose its efficacy and power. I have spoken longer than I should, gentlemen. I am very much obliged to you. [Loud, continued applause, mingled with calls to "Go on!"]

Chapter 18

President Warren G. Harding
Stanley Park, Vancouver, British Columbia
16 July 1923

I may as well confess to you at the outset a certain perplexity as to how I should address you. The truth of the matter is that this is the first time I have ever spoken as President in any country other than my own. Indeed, so far as I can recall, I am, with the single exception of my immediate predecessor, the first President in office even to set foot on politically foreign soil.

True, there is no definite inhibition upon one doing so, such as prevents any but a natural born citizen from becoming President, but an early prepossession soon developed into a tradition, and for more than a hundred years, held the effect of unwritten law. I am not prepared to say that the custom was not desirable, perhaps even needful, in the early days, when time was the chief requisite of travel. Assuredly too, at the present, the chief magistrate of a great republic ought not to cultivate the habit or make a hobby of wandering over all the continents of the earth.

But exceptions are required to prove rules. And Canada is an exception, a most notable exception, from every viewpoint of the United States. You are not only our neighbour, but a very good neighbour, and we rejoice in your advancement and admire your independence, no less sincerely than we value your friendship.

I need not depict the points of similarity that make this attitude of the one toward the other irresistible. We think the same thoughts, live the same lives and cherish the same aspirations of service to each other in times of need. Thousands of your brave lads perished in gallant and generous action for the preservation of our Union. Many of our young men followed Canadian colours to the battlefields of France before we entered the war and left their proportion of killed to share the graves of your intrepid sons. This statement is brought very intimately home to me, for one of the brave lads in my own newspaper office felt the call of service to the colours of the sons of Canada. He went to the front, and gave his life with our boys for the preservation of the American and Canadian concept of civilization ...

I may not address you to be sure, as "fellow citizens," as I am accustomed to designate assemblages at home, but I may and do, with respect and pride, salute you as "fellow men," in mutual striving for common good.

What an object lesson of peace is shown today by our two countries to all the world! No grimfaced fortifications mark our frontiers, no huge battleships patrol our dividing waters, no stealthy spies lurk in our tranquil border hamlets. Only a scrap of paper, recording hardly more than a simple understanding, safeguards lives and properties on the Great Lakes, and only humble mileposts mark the inviolable boundary line for thousand of miles through farm and forest.

Our protection is in our fraternity, our armor is our faith; the tie that binds more firmly year by year is ever-increasing acquaintance and comradeship through interchange of citizens; and the compact is not of perishable parchment, but of fair and honourable dealing which, God grant, shall continue for all time.

An interesting and significant symptom of our growing mutuality appears in the fact that the voluntary interchange of residents to which I have referred is wholly free from restrictions. Our national and industrial exigencies have made it necessary for us, greatly to our regret, to fix limits to immigration from foreign countries. But there is no quota for Canada. We gladly welcome all of your sturdy, steady stock who care to come, as a strengthening ingredient and influence. We none the less bid Godspeed and happy days to the thousands of our own folk, who are swarming constantly over your land and participating in its remarkable development. Wherever in either of our countries any inhabitant of the one or the other can best serve the interests of himself and his family is the place for him to be.

A further evidence of our increasing interdependence appears in the shifting of capital. Since the armistice, I am informed, approximately 2.5 billion dollars has found its way from the United States into Canada for investment. That is a huge sum of money, and I have no doubt it is employed safely for us and helpfully for you. Most gratifying to you, moreover, should be the circumstance that one half of that great sum has gone for purchase of your state and municipal bonds, a tribute, indeed, to the scrupulous maintenance of your credit, to a degree equaled only by your mother country across the sea and your sister country across the hardly-visible border.

These are simple facts, which quickly resolve into history for guidance of mankind in the seeking of human happiness. "History, history!" ejaculated Lord Overton to his old friend. Lindsay, himself a historian; "what is the use of history? It only keeps people apart by reviving recollections of enmity."

As we look forth today upon the nations of Europe, with their armed camps of nearly a million more men in 1923 than in 1913, we can not deny the grain of truth in this observation. But not so here! A hundred years of tranquil relationships, throughout vicissitudes which elsewhere would have evoked armed conflict rather that arbitration affords truly, declared James Bryce,

> the finest example ever seen in history of an undefended frontier, whose very absence of armaments itself helped to prevent hostile

demonstrations"; thus proving beyond question that "peace can always be kept, whatever be the grounds of controversy, between peoples that wish to keep it."

There is a great and highly pertinent truth, my friends, in that simple assertion. It is public will, not public force, which makes for enduring peace. And is it not a gratifying circumstance that it has fallen to the lot of us North Americans, living amicably for more than a century, under different flags, to present the most striking example yet produced of that basic fact? If only European countries would heed the lesson conveyed by Canada and the United States, they would strike at the root of their own continuing disagreements and, in their own prosperity, forget to inveigh constantly at ours.

Not that we would reproach them for resentment or envy, which after all is but a manifestation of human nature. Rather should we sympathize with their seeming inability to break the shackles of age-long methods, and rejoice in our own relative freedom from the stultifying effect of Old World customs and practices? Our natural advantages are manifold and obvious. We are not palsied by the habits of a thousand years. We live in the power and glory of youth. Others derive justifiable satisfaction from contemplation of their resplendent pasts. We have relatively only our present to regard, and that, with eager eyes fixed chiefly and confidently upon our future.

Therein lies our best estate. We profit both mentally and materially from the fact that we have no "departed greatness" to recover, no "lost provinces" to regain, no new territory to covet, no ancient grudges to gnaw eternally at the heart of our national consciousness. Not only are we happily exempt from these handicaps of vengeance and prejudice, but we are animated correspondingly and most helpfully by our better knowledge, derived from longer experience, of the blessings of liberty. These advantages we may not appreciate to the full at all times, but we know that we possess them, and the day is far distant when, if ever, we shall fail to cherish and defend them against any conceivable assault from without or from within our borders.

I find that, quite unconsciously, I am speaking of our two countries almost in the singular, when perhaps I should be more painstaking to keep them where they belong, in the plural. But I feel no need to apologize. You understand as well as I that I speak in no political sense. The ancient bugaboo of the United States scheming to annex Canada disappeared from all our minds years and years ago. Heaven knows we have all we can manage now, and room enough to spare for another hundred millions, before approaching the intensive stage of existence of many European states.

And if I might be so bold as to offer a word of advice to you, it would be this: Do not encourage any enterprise looking to Canada's annexation of the United States. You are one of the most capable governing peoples in the world, but I entreat you, for your own sakes, to think twice before undertaking management of the territory that lies between the Great Lakes and the Rio Grande.

No, let us go our own gaits along parallel roads, you helping us and we helping you. So long as each country maintains its independence, and both recognize their interdependence, those paths cannot fail to be highways of progress and prosperity. Nationality continues to be a supreme factor in modern existence; make no mistake about that; but the day for the Chinese wall, enclosing a hermit nation, has passed forever. Even though space itself were not in process of annihilation by airplane, submarine, wireless and broadcasting, our very propinquity enjoins that most effective cooperation which comes only from clasping of hands in true faith and good fellowship.

It is precisely in that spirit, men and women of Canada, that I have stopped on my way home from a visit to our pioneers in Alaska to make a passing call upon my very good neighbour of the fascinating Iroquois name, "Kanada," glorious in her youth and strength and beauty, on behalf of my own beloved country. I stretch forth both my arms in the most cordial fraternal greeting, with gratefulness for your splendid welcome in my heart, and from my lips the whispered prayer of our famed Rip Van Winkle: "May you all live long and prosper!"

Chapter 19

General Dwight Eisenhower
Canadian Club, Ottawa
10 January 1946

Ever since the war ended in Europe I have been hoping for opportunity to visit Canada. My purpose was deeper than mere desire to renew association with old Canadian friends. I have wanted to come here so that I might, in the heart of their homeland, pay humble tribute to the soldierly virtues of those wartime comrades and, from a more personal viewpoint, give expression to my gratitude for their loyal and faithful adherence through long years of war to the principle and substance of allied unity.

It is beyond the power of any man to add to the luster of the military reputation established by the brave men and women of Canada who served with me in Europe. They have written their own proud record in your hearts and in those of all men wherever freedom is venerated. But it is only simple justice to state that in an allied force numbering in the millions, and in which courage and fortitude were so much the rule as to be taken for granted, assignment of vital battle objectives to the Canadians brought to the High Command only feelings of satisfaction and of confidence. The 1st Canadian Army under General Crerar will always be remembered and respected as an invaluable member of the allied team.

No man could command a force in which your Canadians were included without feelings of deep humility and lasting pride. Because I had that privilege, those men were, for many months, my Canadians, too, and no one can take from me the place they hold in my affection and admiration.

Memory goes back to my first contacts with them in Britain, when they were commanded by General McNaughton. That summer, they carried out the memorable Dieppe operation, in which one of those freak chances of war resulted in a casualty list of saddening proportions. Yet let no one tell you that the Dieppe affair was devoid of valuable results. I know of no other single incident that did so much to confirm convictions that the coastal fortifications in France could be successfully breached on a large scale. Moreover, out of that operation many battle leaders derived valuable lessons that were applied later to the amphibious operations in the Mediterranean, and still later, when we lunged across the Channel for the final invasion.

Canadians first came under my command in Sicily. From that moment onward, we served together in Italy, France, Belgium, Holland and, finally, in Germany. Other stirring pictures come back to me. The Royal Canadian Navy, pressing home the assault against the Normandy beaches! The bold pilots of the Royal Canadian Air Force, riding herd in the skies and covering the battle path of their comrades on the ground all the way from the beach to the Elbe. Great fighters, in great events! They lived history—a bright page of history.

I think I can best express my feelings toward my Canadian comrades by saying that I am truly grateful to the fathers and mothers who sent those men and women to serve in the Allied Command in Europe, and equally grateful to all who, here in their homeland, supported them unstintingly throughout the years of conflict.

Canada points with justifiable pride to a dozen directions in which she made vitally important contributions to allied victory. In carrying on the great air training program, in providing mountains of munitions, in convoying ships through seas infested with submarines, in sending needed cargoes of foodstuffs—in all these and many more, your record needs no embellishment from me.

Throughout this war, our two nations have been drawn together in planning and producing for a common cause. It has been a cooperation that seemed as natural as it was inevitable. Our nations are such good friends that we take neighbourly collaboration as a matter of course. During the two years when you were at war and we were not, some twelve thousand American citizens crossed your border to enter the armed forces of your country. After the [Japanese] attacked us, and the European Axis declared war, 26,000 individuals of Canadian birth entered our own armed forces. These reciprocal acts seem to me spontaneous evidence of the friendship that must forever exist between our two people.

There is other evidence of effective war cooperation between our two countries. Under the far-sighted leadership of Prime Minister Mr. Mackenzie King, and of our late President Roosevelt, common problems were solved by a devotion to [these problems] of common resources. Among these were the defense of Newfoundland and the Maritime Provinces, the development of an air route across Canada to Alaska (since known as the Northwest Staging Route), an air route over Hudson Bay, and the overland Alaskan Highway. A common readiness to venture boldly resulted in the initially hazardous airway across Labrador, Iceland and Greenland which, in a few short years, has made air travel to Europe a commonplace. Cooperation exploited for war purposes the great ports of embarkation at Halifax and Prince Rupert in British Columbia.

We, in the United States, keenly realize that success in these and other vital projects demanded generosity and many concessions on the part of the Canadian government. As a soldier-citizen of your neighbouring country, it is a great privilege to express to you deep and lasting gratitude. The allied victory in Europe stands as a monument to teamwork and to the results of practical understanding between nations. Nowhere was that teamwork more effective than here in our two homelands. Even customs duties were relaxed, and the freest exchange of personnel, material and all types of commodities was permitted across the international border. Through these means, the efficient prosecution of the war was immeasurably increased. As a direct consequence hostilities were shortened!

In addition to Canada's contribution to victory in Europe, our joint operational effort extended to other sections of the globe. A Canadian combat team participated in the Aleutians campaign. Over a long period of time, squadrons of the Royal Canadian Air Force and units of the Royal Canadian Navy operated jointly with United States forces in the North Pacific. Hundreds of American soldiers were trained in Canadian schools during the war, and this practice was pursued, also, in the opposite direction.

In this reminiscent review of the war years, I have refrained from mentioning until now one specific instance when my attention, as a commander, was intensively directed toward the Canadian sector. The first Canadian Army covered itself with honour in the beachhead in the bitter attack beginning February 8, 1945, and in the operation across the Rhine. But the instance in which it produced, from my viewpoint, its greatest climax was when it undertook the hazardous mission of clearing the Scheldt Estuary, key to the great port of Antwerp. Although we had already taken the city and port, they were useless to us while the Germans commanded the approaches. We had to work that port; final victory came directly to depend upon its early usefulness. When Field Marshal Montgomery turned the task over to my old friend, General Crerar, and the Canadians, I knew the task would be brilliantly and expeditiously executed.

It is great accomplishments such as that one which I like to remember. The end of Nazism was in clear view when the first ship moved unmolested up the Scheldt. Yet retrospective satisfaction is saddened always by the memory of brave men whose lives have been spent in the victory, of gallant soldiers whose priceless courage has bought, for us, the peace. There is no way to pay to them and their loved ones an equal devotion, except as we strive as unselfishly and gallantly to maintain the peace as they strove to win it.

The tragic, turbulent years of war ended last May in Germany, last August in the Pacific. Now the victors have set themselves a new and even greater task: to work out a formula and a practical procedure intended to smooth international frictions and to find a way to banish war forever from the world.

I hate war as only a soldier who has lived it can, only as one who has seen its brutality, its futility, and its stupidity. Yet there is one thing to say on the credit side; victory required a mighty manifestation of the most ennobling of the virtues of man; faith, courage, fortitude, and sacrifice. If we can only hold that example before our eyes, moreover, if we can remember that the international cooperation then so generously displayed points the sure way to the success of the United Nations Organization, then the war can never be regarded as a total deficit. I have heard people say that wartime unity was based only on necessity, that now, when necessity is past, we may expect differences which were forgotten in the urgency of a common fear! But the falsity of that contention is clear, because the necessity for cooperation has not passed. Nations that joined together to defeat ruthless enemies have even greater reason to remain united for the peaceful settlement of their differences lest new Hitlers rise to throw the world into a chaos more awful than the shattered countries of Europe present today. That is what we squarely face!

Our two nations have lived as peaceful neighbours for so long that in our own relationships we have totally forgotten the meaning of fears and lusts for conquest that bred the war from which we have just emerged. The ripeness of our friendship is apparent for all to see in a border that marks separate sovereignty, but binds together rather than divides. The secret is nothing other than mutual understanding and respect.

We must not over simplify the problem. We must not delude ourselves into believing that all nations will easily achieve this broad result, or that nothing more is demanded than verbal adherence to beautiful generality. But it can be achieved if every nation realizes that its very survival may depend on its earnest cooperation in the peaceful settlement of disputes. All must learn that in cooperation, there is giving as well as receiving. The one that eternally gives and does not receive will eventually exhaust itself. In the contrary case the recipient becomes nothing but the object of another's bounty. To cooperate, we must give and take in a spirit of mutual, sympathetic understanding. Our two countries have long done it. The United Nations did it in war. The practice must continue and must become universal. When that is done, the fortifications that bristle along borders throughout the world will speedily come tumbling down, and from the hearts of populations will be lifted age old burdens of fear.

Another mistake we must not make is to assume that this crusade for promoting mutual understanding can be successfully conducted exclusively by others: by the world's statesmen and political leaders. Each of us, however humble, has a part to play. Governments may wisely deal with the problems which rise in our concerted search for peace, but in the end it will be the citizens of all countries who must outlaw war. Until the peoples of the world understand and respect the interests of their neighbours, the victory will elude us. Until the peoples of the world embrace the democratic belief that the dignity of the individual is the basis of the success of nations, the world will not find an enduring peace.

I venture to speak of these things because it was my lot to be intimately associated with a great cooperative effort in Europe. Success was ours because each nation was willing to submerge what might have appeared to be its own narrow interests in the common cause. A bright factor in future prospects lies in the fact that since the fighting ended, there have been no futile arguments over the part that any particular one of the United Nations played. Just as each was necessary to victory, all must march together toward peace. Positive action is required. Attack, not defense, is indicated!

We have come through a momentous experience together. If it has been glorious in its achievement, it has been tragic in the lives we had to spend for success. White crosses, standing in regimented clusters throughout a thousand leagues of foreign soil, forever mark the path of victory and the price your nation and mine and our friends have paid for survival. They cry out for peace. They challenge democracy today. I pray, and I firmly believe that in meeting that challenge, your nation and mine will always find themselves in the forefront of the charge.

Chapter 20

Former President Herbert Hoover's Report on the World Famine, CBC Broadcast, Ottawa 28 June 1946

I have been honoured by your invitation to make from Canada the final report upon my food mission to 38 nations. I am glad for this privilege. It gives to me the opportunity to pay tribute to the magnificent service Canada has given to the world. To Canada flows the gratitude of hundreds of millions of human beings who have been saved from starvation through the efforts of this great Commonwealth of the North.

Upon four nations, Canada, the United States, the Argentine and Australia, has fallen 90 percent of the overseas burden of relief to this, the greatest famine in all human history. Over ten million tons of food have been shipped to the 800 million people short of food since this famine became acute. Canada has provided over one fifth of this supply. Without this gigantic flow of overseas food, hundred of millions would have died, and other hundreds of millions would have survived only as permanent physical wrecks. And when we use this impersonal word "people," let us not forget that most of them are women and children. Far beyond our humanitarian responsibilities lay the necessity to save the political and social structure of the world from sinking into a chaos in which recovery and the making of peace would be impossible.

We can see the future more clearly if, for a moment, we look back over our months of effort to drive the wolf from the door of the world. This crisis, of course, had its roots in the degeneration of agriculture and manpower in the war-torn areas. But to this was added the plunder by armies of several million tons of food out of the last harvests in Germany, Eastern Europe and Manchuria. The crisis was further aggravated by the large feeding of bread grains to animals, in the earlier months of the harvest year. But on top of all these disasters has been the unparalleled coincidence of five great droughts: in the western Mediterranean, India, China, South Africa, and a partial failure of crops in the Argentine.

The full realization of the impending calamity came early in March. At once it was evident that there were two quite different problems. The first was the months of acute crisis until the arrival of the northern hemisphere harvests which come in from July to September, and thus renew the depleted world larder. The second is the problem of better organization over the year following the present harvest. My immediate concern was naturally limited to the crisis months. It is essential that this dual nature of the problem be borne in mind; otherwise the issues become confused and the cure chaotic.

In pursuance of President Truman's wishes, I have traveled some 50,000 miles, visiting all of the important famine and food-deficit areas in the world and all of the major food surplus areas excepting South Africa and Australia. I have discussed crops, animals, calories, rations, stocks, ships, railroads, supplies and hunger with the Presidents, the Prime Ministers, and the food officials of each of these nations.

Without any special authority, my function has been mostly advisory – or perhaps persuasive would be a better word. Certainly I am deeply indebted for the most extraordinary welcome and cooperation accorded to my associates and me.

When the potential dangers were realized four months ago, the Combined Food Board estimated that there was an 11 million ton gap in the necessary amounts of cereals to meet the minimum demands of hungry nations—and a similar appalling shortage in fats and other foods. With this gap facing us, it did not seem possible to prevent mass starvation. I felt compelled to say publicly at that time, "Our task is now to minimize the loss of life."

On my return from Europe and Asia a month ago, my colleagues and I felt assured that as of May 1st the gap in the bare subsistence supply of cereals had been reduced from 11 million tons to about 3.6 million tons, with a corresponding reduction in the gaps of fats and other essentials. This reduction was due to the development of new sources of supplies; to substitutions; to the success of our appeal for self-denial in the surplus food countries. The reduction of the gap was due especially to the willing acceptance in the food deficit countries of drastic curtailment of their requested import programs. It meant, for some of them, drastic regimes of bare subsistence.

Our determination has been to hold the lowest of them up to a level of 1,500 to 1,700 calories per person per day. If we could hold these levels, it would at least prevent mass starvation. But even this drastic program was endangered by that tragic gap of 3.6 million tons. If it could not be overcome, we were defeated. But something like the widow's cruise is happening. In the two months since those estimates, the world has developed even further additions to world supplies. The Latin-American states have greatly reduced their import requirements during the crisis months. Especially the Argentine is greatly expanding its contribution of supplies. The other Latin-American states are giving aid. The British government has reduced its pipeline supplies. Larger diversions have been made in India from the surplus provinces to the famine areas. The conservation measures in Canada and the United States are contributing even more largely to our potential exports. The United States harvest has arrived earlier than usual.

From all these gains I am happy to announce to you that it now seems assured that the tragic gap of about 3.6 million tons in minimum supplies with which we were haunted two months ago can now be closed. I am humbly grateful to be the one to make this announcement. But it cannot be emphasized too strongly that this ultimate victory over mass starvation is based upon three assumptions:

First, that the drastic food regimes in the food-deficit countries will be continued during the crisis months until the danger is absolutely over. Second, that the people in the food surplus countries continue their sacrifice in the consumption of wheat and fats during the remaining few months of the crisis. Third, that supplies be shipped overseas in an uninterrupted stream over this period.

The precariousness of the situation is not over. Scarcely any of the major food deficit areas have stocks of as much as 30 days overseas food, even on the basis of much reduced living. If we fail in shipments, mass starvation will be instantly upon us.

It is, at least, reassuring that if we have continued cooperative action of the various nations, mass starvation will be prevented, with one exception. That exception is China, where transportation to the interior and inadequate organization has rendered relief only partially successful. In other famine areas, there will be suffering. We truly need more supplies than are just enough to prevent mass starvation. Many of the old people and the weaker children will fall by the wayside; nevertheless, the great majority of the endangered will be saved. Beyond this saving of human life, the political and social stability of nations (upon which alone peace can be built) will be preserved. For success in preventing mass starvation, credit must first go to the Combined Food Board in which Canada plays so important a part. That board has had the stern task of dividing the world's food between nations upon the agreed programs. UNRRA deserves praise in the limited field it covers, that is, the 20 percent of the people who cannot finance their food imports. And no tribute can be great enough to the magnificent cooperation of the responsible officials in the forty nations that have joined in a gigantic effort to save life.

My present concern is with the immediate crisis months. Naturally, my colleagues and I on this mission have been deeply interested in the food prospects of each nation after the coming harvest. Moreover, hope in the outlook for the next year affects the courage and morale of hungry people to endure for the next few months. More especially is this so as famine has its worst moments just before the new harvest, for then the reserves are gone.

I may say at once that I do not take the extreme pessimistic view of the world supplies, after the coming harvests, which have been expressed in several quarters. We can at least hope there will be no plundering by armies during the next year. We have reason to believe that there will not be five coincident great droughts again in one year. In three of these drought areas, the harvest prospects are very much improved. For instance, it is already estimated that France and North Africa will require 2.5 million tons less of food imports than during the past year. With continued favourable weather, we in North American seem destined to have abundant harvests again.

It must not, however, be thought that all trouble is over. The war-devastated areas will not have fully recovered their ground crops, nor have restored their flocks and herds during the next year. And famine will linger in China and India until November, when the rice crops come. The food situation of the world in the next year will not be easy, but next year in my view will not be one of such dreadful crisis and drastic regimes as the one that we are now in.

To prepare for the next harvest year the United Nations are now setting up the International Emergency Food Council. It will consolidate various world agencies into more effective organization. The selection of one of my colleagues upon this mission, Dr. Dennis FitzGerald, as Secretary General is a complete assurance of efficient action.

But there is a further step beyond the present United Nations proposals which the world sorely needs. This 1,500 to 1,700 calorie bottom level in many areas is dreadfully hard on children. While it will see adults through, the kind of food is not the most suitable for children. Disease and mortality among the little ones are ever the sensitive barometers of starvation and poverty. Several nations have done the best they could by giving the children priority in their meager dairy products; some extra food is given in some schools, and the scattered charitable agencies are doing the best they can in limited areas. But in all, they are only touching the fringe of the problem. Millions of mothers are today watching their children wilt before their eyes. The proof of this is an annual mortality rate in many cities as high as 200 per 1,000 among children under one year of age. The further proof is that there are somewhere from 20 to 30 million physically subnormal children on the continent of Europe. There are other millions in Asia.

After the First World War, we gave a good extra meal a day of restorative food to 10 million undernourished children. I deplore that this special aid for children has had no counterpart through a widespread organization set up after this war. And I repeat that civilization marches forward upon the feet of healthy children. We cannot have recovery of civilization in nations with a legacy of stunted bodies or distorted and embittered minds. I would like to suggest that the redemption of these children be organized at once by the newly created International Emergency Food Council, and that all nations be called upon to contribute to its cost. The job could be done with three or four hundred million dollars, a charge beyond any organized private charity, but not a great sum from the world as a whole.

Mr. Prime Minister, I have held this statement to sober words. I have not tried to describe the grim visage of famine in action. I have not attempted to express the emotion which every decent human being feels in the presence of the scenes of hunger and of sickly children I have witnessed. Nor have I tried to express the sympathy and pride which swells in one's heart for those hundreds of thousands of heroic men and women in the world who are struggling to save these million of human lives. They labour for their countrymen in villages, in cities and in the halls of government. They know that hunger is a destroyer far worse than war. Great as its toll of life may be, yet its destruction of morals, of social and political institutions is infinite.

May I repeat here a statement I have made to men of government in each of these 38 nations? The world has ended a bloody and horrible era of the killing of even women and children. The jeopardy to mankind by famine gives to us an opportunity to change the energies of the world from killing to saving life. These months can bring the glow of a new faith and a new hope for the dawn of a new era to mankind. To succeed is far more than a necessity to economic reconstruction of the world. It is far more than the path to order and peace. It marks the return of the lamp of compassion to the earth. And that is part of the moral and spiritual reconstruction of the world.

Chapter 21

Senator John F. Kennedy
The University of Montreal
4 December 1953

I appreciate this opportunity to speak to you at this celebrated university in this ancient and famous city. The functions of the private university, particularly those that are Roman Catholic, are basic and fundamental today, for its task is a continuing search for the truth, both for its own sake and because only if we possess it can we be really free. Never has been the task of finding the truth more difficult. In the struggle between modern states, "truth" has become a weapon in the battle for power; it is bent and twisted and subverted to fit the pattern of national policy.

Frequently, we in the West are forced by this drumbeat of lies and propaganda to be "discriminating" in our selection of what facets of the truth we ourselves will disclose. Thus the responsibility of a free university to pursue its own disinterested studies is even more important today than ever before. The University of Montreal has succeeded in carrying out this mission, so that today it stands as a bulwark on the North American continent in the battle for the preservation of Christian civilization.

I appreciate also this opportunity to express once again the respect and friendship with which the people of the United States regard their neighbours in Canada. The ties that bind our two nations together are many and indissoluble. We have a similar background in that both of our nations have people from many dissimilar backgrounds. Although this is my first journey to Canada, Canadians are by no means strangers to me ... Perhaps most fundamental of all, the roots of our similarly free political and economic institutions may be traced back to a common seed, and the peaceful maintenance of the Canadian-American border has been a symbol all over the world for those who believe that a just and lasting peace can be achieved.

The bonds between our two countries, then, are beneficial to both. We export professional football players to you; and you export professional hockey players to us. The example of cooperation that Canada and the United States have set in the economic, military, political, cultural and other spheres is one for all the world to admire.

Unfortunately, from time to time tensions arise between the United States and Canada, just as tensions will arise between any close friends.

Today, such tensions have received a disproportionate amount of headline space in the newspapers of both of our countries; disproportionate not because such tensions are unimportant, but because this negative side of the balance sheet is greatly smaller than the positive side which I have previously mentioned. Nevertheless, it is well to understand exactly what these tensions are, and how they might best be reduced. Today, the charged atmosphere of suspicion and fear that has resulted in my country from the external and internal threat of Communist imperialism has caused a number of incidents that have created alarm and resentment among Canadians and Americans alike. The proposed St. Lawrence Seaway has been frequently postponed, much to your disappointment, because of the failure of the United States to get Congressional approval for participation in its construction, and the proposed St. Lawrence Power Project has not yet cleared its final hurdle in the United States Court of Appeals in order that the power authority of the State of New York may join with Canada in the construction of that project.

Perhaps of more importance, several questions have been raised with respect to international trade between the two countries. The US Tariff Commission has held hearings at which American producers requested restrictions on the importation of Canadian oats, fish, lead, zinc, and oil. Bills for the same purpose have been introduced in Congress. Last March, a year long embargo on all Canadian beef cattle, imposed because of a local outbreak of hoof-and-mouth disease, was lifted, after costing Canada about $50 million dollars. Even this problem is not one way. New Englanders may accuse Canadians of "dumping" ground fish fillets, but Canadians are accusing New Englanders of dumping textiles. Canadians have also expressed concern with respect to United States policies for exporting agricultural surpluses; and of course, Canada and the United States are competing for other export markets in Latin America and elsewhere.

It would not be appropriate for me to attempt to analyze each of these many issues and discuss in detail their solutions. But I do maintain that much of the confusion and fear results from the unfounded misunderstandings and misconceptions, which the citizens of each country hold with respect to the other. Perhaps if I explain some of the factors in the United States which give rise to this uncertainty and confusion, it may be of some help to you in understanding the conflicts we read about today.

I make this statement as a member of the United States Senate, one of two parliamentary bodies in the legislative branch of our Federal government. It is frequently difficult for citizens of other countries, particularly those with a parliamentary form of government where responsibility and authority are joined more closely together, even for Canadians with a Federal system of their own, to comprehend the full significance of the difference between the two Houses of Congress, between the legislative branch and the executive branch, and between the Federal and State governments; or to understand that a Congressional Committee is not the same as the United

States government. For example, the editor of the *Montreal Star*, Mr. G. V. Ferguson, wrote in 1952 that Canadians find it hard to understand that the American Congress can successfully frustrate its own administration in the pursuance of international trade objectives. "In Canada," Mr. Ferguson pointed out, "a government remains a government only so long as it can pass its legislative program." Even more recently, Mr. Attlee of Great Britain raised questions concerning the ultimate source of power in the United States.

Our constitutional founders believed that liberty could be preserved only when the motions of government were slow, the power divided, and time provided for the wisdom of the people to operate against precipitous and ill-considered action. The delegates believed that they were sacrificing efficiency for liberty. They believed, in the words of James Madison, who in his middle thirties was the most vigorous figure in Philadelphia that they were "so contriving the interior structure of the government as that its several constituent parts may, by their mutual relations ... be the means of keeping each other in their proper places."

In our constitution, there are limits placed on both the Federal and State Governments, and there is an area of individual liberty protected against both. Like the reign of law, this is a tenet that has roots deep in Graeco-Roman theory, medieval political theory, in Locke and Montesquieu. The system of checks and balances set up in our constitution was, of course, also the result of the necessary compromises between powerful interests in all of the thirteen colonies. The most basic dispute of the Convention was that involving the larger states (Massachusetts, Virginia and Pennsylvania) with the smaller states: Delaware (so small in the words of John Randolph that it was composed of five counties at low tide and three at high), Connecticut, and New Jersey. The larger states possessing a majority of the population and revenue were determined that their influence should be in proportion, while the smaller states were reluctant to sacrifice their confederatory status wherein each state, as sovereign, held veto on action. The result of the Connecticut compromise, "a motley measure" in the words of Alexander Hamilton, is familiar to us all. The representation in the Lower House was based on population, and they alone had the power to initiate legislation dealing with revenue matters, while in the Upper House each state was given an equal vote.

Successive Presidents who have had difficulty with the Senate, including President Eisenhower, would be surprised to have learned what our founders perceived the role of the Senate to be. In a famous anecdote, Jefferson after his return from France once asked Washington at breakfast why he had agreed to a second chamber in Congress. Washington asked him, "Why did you pour that coffee into your saucer?" "To cool it," Jefferson said. "Even so," said Washington, "we pour legislation into the Senatorial saucer to cool it."

There is no doubt that the framers of the Constitution saw the Senate as a sort of privy council to the President, enjoying a different and more intimate relation with the Chief Executive than did the direct representatives of the people. And thus the Senate was given a powerful voice over foreign affairs and the selection of office holders for the Executive Department. Washington tried to make such use of the Senate. Herbert Agar, in discussing the situation writes,

> [Washington] entered the chamber one day and took the vice President's chair, saying he had come for their advice and consent regarding an Indian treaty, and that he had brought with him General Knox, the Secretary of War, who knew all about the treaty. Knox produced the papers which were read; Washington then waited for some advice or consent. The Senate was unwilling to give it in the presence of the President and his cabinet minister. The feeling seemed to be that the Senators were under pressure, and that their dignity was being violated. The Senate did not want information from General Knox; it wanted to be left alone to act in its own fashion.

"We said for him to withdraw," wrote Senator Maclay, "he did so with a discontented air."

A proper understanding of the system of checks and balances would explain to citizens of other countries the many and seemingly conflicting actions which appear on the governmental scene in the United States. A State governor may protest the imports of Icelandic fish, but only the President and the Tariff Commission can restrict such imports, even into that State under present law. The United States Department of Agriculture may protest the importation of Canadian oats, and a United States Senator may introduce a Bill to restrict such imports, but, until the House of Representatives takes initial action to amend the Reciprocal Trades Agreement Act, the final decision rests with the Tariff Commission in the Executive Branch. When Congress failed to approve the St. Lawrence Power Project, the Federal Power Commission authorized the State of New York to build it, but only the Federal Courts can remove all legal objections to that decision. A Senator may broadcast all his suspicions of foreign officials; but he speaks only for himself and not the United States government or our people.

Time has proved that the American Constitution is not, as Macaulay once said, "all sail and no anchor." Sir John Macdonald, speaking in 1865, after the American Constitutional system had received its most severe test in the American Civil War stated,

> It is the fashion now to enlarge on the defects of the Constitution of the United States, but I am not one of those who look upon it as a failure. I think and believe that it is one of the most skillful works that human intelligence has created; [it] is one of the most perfect organizations that ever governed a free people. To say that it has

some difficulties is but to say that it is not the work of omniscience but of human intellect.

Our constitutional system, like that of Canada, was the result of special circumstances existing at the time of our early development. But like yours, it demonstrated confidence in man as a rational being, in the belief that given an atmosphere and time, where truth has an opportunity to compete with error in the market place of ideas; in the long run, the judgment of the great majority of the people can be trusted to come to the right decision.

The rights of the minority were given special protection in the American Constitution. This freedom for the minority was provided through the Bill of Rights, especially the first eight amendments, which wrote into law the inalienable and God-given rights of man, while the 9th and 10th, which dealt with the so-called reserve powers, provided that those powers not exclusively granted to the United States government were held by the various states and the people themselves.

In contrast to the United States, the enumerated powers in the Canadian Constitution are provincial, and the reserve and residual powers in theory are federal. And an additional protection was the establishment of an independent judiciary on equal terms with the executive and legislative branch. John Marshall, the first Chief Justice of the United States Supreme Court, in a series of fundamental decisions (Marbury vs. Madison, which established the right of the Supreme Court to hold as unconstitutional an act of Congress, and McCullough vs. Madison in which the court annulled a state law which conflicted with a federal law), set up the Supreme Court to act as "umpire" in our federal system. This is one of the main adjustive mechanisms in the constitutional framework through the principle of judicial review, which is quite unique in its broad extension and use. For many years, particularly in the early days of the New Deal, the Court was regarded by many, by its constitutional interpretation of the Acts of Congress, as a block to legitimate progress. In recent years, however, the Court has acted generally as a conservator of fundamental values and significantly advanced them in areas, such as racial discrimination.

The boldest conception of the delegates to the American Constitutional Convention was that the Federal government was not superior to the State government; the State and Federal governments each had their share of sovereignty; each operated directly upon its citizens; each was supreme in its field. A famous legal case from the distant past might explain clearly the source of some of our present difficulties. To illustrate the difficulties of comprehending our governmental system, while at the same time illustrating the division of functions in our government, I would like to choose an example — not from the present tensions which mar our near perfect relationship, but rather from an incident which occurred more than 110 years ago. I would remind you of the very famous case of "the People vs. McLeod." In the years 1837 and 1838, there was considerable difficulty along the American-Canadian border, due largely to the overly enthusiastic desires of many American citizens to bring democracy to Canada by force against the British crown. *The Montreal Transcript* for December 23, 1837, summed up the atmosphere as follows:

> The concurrent statements of the Canadian press, the American press, and of private letters, leave no longer any doubt of a hostile feeling along, and within, the American frontier—a cherished hope of perpetuating their own blind prejudices at the expense of the British government, which, with all its noble characteristics, has in their eyes the damning sin of being a monarchy.

In one of a series of incidents along the border, a group of Canadians sought retaliation against an unauthorized raiding party of American citizens and destroyed the steamer Caroline in a New York port. An American citizen was killed; three years later, a Canadian by the name of Alexander McLeod was arrested and imprisoned by the State of New York on a charge of murder. Inasmuch as the British government assumed responsibility for the actions taken as a matter of international relations between the two countries, it was generally agreed by experts in international law that McLeod was being unlawfully detained. At that time, the position of Secretary of State, which corresponds to your Minister of External Affairs, was held by a very famous American, and a former Senator from Massachusetts, Daniel Webster. Mr. Webster, although using the restraint necessary for the support of Congress and public opinion, practically admitted that the arrest and trial of McLeod was improper; and Presidents Harrison and Tyler [who succeeded Harrison upon his death] agreed.

The British and Canadian authorities assumed that this would be an end to the matter, and that their demand for the release of McLeod would be instantly met. Such, however, was not the case. The President, through Daniel Webster, pointed out that the Executive branch of the Federal government was forbidden by the Constitution to interfere with the conduct of the case by the Judicial branch of the State government. They also pointed out that, because of the division of functions between local and federal authorities, they could not require the local prosecuting attorney to dismiss the case. The British ambassador in Washington, Mr. Fox, wrote Secretary of State Webster, however, that his government could not "admit for a moment the validity of the doctrine that the Federal government of the United States has no power to interfere with the matter in question and that the decision thereof must rest solely and entirely with the State of New York" and he talked darkly of further action to free McLeod.

Next, the British wondered, if it was impossible to interfere with the Judicial branch of the State government under existing law, could not the US Administration, as leader of the majority party, obtain action by Congress to change the law. (Of course, Congress cannot change the Constitution, which in our country is supreme over all federal and state statutes.) But

President Tyler did send a message to Congress urging legislation for the removal of such cases from state courts to federal courts, on the grounds that such incidents embarrassed the Federal government in its conduct of international relations. But the President, despite his anxiety to conform to the wishes of the increasingly hostile British, could only request such legislation; and, although it was eventually passed, the House Committee on Foreign Affairs, to whom the McLeod Case was referred, took a very dim view of any action being undertaken with respect to the case by the Executive branch. You might also be interested to know that, although the House of Representatives was anxious to review all of the correspondence and documents in the State Department relating to the case, it could not demand that information, but only request it if, it said by resolution, the President did not feel this to be incompatible with the public interest.

So history presents us with a case 110 years old to remind Americans and Canadians of the dangers in misunderstanding the governmental process of the other country. The McLeod case illustrates the role of the American President and his Secretary of State as the chief spokesmen for my nation in foreign affairs; the role of Congress as the only body with legislative power, a power separate and distinct from that exercised by the President; and the role of states as individual entities within the Federal government, whose jurisdiction in certain matters cannot be infringed by federal action. In addition, the case illustrates the checks and balances that exist not only between the Federal and State governments, but also between the three branches of government, Executive, Legislative and Judicial. Finally and most important today, it illustrates how our system of government can appear to others to speak with one tongue but many voices, and thus create misunderstandings which lead to unnecessary tensions.

Incidentally, I didn't mean to leave Mr. McLeod languishing in jail without telling you the final outcome of his case. His attempt at *habeas corpus*, which the Federal government supported, failed in the New York Supreme Court as the result of a judicial opinion which has been much criticized in international law circles; but as somewhat of an anti-climax, he was subsequently tried by a local court and acquitted by the jury. All of the trouble caused by his arrest was unnecessary.

A great heritage has been passed on to both of us. Our job now, of course, is to maintain it in a changing world, and pass it on with its basic protection for the average citizen, undisturbed. The responsibility of those who now hold elective office is thus especially great. As one who has served several years in our House of Representatives and in the United States Senate, I must admit that the task of representation is not always as simple as it sometimes seems to students of the legislative process. Those of you who aspire to public office should be reminded that it is not always easy to be on the side of the angels. Indeed, on most issues it seems as though the angels are not with us, at least not politically, as the questions that face us do not involve moral issues of right and wrong, but rather the settlement of conflicting claims of powerful interests. For example, though I believe that the St. Lawrence Waterway would benefit substantial sections of my country as well as yours, yet its effect on New England, and particularly on the Port of Boston, which I represent, might be unfortunate. The easy answer on the course to adopt would be for the representative to vote for the national interest, but am I not sent to the Congress to represent the needs of my people. It is not a moral question, nor is the answer obvious as to whether we should vote twenty million dollars more for hospital construction, even though we have at the same time a heavy budgetary deficit. I am not even as convinced as is Mr. Dulles, our Secretary of State, that foreign policy is a moral issue, for if this is not simply a struggle for survival by the powerful states but a crusade against the evils of the materialistic system that the communists espouse, how can we, to defeat Soviet Communism, ally ourselves closely with the communists of Yugoslavia?

If our country's foreign policy were based on moral grounds alone, it would be difficult to understand how we can reconcile our favouring freedom for the people behind the Iron Curtain on the one hand and yet opposing freedom for the people of Morocco on the other, merely because in our case we have air bases there. The point is that the questions on which we vote only rarely involve issues that admit an easy solution. Some politicians vote as the result of hoping to appease political pressures at home and stay in office and become, according to Dryden's *Epilogue to the Duke de Guise*:

> Damned neuters in the middle / way of steering / Are neither fish nor flesh nor / good red herring; / Not Whigs, nor Tories they; nor this / nor that / Nor birds, nor beasts; but just a kind / of bat; / A twilight animal, true to neither / cause / With Tory wings, and Whiggish teeth / and claws;

While others, like Senator Taft in our country, or Sir Wilfrid Laurier or Louis St. Laurent in yours, vote according to their convictions. But their convictions are, after all, the result of their own lives, their environment, their experience and prejudices, their glands and blood pressure, and thus their convictions may bring them to the wrong conclusion, as occasionally did Senator Taft's, while the politicians who supinely follow the wishes of the people may end up voting right, for under our federal system the needs of the individual state must be given recognition, for the sum of the real interests of the separate states, in those cases where they do not conflict, is the national interest. But in the final analysis, the only way to national survival is for our political leaders to accept the viewpoint expressed by Edmund Burke in his famous letter to the electors of Bristol. After stating his position on Britain's relations with the American colonies, he wrote:

> Gentlemen, you have my opinion on the present state of affairs ... I feel warmly on this subject and I express myself as I feel ... Flattery and friendship are very different things and to mislead them is not to serve

them. I cannot purchase the favour of any man but counsel him from what I think is his ruin.

We cannot afford the luxury of irresponsibility in national affairs. Today our economic and political system is competing with that of the Communists. In 50 years the Communists have moved outward with unparalleled swiftness so that now they control over one third of the world's population, and their shadow hangs over the lives of many millions of men in the free world. Their economic system, rigidly controlled, devoted completely to the aggrandizement of the state, is steadily closing the gap in productive supremacy that once we enjoyed. The troubles and pressures of the 18th century, when our country began, pale in significance with those we now face, for basically challenged are all of the suppositions upon which our founders based our government: that there are inalienable rights; rights granted by God and not by the state; that man is a political being; that he is rational; that the state is organized for his welfare and to protect his rights; that rule by the majority is not only more just, but more efficient. Unless we can prove again the truth of these fundamentals, then time will continue to serve the cause of our enemies.

In conclusion, I would like to address a brief word to the present relations of our two great countries. I am not attempting to minimize the disputes that have caused an unfortunate amount of resentment and distrust on the part of both Canadian and American citizens; neither am I able to offer a simple formula for the solution of these problems. But I know that I speak for the great majority of American people when I say to you that the United States highly values her fraternal friendship and association with Canadians. If you and I, the citizens and officials of our two great nations, and the press, can all emphasize these positive values and traditions which insure the continued amity of the United States and Canada, then there will be less danger of a deterioration in our relationship resulting from temporary insignificant or politically inspired controversies. If the United States and Canada, with their common language, common history, common economic and political interests and other close ties cannot live peacefully with one and other, then what hope is there for the rest of the world? We have a responsibility to demonstrate to all peoples everywhere that peaceful and stable existence by powerful countries, side by side, can remain a permanent reality in today's troubled world.

It is my hope that the people of Canada, by their careful judgment and clear-thinking stability, will refuse to permit the pressures of the day to weaken those foundations laid a century ago. Let us put away the misunderstandings and misconceptions that give rise to uncertainty and confusion at the present time, just as they did over one hundred years ago; then our two nations will continue to grow in friendship, to grow in prosperity, and to grow in peaceful and democratic achievement.

Chapter 22

President Richard Nixon
Rideau Hall, Ottawa
13 April 1972

This trip to Canada has been one which has been very much in our minds, and to which we have been looking forward for many months: as a matter of fact, since entering office. It has given us a chance already to see old friends like former Prime Minister Mr. [John] Diefenbaker whom we met in Washington when I was vice President of the United States, and to renew acquaintances with others with whom we have worked during the period that I have served as President of the United States. And I would say one of the real pleasures of this trip has been the opportunity to know better—I have met him once before—His Excellency, our host tonight, the Governor General [Roland Michener].

The Prime Minister and I have had an opportunity to have chats on several occasions, and we had one particularly interesting interlude on the last occasion that I visited Canada very briefly, when we celebrated the tenth anniversary of the inauguration of the St. Lawrence Seaway. Governor [Nelson] Rockefeller [of New York] was our host on the American side that day ... Governor Rockefeller, with his great, expansive charm, was introducing the various guests. He said, "Secretary and Mrs. Rogers," and they stood up, "the President of the United States and Mrs. Nixon," "the Prime Minister and Mrs. Trudeau." That was in 1969. (Prime Minister Pierre Elliott Trudeau was not married until March 1971). Fortunately, I spoke after he did, and I was able to save the situation somewhat by saying that the governor was simply meaning to be prophetic. I didn't realize what a good prophet the governor was.

But I think, as far as the Prime Minister is concerned, and Mrs. Trudeau, whom we have had the privilege and honour of meeting for the first time tonight, that the Prime Minister has proved that he is a very effective political leader. He has shown his devotion by his marriage to the great interest in beautification in Canada. And also, he is doing something about under-population [The first child of Pierre and Margaret Trudeau, Justin, was born on 25 December 1971].

Could I say just a few words now that will not be in the formal sense in which I will be speaking tomorrow, when I will be privileged to address the Parliament, but which will try to let those here in this company, and those who may be hearing what we say over this electronic device, provided the unions are not boycotting it (that is another thing we have in common) but in any event, may I tell you what one American and his wife, what we have in common with Canada and why we feel especially close to Canadians?

My secretary, many years ago when I was a young, practicing lawyer, was then an American, but she was very proud that she had been born in Canada. And as a result, after my wife and I were married, about 30 years ago (you wouldn't know it, but it was that long ago) but in any event, the year that we were married, we, with another couple, drove on a vacation to Canada. We were in Victoria and British Columbia, and brought back many pleasant memories of our first visit to Canada. It was because my secretary recommended that we go there, and we had no regrets. Then I recall in the year 1942, just before World War II came along ... and before going overseas, we had saved a little money and we had some time for a vacation, and we took the train to Quebec, and I shall never forget those three days that we had, and my wife will never forget, in Quebec: The [Chateau] Frontenac, that magnificent view from the promenade down over the river, but more, the warmth and friendship of the people that we met on that occasion.

Then there have been other occasions through the years. When we first came to Congress in 1946, and the next year, 1947, we had a few days off and we drove up the eastern part of the United States through the beauty of New England in the summertime, and we learned to know Nova Scotia and St. John, that side of Canada. Then, during the years out of office, I, of course, had the opportunity to visit Ottawa on one occasion, Toronto on another occasion, and Montreal.

But there was one particular occasion that I think stays in my mind more than all the others. I have been to Picton. Now, most Americans will not know what Picton is, but you Canadians will know. Or maybe you don't. But in the year 1957, the Secretary of State and I—I was then vice President and he was attorney general of the United States—were invited by the publisher of the Rochester paper, Mr. Paul Miller, to sail across Lake Ontario, and to go over to the Canadian side and see the beauties of Canada. It was to be a wonderful trip. I didn't realize that even on Lake Ontario one could get seasick, but finally when I saw Canadian soil, believe me, it was the most welcome soil I ever stepped on.

But the incident which I would like to leave on this occasion with our friends from Canada was what happened in Picton that day. It was a Saturday night. We had played golf earlier in the day. We were still in sports clothes in sports jackets, and we decided to go to one of the local pubs, just as we were. We went in and sat down. At the time, we had no Secret Service with us, and the waiter looked us all over, and in some way he seemed to think he recognized me, but he wasn't sure. We noted, or Secretary Rogers at least noted (he was then attorney general and is supposed to note such things), that the waiter was talking to the bartender after serving us. The bartender was looking over and saying, "No, it can't be, it can't be."

After we had finished (he was a very polite waiter), after we had finished and were ready to leave, the waiter came up and said, "Sir, if you don't mind, I have a bet with the bartender, and you can help me win it or I might lose it." I said, "What is the bet?" He said, "I bet him five dollars that you are vice President Nixon." I said, "Well, call him over and we will confirm it." So the bartender came over and said, "Is it true?" I said, "Yes." He said, "I would never have believed it." He gave him the five dollars, and as we started to move on, I heard him mumble to the waiter, "You know, he doesn't look near as bad in person as he does in his pictures."

Now, that little story tells us something about why this trip is important and why it is quite necessary. Maybe none of us look quite as bad in person as we may in our pictures, and we Canadians and Americans, because we are only an hour and ten minutes apart by air, must never miss the opportunity to see each other in person, to discuss our differences, maybe to continue them but at least to discuss them, and to maintain the individual dignity, the parallel courses to which the Governor General has referred so eloquently just a few moments ago.

I said, when I arrived at the airport, that the example that we in Canada and the United States have set is one which all the world could well look to and perhaps in years ahead might well follow: two nations, very much alike but also very different, and very proud; proud of what we are like and proud of how we are different but two nations living together in peace, discussing differences, not fighting about them. And as I thought tonight of how I could relate that particular thought to this occasion, I looked at this room (in this respect I must admit I am a bit old fashioned; I like a room like this: the high ceilings, the sense of history, all that has happened here) and I think of other great rooms around the world where this same sense of history fills us.

I had the privilege in 1958 of speaking in Guild Hall in London, and I remembered tonight some of the great speeches that have been made there: one by President Eisenhower at the end of World War II, and many others. Perhaps the most eloquent speech, and the briefest speech ever made in Guild Hall was one made by a British Prime Minister 150 years ago. After Nelson's victory at Trafalgar, William Pitt was toasted as the savior of Europe. He rose to respond. He answered in these words: "For the honour you have done me, I return you many thanks. But Europe will not be saved by any single man. England has saved herself by her exertions, and will, I trust, serve Europe by her example."

Tonight I think we could well say the world will not be saved by any single nation, but Canada and the United States, by their example, can contribute enormously to a new world in which nations can live together in peace, friendship, and understanding, maintaining their dignity, maintaining their individuality. This is the example which Canadian-American friendship stands for, and it is one of which all of us can be very proud.

Chapter 23

President Jimmy Carter on the Return of Six
Americans From Iran Telephone Discussion with
Prime Minister Joe Clark
31 January 1980

President Carter: Mr. Prime Minister, good morning to you.

[The Prime Minister responds.]

... I called—as you know, we've had a series of communications back and forth privately, sometimes almost in verbal code, on the telephone and otherwise —but I wanted to call, now that our six Americans are back in this country and safe, publicly and on behalf of all the American people, Joe, to thank you and Ambassador Taylor and the Canadian government and people for a tremendous exhibition of friendship and support and, I think, personal and political courage.

You've probably seen the outpouring of appreciation that has come from the American people on their own volition. And it's typical of the way we all feel. I might point out that the congressional parliamentarians tell me that the action taken by our Congress yesterday toward the Canadian government is the first time in the history of our nation that the Congress has ever expressed its thanks personally to another government for an act of friendship and heroism. And I just wanted to relay that historical note to you as well.

[The Prime Minister responds.]

Well, I thank you. I don't believe that the revelation of their departure will be damaging to the well-being of our other hostages. You're nice and very perceptive to express that concern. I think it was a remarkable demonstration of mutual trust that the fact of the existence of those Americans was kept confidential so long, and the fact that it was not revealed publicly until after they'd already left, is very good. But Joe, good luck to you. And I hope that you'll not only send a copy of my letter to Ambassador Taylor but also publicly express to the people of Canada my deep appreciation, both to you, to Ambassador Taylor, to all of the embassy officials, and indeed to your whole country. We are deeply grateful for this, a new demonstration of the closeness that is very beneficial to us.

[The Prime Minister responds.]

Same to you, Joe. Have a good 1980. Goodbye.

President Carter to reporters: Well, he's very nice. He expressed his hope that the revelation of their departure was not in any way going to endanger our own hostages still being held, and pointed out accurately that they've been very supportive of us from the very beginning of the Iranian crisis.

Prime Minister Joe Clark to reporters while on the campaign trail

1 February 1980

Reporter: Mr. Clark, I wonder if you could tell us if President Carter made any reference to the release of the news [about the escape of the hostages] coming from a Canadian journalist in Washington, and the fear that many people have expressed, that the fact that this news has come out might in some way endanger the 50 hostages still being held in Tehran?

Prime Minister Clark: No, the President did not raise that matter, although I raised the matter directly. I told him that the only concern I had about the entire episode was that I would not want the release of the news at this time to jeopardize the safety or the security of the Americans still held hostage. He said that in his judgment the publication of the news at this time did not jeopardize the Americans who are still hostages and that there should be no undue concern about their situation being adversely affected by the fact that good journalists did their job and had the news out.

Editor's Note: Former Prime Minister Clark graciously allowed the editor access to his private papers, currently restricted to researchers, in Library and Archives Canada for the purpose of searching for any notes or Canadian records of his side of this historic telephone call from President Carter. While no private notes were discovered, this search, undertaken by the LAC's Maureen Hoogenraad, did locate a transcript of Prime Minister Clark's press conference of 1 February 1980, from which I have been able to give readers at least some detail of our Prime Minister's side of part of the conversation with President Carter. The editor would like to publicly acknowledge and thank Mr. Clark and Ms. Hoogenraad for their assistance.

Chapter 24

President George H.W. Bush at the Air Quality [Acid Rain] Agreement Signing Ceremony
West Block, Parliament Hill, Ottawa
13 March 1991

This agreement that we're fixing to sign is added proof that the challenges we face require a new partnership among nations. Last year at the Houston economic summit, we agreed to give this effort real priority. Our negotiators gained momentum with the passage in the US of our landmark environmental legislation, the Clean Air Act of 1990. Credit for this accord belongs to the EPA in our country, its able administrator, Bill Reilly, who is with us today. And of course, credit goes to the negotiators on both sides for the spirit in which they completed this task. Let me thank our special negotiator, Dick Smith, and his colleagues, as well as their counterparts across the table on the Canadian side for a job well done.

Beyond our common interest in our shared environment, this agreement says something about our overall relationship. The fact that Canada and the United States were able so quickly to craft a wide-ranging and effective agreement on such a complex subject says a lot about the extraordinarily strong relationship between our two countries.

Mr. Prime Minister [Brian Mulroney], I do recall our own discussions on environmental issues, and especially our meeting before I became President back in January of 1987. I made a comment then that made its way into more than a few Canadian news reports, that I'd gotten "an earful" from you on acid rain. That was the understatement of the year [laughter]. So now, I came up here to prove to you that I was listening, and that all of us on the American side were listening. And again, we appreciate your strong advocacy; your articulate advocacy of this principle that I think will benefit the American people, the Canadian people. And I like to think it goes even beyond the borders of our two great countries.

So, thank you very much. The treaty that we sign today is testimony to the seriousness with which both our countries regard this critical environmental issue. And here is one that did take "two to tango". Here is one where each had to come give a little and take a little, and it's been worth it. And I think we're doing something good and sound and decent today.

Chapter 25

Former President George H.W. Bush on The Thrill of Fishing in Arctic Canada, *Deh Cho Drum*, Fort Simpson, Northwest Territories
31 August 1997

I love fishing the Tree River. Way above the treeline, the fast-flowing Tree River pours its rushing green-grey waters into the Arctic Ocean, about a mile or two from where I fished for char. As the waters race over the boulders and rocks, you can catch an occasional glimpse of the majestic char, struggling to continue their fight against the current, their quests to reach their destiny, up-river quest. If thirsty, you can cup your hands and drink of these pristine waters. Yes, there are some mosquitoes around, but not enough to detract from the joys of fishing. Even a mild breeze seems to keep the critters away.

This year the weather was perfect. We fished in T-shirts, needing a sweater or jacket only in the early morning or late afternoon. The weather up there is variable, and it can get wet and very cold even in August, but not this year. There were a lot of char in those fast-running waters, a lot of big, strong fish. My 13 year old grandson, Jeb, from Miami, Fla., got a 25- to 30-pound fish on his Magog Smelt fly, a brown, wet fly that was very productive over the course of our whole trip. He fought the fish for 45 minutes, following our guide Andy's instruction to perfection. The big red, finally tiring, came into the shallow waters just above some rapids, and then, with one ultimate surge of energy, he flipped over the edge of the pool into the white-water rapids, broke the 20-pound test tippet, and swam to freedom. My grandson, not an experienced fly fisherman, had fought the fish to perfection. He did nothing wrong. All the fishing experts who were watching told him so, but those big fish are strong and tough and they never give up.

I had 43 fish on my fly rod, only to bring two into the shore. Don't laugh; I was proud to have kept the fly in the water, kept on casting, having the thrill of having that many fish, even for a moment, on my No.9 rod. I used an L.L. Bean reel. As for flies, I found that the Mickey Finn, the Blue Charm and the Magog Smelt all worked well. So did some others, the names of which escape me even as I write. I tried some dry flies but they produced zilch in the way of action. I found that I got most of my fish on when the fly was drifting down stream, though I got two or three hits the instant the fly hit the water. One pool was narrow, right next to the fastest part of the river.

I'd throw the fly out into the white-capped waves and it would be rushed by the current into the pool. When it left the raging water and hit the more placid pool, the fish would strike.

Miscellaneous observations: I did better on getting the fly unhooked from the rocks this year, though I did lose a tiny number of flies when they were claimed by some especially craggy rocks. I learned that the way to get lots of fish on the line is to keep the hook in the water. Obvious. Well, maybe, but a lot of fishermen seem to hang out waiting for someone else to catch one before they'd do serious fly casting. The rocks were very slick and, at 73 years of age, my balance is less than perfect. Put it this way: I can't turn very well and I slip a lot. The felt-bottom boots help. Better still are the felt bottom boots with little, diamond-hard spikes.

I fish a lot, but my advice is "get a good guide." I had one in Andy, who in a very gentlemanly way pointed out mistakes and helped me in every way. He was a good net man, a great fly adviser, and he got as big a kick when I got a fish as if he had taken it himself. Last observation: I found myself getting intolerant of those fishermen using hardware. There is something more sporting, more competitive, more difficult, more challenging about using a fly rod.

I know that the *Deh Cho Drum* paper is not quite the size of Toronto papers or the *New York Times*, but you know what? I bet the 800 or 900 readers of your paper know a hell of a lot more about fishing than the readers of those big city papers. That made me hesitant about sharing these amateurish observations with you. But, on the other hand, maybe your readers will better be able to sense the exhilarating joy I felt when standing out there knee deep in the ice cold waters of the Tree River pools, communing with nature, counting my blessings, thanking God, and catching some char, too.

I am a very happy and a very lucky man now. Because of time spent fishing and the chance that fishing gives me to relax and think freely, now more than ever I see clearly just how blessed I really am. I served my country. I have a close family and a wonderful wife to whom I have been married for 52 and a half years, and yes, I went to the Tree River and caught char. Tight lines to all you fisherman!

Submitted by this most enthusiastic amateur, to whom Canada has given such joy.

Chapter 26

President William J. Clinton at a Dedication Ceremony for the New US Embassy in Canada Ottawa, Canada
8 October 1999

It is no surprise that the word "multicultural" actually comes from Canada. For two centuries, you have shown the world how people of different cultures can live and work together in peace, prosperity, and mutual respect in a country where human differences are democratically expressed, not forcefully repressed. Earlier this year, we in the United States were pleased to see Canada's rich tradition of democracy deepen with the creation of the new territory of Nunavut. We are proud to be your partners and allies. And we deeply value our relationship with a strong, united, democratic Canada.

Of course, as any two nations as complicated as ours are, we have our differences, and we don't always see eye to eye. It's kind of interesting to watch Jean Chrétien and me get in an argument. It's kind of like getting in an argument with your brother, you know? You have to do it every now and then just to keep in practice [laughter]. When we do have our differences, we try to approach them in good faith and directly, as true friends must. And we have shown that when we work together, on nearly every issue we can reach agreement ...

Let me say to all of you ... as we move into this new world of the 21st century; as we contemplate whether our children and grandchildren live to be 100 years or more because of the decoding of the human gene; as we imagine whether poor people across the world, from Africa to Latin America to Asia, will be able to skip 50 years of economic development because of the availability of the Internet and the cell phone and the rapid transfer of knowledge; as we imagine all the glories of modern technology in the modern world, that it is well to remember that for all this race to tomorrow in technology, the deepest problem the world faces today is the most primitive problem of human nature, the fear of the other, people who are different from us.

What have we done, Jean and I, since we've been in our respective positions around the world? We tried to stop people from killing each other in Bosnia and Kosovo because of religious and ethnic differences. I spent an enormous amount of time trying to help the people in the land of my forbears in Northern Ireland get over 600 years of religious fights. And every time they make an agreement to do it, they're like a couple of drunks walking out of the bar for the last time. When they get to the swinging door they turn around and go back in and say, "I just can't quite get there." It's hard to give up these things. Look at the Middle East; for all of our progress, it is so hard for them because of millennial differences. Why were all those people slaughtered in Rwanda?

When we have differences here in our homes, in our neighbourhoods in Canada and in the United States, it is well to remember that the effort we are making to remind our own citizens that our common humanity is always more important than the things which divide us. They make life more interesting, our differences, but we must constantly reaffirm that.

Canada and the United States, I think, have a special responsibility to the new millennium. It would be tragic if all the dreams that we share for our children and our grandchildren's future, if all the potential of the modern world, were to still keep crashing on the rocks of mankind's oldest failing. Let us show the world we don't need to be afraid of people who are different from us. We can respect them. We can differ honestly. But always, always, we must reaffirm our common humanity. That, to me, is the true story of our long friendship, which this magnificent building embodies. And now, it is with great pride and privilege that I declare this embassy officially open, in service to the people of the United States and in friendship to our greatest neighbour and ally, the people of Canada. May God bless the people of Canada and the United States of America ...

Chapter 27

President William J. Clinton to the Forum of Federations Conference Mont-Tremblant, Quebec
8 October 1999

Today I would like to talk briefly about the ways we in the United States are working to renew and redefine federalism for the 21st century; then, how I see the whole concept of federalism emerging internationally; and finally, how we—how I think, anyway—we should judge the competing claims of federalism and independence in different contexts around the world.

First, let me say we are 84 days, now, from a new century and a new millennium. The currents of change in how we work and live and relate to each other, and how we relate to people far across the world, are changing very rapidly. President Franklin Roosevelt once said that new conditions impose new requirements upon government and those who conduct government. We know this to be the case not only in the United States and Canada, Great Britain and Germany, Italy and France, Mexico and Brazil, but indeed, in all the countries of the world. But in all these places there is a federalist system of some form or another. We look for ways to imbue old values with new life, and old institutions with new meaning.

In 1992, when I ran for President, there was a growing sense in the United States that the compact between the people and their government, and between the states and the federal government, were in severe disrepair. This was driven largely by the fact that our federal government had quadrupled the national debt in 12 years, and that had led to enormous interest rates, slow growth, and grave difficulties on all the states of our land which they were powerless to overcome. So when the Vice President and I ran for national office, we had no debate from people who said, "Look, this is a national priority and you have to deal with it." But we talked a lot to governors and others about the necessity to create again what our founding fathers called "the laboratories of democracy". We frankly admitted that no one knew all the answers to America's large welfare caseload, to America's enormous crime rate, to America's incredible diversity of children and challenges in our schools. And so we said we would try to give new direction to the nation and deal with plainly national problems, but we would also try to build a new partnership that would make all of our states feel more a part of our union and more empowered in determining their own destiny.

Now, people develop this federalist system for different reasons. It came naturally to the United States because Great Britain set up colonies here as separate entities. And the states of our country actually created the national government. So we always had a sense that there were some things the states were supposed to do and some things the federal government was supposed to do.

Our founding fathers gave us some indication in the Constitution, but the history of the United States Supreme Court is full of cases trying to resolve the whole question of what is the role and the power of the states, as opposed to what is the role and the power of the national government in ever-new circumstances. There are different examples elsewhere. For example, in the former Yugoslavia, federalism was at least set up to give the appearance that all the different ethnic groups could be fairly treated and could have their voices heard.

So in 1992, it appeared that the major crisis in federalism was that the states had been disempowered from doing their jobs because the national economy was so weak, and the fabric of the national society was fraying in America. But underneath that, I knew that once we began to build things again, we would have to resolve some very substantial questions, some of which may be present in your countries, as well. We set about to work, the Vice President and I, in an effort which I charged to him, to attempt to redefine the mission of the federal government. And we told the people of the United States that we actually thought the federal government was too large in size, that it should be smaller but more active, and that we should do more in partnerships with state and local governments and the private sector, with the ultimate goal of empowering the American people to solve their own problems in whatever unit was most appropriate, whether it was an individual citizen, the family, the community, the state, or the nation. And we have worked at that quite steadily. Like Canada, we turned our deficit around and produced a surplus. We also shrank the size of the federal government. The size of the United States federal government today is the same as it was in 1962, when John Kennedy was President, and our country was much, much smaller.

In the economic expansion we have been enjoying since 1993, the overwhelming majority of the jobs that were created were created in the private sector. It's the largest percentage of private sector job creation of any economic expansion in America since the end of World War II. Meanwhile, many of our state and local governments have continued to grow in size, to meet the day-to-day demands of a lot of the domestic issues that we face in our country. And I think that is a good thing.

In addition to shrinking the size of government, we've tried to empower the states to make more of their own decisions. For example, the Department of Education has gotten rid of two-thirds of the rules it imposed on states and school districts when I became President. Instead, we say, "Here are our national objectives. Here is the money you can have. You have to make a report on the progress at meeting these national objectives, but we're not going to tell you how to do it anymore." And it's amazing what you can do if you get people to buy into national objectives with which they agree, and you stop trying to micromanage every instance of their lives and their daily activities. So we found some good success there.

We've also tried to give the states blanket freedom to try more new ideas in areas where we think we don't have all the answers now, from health policy to welfare reform, from education to fighting crime. We have always felt this has been easy in the United States, though, compared to a lot of places, because we've had this history of believing, from the time of our founders, that the national government would never have all the answers, and that the states should be seen as our friends and our partners because they could be laboratories of democracy. They could always be out there pushing the envelope of change. And certain things would be possible politically in some places that would not be possible in others, and we have been very well served by that. It has encouraged a lot of innovation and experimentation. Here is the problem we have with the basic business of government and federalism today. In the 21st century world, when we find an answer to a problem, very often we don't have time to wait for every state to agree that that's the answer. So we try to jumpstart the federalist experience by looking for ideas that are working and then embodying them in federal legislation and giving all the states the funds and other support they need to do it.

Why do we do this? Well, let me give you one example. In 1787, in the United States, the founding fathers declared that all the new territories would have to set aside land for public schools, and then gave the responsibility for public education to the states. Then, in the next few years, a handful of states mandated education. But it took more than 100 years for all of our states to mandate free public education for all of our children. That was 19th century pace of change. It's inadequate in the 21st century. So I have tried to do what I did as a governor. If something is working in a state, I try to steal it, put it into federal law, and at least give all the states the opportunity and the money necessary to implement the same change ...

Since our Ambassador is a native of Georgia, I'll give you one example. One of my goals is to make universal access to colleges and universities in America, and we now have something called the HOPE scholarship, modeled on Ambassador Giffin's home state program, which gives all students enough of a tax subsidy to at least afford the first two years of college in America, because we found in a census that no matter where you come from in the United States, people with at least two years of education after high school tended to get jobs where their incomes grew and they did better. People with less than that tended to get jobs where their incomes stayed level or declined in the global economy.

Now, we've also tried to make dealing with Washington less of a problem. We've ended something that was very controversial, at least prospectively, called unfunded mandates, where the federal government would tell the states they had to do something and give them about five percent of the money it cost to do it. That, I think, is a problem in every national federal system. We continue to give the states greater freedom and flexibility. And this summer I signed a new executive order on federalism which would reaffirm, in very specific ways, how we would work in partnership and greater consultation with state and local officials.

Federalism is not a fixed system; it, by definition, has to be an evolving system. For more than 200 years, the pendulums of powers have swung back and forth one way or the other. And I do want to say, for those of you who may be looking outside in, thinking the Americans could never understand our problems, that they don't have any problems like this, that it is true that, by and large, in our state units we don't have people who are of just one racial or ethnic or religious group. But to be sure, we have some of that. I'll give you one example that we're dealing with today.

The United States Supreme Court has to decide a case from the state of Hawaii in which the state has given native Hawaiians, Pacific Islanders, and only them, the right to vote in a certain kind of election. And someone in Hawaii has sued them, saying that this violates the equal protection clause of the United States Constitution. We disagree because of the purpose of the election. But you can see this is a federalist issue. We basically said the national government would give that to the states, the states want to do it this way; then a citizen says, "No, you can't do that under national law."

Another example that causes us a lot of problems in the West; what happens when the federal government actually owns a lot of the land and the resources of a state? The national government is most unpopular in America in states like Wyoming or Idaho, where there aren't very many people; there are a lot of natural resources. Cattlemen, ranchers have to use land that belongs to the federal government, and we feel that we have to protect the land for multiple uses, including environmental preservation as well as grazing or mining or whatever. And so it's an impossible situation. It's very funny: in these states, when we started, the federal government was most popular in the areas where we own most of the land, because we built dams and channeled rivers and provided land for people to graze their cattle. And within 50 years, the federal government has become the most unpopular thing imaginable. Now, I used to go to Wyoming on vacation just to listen to people tell me how terrible the job I had was [laughter]. But it's a problem we have to face.

And let me say one other thing I think might be interesting to you; the Democratic Party and the Republican Party in the United States tend to have different ideas about federalism, depending on what the issue is, which is why it's always good to have a dynamic system. For example, we Democrats, once we find something working at the local level that advances our social policy, or our economic policy, we want to at least make it a national option, if not a national mandate. When I became President, crime was [generally] going up, but there were cities where crime was going down. I went [to some cities] and found out why it was going down. And it was obvious to me that we didn't have enough police officers preventing crime in the first place, so I said we're going to create 100,000 police at the national level and give them to the cities. The Conservatives were against that. They said, "You're interfering with state and local rights, telling them how to fight crime." Of course, I wasn't; I was giving them police. They didn't have to take them if they didn't want them [laughter]. And it turned out they liked it quite well; we have the lowest crime rate in 26 years. But there was a genuine federalism dispute.

Now we're having the same dispute over teachers. We have the largest number of children in our schools in history, and lots of evidence that smaller classes in the early grades yield permanent learning gains to children. So I said, now let's put 100,000 teachers out there. And they say I'm trying to impose this terrible burden on state and local governments, sticking my nose in where it doesn't belong. On the other hand, in the whole history of the country, personal injury law (including economic injuries) and commercial law have always been the province of state and local government except for things like securities, stocks, bonds, things that required a national securities market. But many people in the Republican Party believe that since there is essentially a national economy and an international economic environment, we should take away from the states all their states' rights when it comes to determining the rules under which people can sue businesses. And they really believe it. And I have agreed with them as it applies to securities litigation, because we need a national securities market. But I have disagreed with them as it applies to other areas of tort reform where they think it's a bad thing that there are state rights. And I say this not to attack the other party, but only to illustrate to all of you that in whatever context you operate, there will always be differences of opinion about what should be done nationally and what should be done at the state level. That cannot be eliminated. The purpose of federalism, it seems to me, is to, number one, take account of the genuinely local feelings which may be, in the United States, a result of economic activities and ties to the land and history; or it may be, in another country, the result of the general segregation of people of various racial, ethnic, or religious groups into the provinces in the federal system.

So the first process is to give people a sense of their identity and autonomy. And then you have to really try to make good decisions so that the system works. I mean, in the end, all these systems only have integrity if the allocation of decision-making authority really produces results that people like living with, so they feel that they can go forward.

Now, let me just discuss a minute what is sort of the underlying tension here that you see all across the world, which is, what is the answer to the fact that, on the edge of a new millennium, where we would prefer to talk about the Internet, the decoding of the human gene, and the discovery of billions of new galaxies in outer space, those of us in politics have to spend so much time talking about the most primitive slaughter of people based on their ethnic, racial or religious differences?

The great irony of the turning of the millennium is that we have more modern options for technology and economic advance than ever before, but our major threat is the most primitive human failing: the fear of the 'Other' and the sense that we can only breathe and function and matter if we are somehow free of the necessity to associate with and deal with, and maybe even under certain circumstances subordinate our own opinions to the feelings of people who are different from us, a different race, a different religion, a different tribe. And there is no answer to this that is easy. But let me just ask you to look [at] the former Yugoslavia, where we, Prime Minister Chrétien and I and our friends, are trying to preserve a Bosnian State, which serves Croatians and Muslims, after four years of horrible slaughter, until we stopped it in 1995, or in Kosovo, where we're exploring whether Kosovo can continue to be an autonomous part of Serbia, notwithstanding the fact that the Serbs ran all of them out of the country and we had to take them back.

Why did all this happen? Partly because it was an artificially imposed federalism. Marshal Tito was a very smart man who basically said, "I'm going to create federalism out of my own head. I'm going to mandate the participation of all these groups in government. And I'm going to forbid my government from talking about ethnic superiority, or oppression, or problems." He wouldn't even let them discuss the kind of ethnic tensions that are just part of the daily life in most societies in this world. And it all worked until he died. And then it slowly began to unravel.

So one of the reasons you have all these people clamoring for the independence of ever-smaller groups is that they had a kind of phony federalism imposed from the top down. So the first lesson I draw from this is that every federalist system in the world today (a world in which information is widely shared, and economic possibilities are at least always, to some extent, based on global forces, certainly in terms of how much money you can get into a country) must be real. There must be some real sense of shared authority. And people must know they have some real range of autonomy for decisions. And it must more or less correspond to what they perceive they need to accomplish. On the other hand, it seems to me that the suggestion that a people of a given ethnic group or tribal group or religious group can only have a meaningful communal existence if they are an independent nation - not if there is no oppression, not if they have genuine autonomy - but they must be actually independent, is a questionable assertion in a global economy, where cooperation pays greater benefits in every area of life than does destructive competition.

Consider, for example, the most autonomous societies on earth, arguably, the tribes still living in the rainforests on the island of New Guinea. There are 6,000 languages still existent in the world today, and 1,000 of them can be found in Papua New Guinea, and Irian Jaya, where tribes living 10 or 20 miles from one another have complete self-determination. Would you like that? On the other hand, consider the terrible problems of so many African peoples where they're saddled with national borders drawn for them at the Conference of Berlin in 1885, that took no reasonable account of the allocation of the tribes on certain lands and the history of their grazing, their farming, their moving.

So how to work it out? There is no answer. We have to provide a framework in which people can work it out. But the only point I want to make to you today (I don't want to beat this to death, because we could stay here for a week discussing this) is that at the end of World War I, the European powers and America sort of withdrew, so we have to share part of the blame. Our record is not exactly spotless in how we went about carving up, for example, the aftermath of the Ottoman Empire. And so we have spent much of the 20th century trying to reconcile President Woodrow Wilson's belief that different nations had the right to be free—nations being people with a common consciousness—that they had a right to be a state ... If every racial and ethnic and religious group that occupies a significant piece of land not occupied by others became a separate nation—we might have 800 countries in the world and have a very difficult time having a functioning economy or a functioning global polity. Maybe we would have 8,000 ...

So that doesn't answer any specific questions. It just means that I think when a people think it should be independent in order to have a meaningful political existence, serious questions should be asked: Is there an abuse of human rights? Is there a way people can get along if they come from different heritages? Are minority rights, as well as majority rights, respected? What is in the long-term economic and security interests of our people? How are we going to cooperate with our neighbours? Will it be better or worse if we are independent, or if we have a federalist system?

I personally believe that you will see more federalism rather than less in the years ahead, and I offer, as exhibit A, the European Union. It's really a new form of federalism, where the States (in this case, the nations of Europe), are far more important and powerful than the federal government, but they are giving enough functions over to the federal government to sort of reinforce their mutual interest in an integrated economy and in some integrated political circumstances. In a way, we've become more of a federalist world when the United Nations takes a more active role in stopping genocide in places in which it was not involved, and we recognize mutual responsibilities to contribute and pay for those things.

So I believe we will be looking for ways, over and over and over again (the Prime Minister and I have endorsed the Free Trade Area of the Americas), we'll be looking for ways to integrate our operations for mutual interest, without giving up our sovereignty. And where there are dissatisfied groups in sections of countries, we should be looking for ways to satisfy anxieties and legitimate complaints without disintegration, I believe. That's not to say that East Timor was wrong. If you look at what the people in East Timor have been through, if you look at the colonial heritage there, if you look at the fact that the Indonesians offered them a vote, they took it, and nearly 80 percent of them voted for independence; it seems that was the right decision there.

But let us never be under the illusion that those people are going to have an easy path, assuming that those of us who are trying to support and help them; assuming we can stop all the pro-integrationist militias from oppressing the people, and we can get all the East Timorese back home, and they'll all be safe. There will still be less than a million of them, with a per capita income among the poorest in the world, struggling to make a living for their children in an environment that is not exactly hospitable. Now, does that mean they were wrong? No. Under the circumstances they faced, they probably made the only decision they could have. But wouldn't it have been better if they could have found their religious, their cultural, their ethnic and their economic footing—and genuine self-government—in the framework of a larger entity which would also have supported them economically? And reinforced their security instead of undermined it? It didn't happen; it's too bad.

But I say this because I don't think there are any general rules; I think that, at the end of World War I, when President Wilson spoke, there was a general assumption, because we were seeing empires break up (the Ottoman Empire, the Austro-Hungarian Empire; there was the memory of the Russian Empire; British colonialism was still alive in Africa, and so was French colonialism) and at that time, we all assumed, and the rhetoric of the time imposed the idea that the only way for people to feel any sovereignty or meaning was if they were independent. And I think we've spent a lot of the 20th century minimizing the prospects of federalism. We all have recoiled, now, so much at the abuse of people because of their tribal, racial, and religious characteristics, that we tend immediately to think that the only answer is independence.

But we must think of how we will live after the shooting stops, after the smoke clears, over the long run. And I can only say this, in closing; I think the United States and Canada are among the most fortunate countries in the world because we have such diversity; sometimes concentrated, like the Inuit in the north; sometimes widely dispersed within a certain area, like the diversity of Vancouver. We are fortunate because life is more interesting and fun when there are different people who look differently and think differently and find their way to God differently. It's an interesting time.

And because we all have to grow and learn when we confront people who are different than we are, and instead of looking at them in fear and hatred and dehumanization, we look at them and see a mirror of ourselves and our common humanity. I think if we will keep these questions in mind: what is most likely to advance our common humanity in a smaller world? What is the arrangement of government most likely to give us the best of all worlds, the integrity we need, the self-government we need, the self-advancement we need, without pretending that we can cut all the cords that bind us to the rest of humanity? I think more and more and more people will say, "This federalism, it's not such a bad idea."

Chapter 28

President George W. Bush
Halifax, Nova Scotia
1 December 2004

Three years ago, Halifax and other towns and villages, from Newfoundland to Manitoba to the Northwest Territories to British Columbia, welcomed, as the Prime Minister (Paul Martin) mentioned, more than 33,000 passengers on diverted flights. For days after September the 11th, Canadians came to the aid of men and women and children who were worried and confused and had nowhere to sleep. You opened your homes and your churches to strangers. You brought food, you set up clinics, you arranged for calls to their loved ones, and you asked for nothing in return. One American declared, "My heart is overwhelmed at the outpouring of Canadian compassion. How does a person say thank you to a nation?" Well, that's something a President can do. And so let me say directly to the Canadian people and to all of you here today who welcomed Americans, thank you for your kindness to America in an hour of need. That emergency revealed the good and generous heart of this country and showed the true feelings of Canadians and Americans toward each other. The affection that appeared in an instant will always be there, and it runs deep. Beyond the words of politicians and the natural disagreements that nations will have, our two peoples are one family ...

Canada represents America's most vital trade relationship in the whole world, and we will do all that is necessary to keep that relationship strong. Yet, our ties go deeper than trade. Our community of values reaches back centuries. Canada and the US may have disagreed on the wisdom of separating from the Crown, but we've always agreed on the great principles of liberty derived from our common heritage. We believe in the dignity of every human life, and we believe in the right of every person to live in freedom. We believe in free markets, humanized by compassion and fairness. We believe a diverse society can also be united by principles of justice and equality. The values we hold have made us good neighbours for centuries, and they will keep us strong allies and good friends for the centuries to come. These shared convictions have also led our great democracies to accept a mission in the wider world. We know it is not possible to live in the quiet isolation of our peaceful continent, hoping the problems and challenges of other nations will pass us by. We know there can be no security, no lasting peace in a world where the proliferation of terrorism, genocide and extreme poverty go unopposed. We know that our own interests are served by an international system that advances human rights and open societies and free trade and the rule of law and the hope that comes from self-government. Both Canada and the United States have accepted important global duties, and we will meet those responsibilities for our own benefit and for the good of mankind.

Canada's leadership is helping to build a better world. Over the past decade, Canadian troops have helped bring stability to Bosnia and Kosovo. Canada's willingness to send peacekeepers to Haiti saved thousands of lives and helped save Haiti's constitutional government. Canadian troops are serving bravely in Afghanistan at this hour. Other Canadians stand on guard for peace in the Middle East, in Cyprus, Sudan, and the Congo ...

Our nations play independent roles in the world, yet our purposes are complementary. We have important work ahead. A new term in office is an important opportunity to reach out to our friends. I hope to foster a wide international consensus upon three great goals. The first great commitment is to defend our security and spread freedom by building effective multinational and multilateral institutions and supporting effective multilateral action.

The tasks of the 21st century, from fighting proliferation [sic], to fighting the scourge of HIV and AIDS, to fighting poverty and hunger, cannot be accomplished by a single nation alone. The United States and Canada participate together in more multilateral institutions than perhaps any two nations on earth, from NATO in Europe to the OAS in the Western Hemisphere to APEC in the Pacific. Canada and the United States are working with a coalition of nations through the Proliferation Security Initiative to stop and seize shipments of weapons of mass destruction materials and delivery systems on land and at sea and in the air.

America always prefers to act with allies at its side. We're grateful to Canada for working closely with us to confront the challenges of Iran and North Korea. Multilateral organizations can do great good in the world. Yet the success of multilateralism is measured not merely by following a process but by achieving results. The objective of the UN and other institutions must be collective security, not endless debate. For the sake of peace, when those bodies promise serious consequences, serious consequences must follow. America and Canada helped create the United Nations, and because we remain committed to that institution, we want it to be more than a League of Nations. My country is determined to work as far as possible within the framework of international organizations, and we're hoping that other nations will work with us to make those institutions more relevant and more effective in meeting the unique threats of our time.

Our second commitment is to fight global terrorism with every action and resource the task requires. Canada has taken a series of critical steps to guard against the danger of terrorism. You have created the Department of Public Safety and Emergency Preparedness. You've toughened your anti-terror laws. You're upgrading your intelligence. I want to thank the government for all those constructive and important decisions. Our two countries are working together every day—every day—to keep our people safe. That is the most solemn duty I have and the most solemn duty the Prime Minister has. From the Smart Border Accord to the Container Security Initiative to the joint command of NORAD, we are working together. I hope we'll also move forward on ballistic missile defense cooperation to protect the next generation of Canadians and Americans from the threats we know will arise.

The energetic defense of our nations is an important duty. Yet defense alone is not a sufficient strategy. On September the 11th, the people of North America learned that two vast oceans and friendly neighbours cannot fully shield us from the dangers of the 21st century. There's only one way to deal with enemies who plot in secret and set out to murder the innocent and the unsuspecting: we must take the fight to them. We must be relentless and we must be steadfast in our duty to protect our people. Both of the countries have learned this lesson. In the early days of World War II, when the United States was still wrestling with isolationism, Canadian forces were already engaging the enemies of freedom from the Atlantic, across the Atlantic. At the time, some Canadians argued that Canada had not been attacked and had no interest in fighting a distant war. Your Prime Minister, Mackenzie King, gave this answer: "We cannot defend our country and save our homes and families by waiting for the enemy to attack us. To remain on the defensive is the surest way to bring the war to Canada. Of course, we should protect our coasts and strengthen our ports and cities against attack, but," the Prime Minister went on to say, "we must also go out and meet the enemy before he reaches our shores. We must defeat him before he attacks us, before our cities are laid to waste." Mackenzie King was correct then, and we must always remember the wisdom of his words today.

Chapter 29

President Barack Obama - Prime Minister Stephen Harper
Press Conference Parliament Hill, Ottawa
19 February 2009

Prime Minister Stephen Harper: It is a great pleasure to welcome President Obama to Canada. We are deeply honoured that he has chosen Canada for his first foreign visit since taking office. His election to the presidency launches a new chapter in the rich history of Canada-US relations. It is a relationship between allies, partners, neighbours, and the closest of friends; a relationship built on our shared values: freedom, democracy, and equality of opportunity epitomized by the President himself.

Our discussions today focused on three main priorities. First, President Obama and I agree that Canada and the United States must work closely to counter the global economic recession by implementing mutually beneficial stimulus measures, and by supporting efforts to strengthen the international financial system. We concur on the need for immediate, concerted action to restore economic growth and to protect workers and families hit hardest by the recession through lowering taxes, ensuring access to credit, and unleashing spending that sustains and stimulates economic activity.

Second, President Obama and I agreed to a new initiative that will further cross-border cooperation on environmental protection and energy security. We are establishing a US-Canada clean energy dialogue which commits senior officials from both countries to collaborate on the development of clean energy science and technologies that will reduce greenhouse gases and combat climate change.

Third, the President and I had a productive discussion about our shared priorities for international peace and security, in particular, our commitment to stability and progress in Afghanistan. This has been a very constructive visit, revealing to both of us a strong consensus on important bilateral and international issues. President Obama, I look forward to working with you in the months ahead to make progress on these issues, and build on the long and deep friendship between our two countries and our two peoples.

President Obama: Thank you. Well, it is a great pleasure to be here in Ottawa. And Prime Minister Harper and I just completed a productive and wide-ranging discussion on the many issues of common concern to the people of the United States and Canada.

I came to Canada on my first trip as President to underscore the closeness and importance of the relationship between our two nations, and to reaffirm the commitment of the United States to work with friends and partners to meet the common challenges of our time. As neighbours, we are so closely linked that sometimes we may have a tendency to take our relationship for granted, but the very success of our friendship throughout history demands that we renew and deepen our cooperation here in the 21st century. We're joined together by the world's largest trading relationship and countless daily interactions that keep our borders open and secure. We share core democratic values and a commitment to work on behalf of peace, prosperity, and human rights around the world. But we also know that our economy and our security are being tested in new ways. And the Prime Minister and I focused on several of those challenges today.

As he already mentioned, first we shared a commitment to economic recovery. The people of North America are hurting, and that is why our governments are acting. This week I signed the most sweeping economic recovery plan in our nation's history. Today the Prime Minister and I discussed our respective plans to create jobs and lay a foundation for growth. The work that's being done by this government to stimulate the economy on this side of the border is welcomed, and we expect that we can take actions in concert to strengthen the auto industry, as well. We know that the financial crisis is global, and so our response must be global. The United States and Canada are working closely on a bilateral basis and within the G8 and G20 to restore confidence in our financial markets. I discussed this with Prime Minister Harper, and we look forward to carrying that collaboration to London this spring.

Second, we are launching, as was mentioned, a new initiative to make progress on one of the most pressing challenges of our time: the development and use of clean energy. How we produce and use energy is fundamental to our economic recovery, but also our security and our planet. And we know that we can't afford to tackle these issues in isolation. And that's why we're updating our collaboration on energy to meet the needs of the 21st century. The clean energy dialogue that we've established today will strengthen our joint research and development. It will advance carbon reduction technologies and it will support the development of an electric grid that can help deliver the clean and renewable energy of the future to homes and businesses, both in Canada and the United States. And through this example, and through continued international negotiations, the United States and Canada are committed to confronting the threat posed by climate change.

In addition to climate change, Prime Minister Harper and I discussed the need for strong bilateral cooperation on a range of global challenges, one of the most pressing being Afghanistan. The people of Canada have an enormous burden there that they have borne. As I mentioned in an interview prior to this visit, those of us in the United States are extraordinarily grateful for the sacrifices of the families here in Canada of troops that have been deployed and have carried on their missions with extraordinary valour. You've put at risk your most precious resource: your brave men and women in uniform. And so we are very grateful for that. There is an enduring military mission against al Qaeda and the Taliban in Afghanistan and along the border regions between Afghanistan and Pakistan, but we also have to enhance our diplomacy and our development efforts. And we discussed this in our private meetings. My administration is undertaking a review of our policy so that we forge a comprehensive strategy in pursuit of clear and achievable goals. And as we move forward, we intend to consult very closely with the government here in Canada to make certain that all our partners are working in the same direction. In April, we'll have a broader dialogue with our NATO allies on how to strengthen the alliance to meet the evolving security challenges around the world. And finally, we look forward to the Summit of the Americas. My administration is fully committed to active and sustained engagement to advance the common security and prosperity of our hemisphere. We will work closely with Canada in advancing these goals, and look forward to a meaningful dialogue in Trinidad. As I've said, the United States is once again ready to lead. But strong leadership depends on strong alliances, and strong alliances depend on constant renewal. Even the closest of neighbours need to make that effort to listen to one another, to keep open the lines of communication, and to structure our cooperation at home and around the world. That's the work that we've begun here today. I'm extraordinarily grateful to Prime Minister Harper for his hospitality, his graciousness, and his leadership. And I'm looking forward to this being the start of a continued extraordinary relationship between our two countries.

Part Four

Speaking About Canada in Washington

It will surprise no one that much of the most significant rhetorical material concerning the relationship between Canada and the United States, at the highest levels of our joint governments, has taken place in the American capital city during the past 100 years. Canadian Prime Ministers, for example, have been the frequent guests at official State Dinners at the White House over the decades. Both Presidents and Prime Ministers have left history a series of rhetorical gems, from these dinners and other Washington appearances, some of which will be found below. Presidents have, as well, taken to the airwaves during Radio Addresses to discuss joint Canada-U.S. concerns. For Canadian leaders, however, Prime Ministers Brian Mulroney, Pierre Trudeau and Governor General Vincent Massey are in a class of three. They are the only Canadians to have been invited and to have accepted an invitation to address the US Congress.

Almost two decades after he stood before Congress in April of 1988, Mulroney remembered the event as one of the most daunting venues he had experienced. "Though I had been making speeches since I was teenager, I have to admit I was nervous," he wrote in his 2007 *Memoirs*. "It was not my intention to seek out headlines back home by being strident or unduly aggressive. This event was much too important for that."[4]

As people around the world know from either visiting the US Capitol Building in Washington, or from watching Presidents deliver their State of the Union addresses, the American House of Representatives is one of the world's grandest democratic chambers. Trudeau spoke at the same spot in 1977, and, like Mulroney, did not disappoint his audience. Trudeau's speech came after the election of the separatist Parti Quebecois in November 1976. Americans were suddenly faced with the possibility that their peaceful neighbour to the north would split into fragments while they stood helplessly by without fully understanding the reasons behind Canada's unity crisis.

"I say to you with all the certainty I can command that Canada's unity will not be fractured," Trudeau thundered before the Congress. "Revisions will take place. Accommodations will be made. We shall succeed." Even today, more than 30 years after Trudeau's address, the force of his words can be felt:

> Most Canadians understand that the rupture of their country would be an aberrant departure from the norms they themselves have set,

> a crime against the history of mankind; for I am immodest enough to suggest that a failure of this always-varied, often illustrious Canadian experiment would create shock waves of disbelief among those all over the world who are committed to the proposition that among man's noblest endeavours are those communities in which persons of diverse origins live, love, work, and find mutual benefit.

Though Mulroney and Trudeau had much different styles, both men made the most of their unique addresses in Washington. Mulroney, who would, three years later, sign the historic acid rain accord with the United States which has done so much to rid the continent of this environmental scourge, spoke over the head of the reluctant environmentalist in the White House, Ronald Reagan, when continuing his crusade against acid rain:

> I ask you this very simple proposition. What would be said of a generation of North Americans that found a way to explore the stars, but allowed its lakes and forests to languish and die? The one thing acid rain does not do is discriminate. It is despoiling your environment as inexorably as it is ours. It is damaging your environment from Michigan to Maine, and threatens marine life on the eastern seaboard. It is a rapidly escalating ecological tragedy in this country as well as ours.

Vice President George H.W. Bush was sitting behind Mulroney that day, in his capacity as the chief presiding officer of the US Senate. Less than a year later, when it was his turn to stand behind that very podium in Washington as America's 41st President, he pledged that America would begin to get its house in order and would become Canada's true partner in the fight against acid rain. The success of the treaty both leaders later signed is arguably the greatest bilateral mark jointly left on North American history.

It was fitting that Massey is the first, and so far the only, Governor General to address the Congress. His stellar career, before becoming the Queen's Representative to Canada, included his service as the first ever Canadian Ambassador to Washington. Massey took up this post in the 1920s, during the Calvin Coolidge era in the US.

All three men rose to the task when granted this rare invitation. And all three, in different ways, and by highlighting different aspects of the complex relationship that is a reality of Canadian-American relations, have made Canadians proud.

In June 2004, Mulroney, by now out of office for 11 years, became the first foreign leader to speak at a Presidential state funeral south of the border. Mulroney's eulogy to Reagan, delivered at Washington's National Cathedral, was carried live over US television networks. Our 18th Prime Minister worked in the words of Canadian Father of Confederation and poet, Thomas D'Arcy McGee, in delivering this eulogy:

In one of his poems, McGee, thinking of his birthplace [in Ireland] wrote poignantly: 'Am I remembered in Erin? I charge you speak me true. Has mane a sound, a meaning in the scenes my boyhood knew?' Ronald Reagan will not have to worry about Erin because they remember him well and affectionately there. Indeed they do. From Erin to Estonia, from Maryland to Madagascar, from Montreal to Monterey, Ronald Reagan does not enter history tentatively. He does so with certainty and panache.

And so the Canadian-American relationship moves forward still. While there will always be challenges to be faced and disputes to settle, citizens of both nations should always recall the example we set before the world. Canadians and Americans, as Mulroney said, move forward "with certainty and panache," and always will. Voices from our joint history demand it.

Arthur Milnes

Chapter 30

Governor General Vincent Massey's Address to the
US Congress Washington, D.C.
4 May 1954

To say that you in the United States and we in Canada have much in common is a venerable platitude. Living as we do side by side on the same continent, our resemblances are many. We have, too, similar views on fundamental things. Among our common characteristics, one of the greatest, I believe, is our dislike of regimentation, our respect for the differences which lend colour to everyday existence. We believe that each man should lead his own life; that each group of men should preserve its own customs. It is not surprising, therefore, that for all that we have in common, you and we should each preserve certain habits and traditions that we cherish because they belong to us. We know it is not your wish to have on your borders a mere replica of your own country, but rather a self-respecting community faithful to its own ways. We are thus better neighbours, because self-respect is the key to respect for others. On our side of the border you will find a country in which parliamentary government has been, we believe, successfully married to a federal system; a country whose people cherish two languages and two cultures—English and French; a land which has inherited from the mother countries in the Old World many forms and customs which have been happily fitted into life in the New. These ways of ours you respect because they are ours, just as we respect your ways because they are yours. Thus, in the words of the Treaty of Amity, Commerce, and Navigation, which laid the foundation of our present concord as long ago as 1794, we "promote a disposition favourable to friendship and good neighbourhood."

In Canada, we are indeed fortunate in our neighbourhood. We have a warmhearted neighbour. This, your people have shown us over the years. There are countless bodies in this country in which, through your invitations, Canadians share membership with their American friends. We are not unmindful of what we owe to your great universities and foundations. Let me say, too, that we are ever conscious of the warmth of the hospitality we receive when we are your guests.

We have a powerful neighbour. Your massive strength, economic and military, excites a sense of wonder at its magnitude. The dedication of this power to the cause of freedom evokes the gratitude of all who love freedom everywhere. Your Canadian neighbours know that when you assumed the grave responsibilities you bear today, it was not of your choosing. And for what you have done, we honour you.

We have a friendly neighbour. There is no need to enlarge on the traditions of neighbourly good sense, which for so long have marked our relations. We can only hope that they may be reflected elsewhere in this troubled world ...

I have talked about us as your neighbours. I have said little about ourselves as your partners. You and we work together in the international community. Along with kinsmen and friends across the seas, we are allies in defense of the things we value. And, if I may say so, I think that we in Canada, like you, have given proof that those values must be actively and zealously defended. Thus in the far north, we are working with you to strengthen the defenses of this continent on our territory and on yours. In Korea, there has been, from an early stage, a brigade group of Canadian troops. They are now standing guard against the possibility of renewed attack. Twelve squadrons of the Royal Canadian Air Force and a further Canadian brigade group are stationed in Europe. Such formations, I need hardly say, should naturally be related in our minds to the size of the population that provides them.

We are also supplying our European friends with mutual aid on a considerable scale. Canada, too, is giving help under the Colombo plan to the countries of southern Asia. We believe—as you do—that the problems of our time cannot be solved by military strength alone. The line can be held only by the deployment of force, but the objective—peace—can be won only by the quality of infinite patience. In our collaboration, we may not always agree on every detail of the plans we must discuss together, but there is no difference between us on the fundamental aims that we pursue; we may differ now and then on the "how's" but, never on the "whys." You may depend upon us as faithful friends and comrades.

Chapter 31

Toasts by President Lyndon B. Johnson and
Prime Minister Lester B. Pearson
Washington, D.C.
22 January 1964

President Johnson: The Prime Minister asked me if I was going to make a speech and I told him I was going to attempt to: not over three minutes in length, but I would expect loud and vociferous applause.

I choose to feel that this is not just a meeting today between two heads of government, but rather a reunion of neighbours who meet around the dining table in friendship and with affection. Mr. Prime Minister, we in this country are proud of your achievements and we are joined in your purpose. We have applauded your craftsmanship and approved of your leadership from your major role in the creation of the United Nations to your winning of the Nobel Peace Prize and even your performance as defenseman on the Oxford hockey team ...

Mr. Prime Minister, I remember so well that the largest American hero of his time, Franklin D. Roosevelt loved so warmly the greatest Canadian of his era, Mackenzie King and, indeed, you may have been present on the occasion in Quebec in 1943 when President Roosevelt said to Prime Minister Mackenzie King, "My old friend, your course and mine have run so closely and affectionately during these many long years that this meeting adds just another link to the chain."

Mr. Prime Minister, may I take the liberty and may I be presumptuous enough to suggest that our friendship may run this same cheerful course that was so stoutly started by our great predecessors and so cordially continued by ourselves. I believe, Mr. Prime Minister, that we have built, here on your first visit, the intimacy and the candour that belong to two good and old friends. As I suggested this morning, as we walked out on the porch to observe this beautiful sunny day, that whenever we have anything to say to each other, let us just pick up the telephone and say it, whether it be to discuss a problem or simply to ask, "How are you getting along up there?" So if you would join me now, I would like to ask you to rise and raise your glass, and let us toast at this high moment Lester B. Pearson, "Mike" Pearson, the Prime Minister of Canada, a loyal neighbour, a durable ally, hockey star, and a good and most understanding friend.

Prime Minister Pearson:

The particular triumph of the Canadian-American relationship is that we have had difficulties and that we have solved them and we are going to have more in the future, but we are going to solve them, too. It is easy to keep the peace when you have nothing to row about. But rows without wars, that means something. That is the symbol of our relationship. I remember saying some years ago in Toronto (I was Secretary of State for External Affairs at that time, and got a great deal of criticism), that the days of easy and automatic relations between our countries are over. So they are. I don't know how easy or automatic they used to be, but I know that in the future we are going to have problems and difficulties.

There are no two countries where the relations are more important to each other economically and in every other way than those between our two countries, but I am not frightened about this kind of thing because I have absolute confidence that, with the kind of friendly understanding which we have, we will be able to face these problems and we will be able to solve them.

We in Canada are very, very sensitive, indeed, about the development of our own Canadian identity building up in the northern half of this continent, a nation which stands on its own feet as much as any nation, any nation anywhere, can stand on its own feet these days. You may at times think we are perhaps a little too sensitive, but we do appreciate, we do realize, that in our relations with the United States, why, we will have our bilateral difficulties. We do realize that in this country, you are bearing the greatest burden that any country at any time ever had to bear, the burden of maintaining peace and establishing security and insuring progress in a nuclear outer space atomic age.

I was talking (and I don't know whether I perhaps should say this) but I was talking last week to General de Gaulle in Paris. We had a very happy visit there and we were very warmly received by the country which, after all, is the other mother country of Canada ... General de Gaulle said, "You are always boasting, you Canadians, that you know the Americans better than anyone else." Which is true. We really should. "What do you really think of them?" I was trying to find words to express at the same time my admiration and anxiety about the United States, and I said, "Well, General de Gaulle, as I have often put it in speeches in Canada, my feeling about the United States is this: To live alongside this great country is like living with your wife. At times it is difficult to live with her. And all times it is impossible to live without her."

Chapter 32

Lyndon B. Johnson with Prime Minister Pearson at the
Columbia River Treaty International Peace Arch
Blaine, Washington
16 September 1964

There are many reasons why my first trip abroad as President should be to Canada. In 1839, J. Pinckney Henderson, the Representative of the Republic of Texas to France and to England, wrote that Great Britain might delay its recognition of the new republic for fear of the impact in Canada. But Canada remained loyal. Great Britain recognized Texas, and that recognition helped open the door to American union for Texas. Had that not happened, Mr. Prime Minister, had Texas stayed independent, classical diplomacy suggests that we might very well today be concluding a treaty of mutual defense against the American influence. As a Texan, I can sympathize with the problems of living beside a wealthy and powerful and pervasive neighbour. That is just how the rest of the United States feels about Texas.

More than three years ago, President Kennedy came to Canada. He told your Parliament his trip was "an act of faith." He said it was faith in our capacity to meet common problems, and in our common cause of freedom. Well, my trip today is a fulfillment and a renewal of that act of faith. It is both a resolution of a common problem, and a strengthening of freedom's cause.

Lord Durham, in the famous report that laid the foundation for modern Canada, spoke of the possibility of establishing "partners in a new industry, the creation of happy human beings." That partnership is the purpose of this treaty that we have signed today. It will supply new electric power to millions of my countrymen. It will supply revenues to Canada ... It joins common purpose to common interest in pursuit of the welfare of the free people who share our continent.

My country is grateful for the spacious spirit with which this generous design was conceived and with the way it was carried out, even down to the last quarter. It is another landmark in the history of one of the oldest and one of the most successful associations of sovereign governments anywhere in the world. What is the secret of this success? It begins with a truth: the only justifiable object of government is the welfare of individual men and women. It is a simple truth. But had others shared it with us, the world would have been spared many dark years. With this as the animating design, our partnership has been built on four pillars. And the success of that structure might well serve as a model to the world.

The first pillar is peace.

The second pillar is freedom.

The third pillar is respect. One of my predecessors, Woodrow Wilson, said, "You cannot be friends upon any other basis than upon terms of equality." We maintain with each other the relationship that we seek for all the world: cooperation amid diversity.

Pericles said of a state that was much smaller than yours, "We have forced every sea and land to be the highway of our daring." In the founding of the United Nations, in the Middle East, in the Congo, in Southeast Asia, the world has responded to Canadian daring. You have followed not the highway of empire which helped destroy Athens, but you have followed the more difficult path to peace which can save the world. And you have been a principal architect, Mr. Prime Minister, of that profound achievement.

The fourth pillar is cooperation. This agreement is the latest in an impressive list. We have disarmed our border; we have shared the costs of defense; we have divided power at Niagara; we have built the St. Lawrence Seaway; we have resolved scores of other problems.

Difficulties that divide others have united us. The reason is plain. We share interest and we share purpose. We come to the council table advised by reason, aware of each other's problems, anxious to find final agreement. You told us, Mr. Prime Minister, "As good neighbours we must be able to sit down and discuss problems realizing that solutions will not be found without hard work and without give and take on both sides." We both have problems we must solve within our borders. My country has a war to win on poverty. We must find justice for men of all races. We must crush the forces of division which gnaw at the fabric of our union. You have your own difficulties. We watch, with friendly confidence in your capacity to merge differences in the grand dream of Canadian design. But there is also much, Mr. Prime Minister, which we share.

In the world, we seek peace, and mounting fulfillment for man. Here we work together, from ocean to ocean, in resources and science, to enrich the life of our two peoples, to elevate the quality of our two societies. Franklin D. Roosevelt once said, "Democracy is the form of government which guarantees to every generation of men the right to imagine and to attempt to bring to pass a better world." That has been the story of your life, Mr. Prime Minister. It is also the strength of our two countries. And I believe that future generations will have cause for gratitude that two great democracies — Canada and the United States—shared the most generous continent that God has ever granted to man.

Chapter 33

Toasts by President Richard M. Nixon and Prime Minister Pierre Trudeau, The White House
24 March 1969

President Nixon: In any new administration, every moment becomes a historical moment when it occurs. And this, Mr. Prime Minister, is a historical moment in this room because this is the first State Dinner that has been held in this room since the new administration came to office ...

If it will not be embarrassing to the Prime Minister, I would like to say a personal word about him. And don't be worried. I can assure you that having sometimes been in this position myself of wondering what was coming up next, I will be careful with what I say. But I was thinking of those many accolades that as an American, and particularly as an American political leader, we could pass on to you. I can refer to the fact that you are a distinguished political philosopher. I could refer to the fact that you are a distinguished member of the bar, eminently successful. But since this is a room in which there are many from political life, what is the most impressive factor in your achievements to date is your political leadership.

When I think that the Prime Minister entered politics in 1965 and within four years became the head of government, believe me, for one for whom it took 22 long years to get here, we have, sir, for you the greatest respect for that political leadership which you have provided. I do not need to say—and I do not say this simply because you are here—that you have been for your own people a very exciting personality, as you have been for the people of the United States. We are glad to get to know you better. We are happy to exchange views with you. We particularly appreciate the opportunity to get the benefit of your thinking not only on the bilateral problems which we usually work out effectively and successfully, but on the great problems that will determine the future of all of us who live on this planet.

I was delighted in the long talk that I had with the Prime Minister today to find that here was a man who had the vision to see beyond the next election and to see what kind of continent we would have 25 years from now, 30 years from now. And on that great issue there can be no difference, fundamentally, in the goals that we, the people of the United States and the people of your country, seek.

Prime Minister Trudeau:

You do me great honour, Mr. President, in drinking to my health. And the kind words you have spoken about me are all the more welcome and moving that they come not only from the head of the country which is Canada's best friend and ally, but they come from a man who has shown through his years in politics (22, you said, Mr. President; that is about six times longer than myself, but then your country is ten times greater so it probably works out) a man who has shown that he could occupy many of the elective offices of his land and who now holds the highest elective office in his country, your country, the greatest, the most powerful on earth, a man who has served his country well with devotion, with knowledge, with wisdom, with fortitude, with courage, a man who has been persistent, a man who has been sincere and faithful.

For these reasons, sir, I thank you for your welcome. And I want to say that, being one of Gaelic descent, I have particular affinity for things American as I think the Americans have for things French and Gaelic. There is a saying, I know, in your land that every good American when he dies goes to Paris. I would suggest, Mr. President, that many of your fellow countrymen have not waited until they die nor until they are good to find Paris. But I would be remiss in my duty if I didn't suggest that there is a very easy and pleasant alternative much closer at hand, Montreal, which welcomes all Americans and which would welcome you, Mr. President. I hope you will be visiting our country as soon as your office permits. I can assure you, you will be very welcome there. I can't guarantee that there will be no trouble. I can't guarantee it for myself. But as one new politician to a more mature one, I can tell you that we will take our chances together. And I think that the Canadian people will show you how much they respect and admire the President of the United States of America.

Every year many Americans come to Canada and the same number, more or less, of Canadians come to the United States: 70 million border crossings last year, Mr. President. We all come to the United States in pursuit of happiness of one kind or another. When I was a student and a younger man I pursued a different kind of happiness. We come here, though, also to seek knowledge, to learn from your greater technology, from your great advances in science, from your great universities; we learn also from the hospitality of your people and from the great ideals and institutions that the leaders of your country have set up as models for humanity over the years. We learn these things and we respect you for that. As one man who is a former Harvard graduate and coming to Washington at the beginning of a new administration, I can promise that I will stay less long than some others. But I will say that many of the things that I learned in one of your great schools was about this fine sense of balance that the Americans had shown in their ideals and in their institutions, and how from the very early days they tackled and solved this problem of eternal conflict between liberty and the rule of law, between the need for authority and the need for individual freedoms, how they tackled the problem of the individual wanting to be alone and yet needing society, and how over, the decades and over the years, your country has been able to adapt and meet these changes.

And I think all foreign students of your country come to admire most this great vitality, this toughness, this resilience of your great society ... rather than be too influenced by its mother country, of course, you had a rather violent parting with your mother country, Mr. President. But we are perhaps in Canada a little bit too inclined to borrow from England and borrow from France. But you went out on your own and you invented this great institution of modern federalism, and you found this balance in your institutions between freedom and order. That is why today, when we see the mighty upheavals in your society, we know you will meet them. We know you will find solutions, and because you are so far ahead of other industrial societies, we know that we will be able to learn from the lessons that you will give other nations who are trying to acquire this great industrial status. We will learn from your errors. We will learn from your successes. And we know we will always have a helping hand in the United States.

There have been for so many years now, Mr. President, no tensions between our countries. It was your first President, George Washington, in his farewell address, who said that passionate relationships between one country and another engendered a host of evils. Well, for a long time there have been no passionate relationships between our countries. There have been relationships based on discussion, on reason, on, as you put it this morning, sir, in welcoming me, the excitement of diversity. But always we have solved these through discussion, through reasonable men getting together and sometimes reasonable women getting together asking ourselves about our problem and seeking the best solution for everyone concerned ... It was a Frenchman, de Tocqueville, who first described, I think in a very able way, the kind of delicate balance that the United States' ideals and institutions were able to put forward. And he had a phrase, si vous me permettez de traduire un peu librement, which went about like this: That you don't receive truth from your enemies, and your friends are rarely willing to offer it. "It is for this reason," he said, "that I have written these books." Well, Mr. President, we are the kind of friends who do tell the truth to each other. We have told it this morning. I am sure we will tell it in the future. We find that this kind of relationship is the only basis on which nations of the world can live in peace together—in understanding.

Chapter 34

President Gerald R. Ford Announcing Plans from the White House for an Economic Conference in Puerto Rico
Washington, D.C.
3 June 1976

I am pleased to announce this morning that the leaders of six other major industrialized nations have accepted the invitation of the United States to attend a summit conference later this month. The conference will be held June 27 and June 28 in the Commonwealth of Puerto Rico. In addition to the United States, Canada, France, West Germany, Italy, and Japan, as well as the United Kingdom will be represented. I have invited them to participate in this meeting because it is vital that the leaders of the industrialized democracies continue a process of close consultation as well as cooperation on the broad range of challenges as well as opportunities in all fields of common interest. In the past, world leaders have met to deal with crises, but today's complex problems require that leaders meet to avoid them. Last fall when we met in Rambouillet, France [Canada had not been invited] we agreed to extensive cooperation in order to sustain the economic recovery. This has meant less inflation and more jobs for millions and millions of people throughout the world.

Now we must meet again to chart a course that will keep the recovery moving forward at a healthy and sustained rate. There will be many other subjects of international significance on the agenda in Puerto Rico, including financial, monetary, and trade issues. But the issue at the heart of the discussions is to determine what our nations can do, working together, to create a more prosperous and secure future for all of our citizens.

Chapter 35

Prime Minister Pierre Elliott Trudeau's Address to the US Congress Washington, D.C.
22 February 1977

For much more than a century, individual Canadians, in countless ways and on countless occasions, have expressed to Americans their friendship. Today, as Prime Minister, I am given the opportunity to express those feelings collectively before the elected representatives of the American people. I do so with pride, and with conviction … The friendship between our two countries is so basic that it has long since been regarded by others as the standard for enlightened international relations. No Canadian leader would be permitted by his electorate consciously to weaken it. Indeed, no Canadian leader would wish to, and certainly not this one. Simply stated, our histories record that for more than a century millions upon millions of Canadians and Americans have known one another, liked one another, and trusted one another. Canadians are not capable of living in isolation from you anymore than we are desirous of doing so. We have benefited from your stimulus; we have profited from your vitality.

Throughout your history, you have been inspired by a remarkably large number of gifted leaders who have displayed stunning foresight, oft-times in the face of then-popular sentiments. In this city, which bears his name, on the anniversary of his birthday, George Washington's words bear remembering. In a message familiar to all of you in this chamber, he said: "It is of infinite moment that you should properly estimate the immense value of your national union to your collective and individual happiness."

At a moment in the history of mankind when men and women cannot escape from the knowledge that the only hope for humanity is the willingness of people of differing complexions and cultures and beliefs to live peaceably together, you have not forgotten Washington's high standards. You have chosen to declare your beliefs in the protection of minorities, in the richness of diversity, in the necessity of accommodation. You have contributed new fibre to that seamless fabric we call the history of mankind: that stumbling, incoherent quest by individuals and by nations for freedom and dignity. Liberty and the pursuit of happiness have not been theoretical concepts for Americans, and nor have they been regarded as elusive goals. You have sought each with vigour, and shared with all mankind the joy and the creativity which are the products of freedom. You have illustrated throughout your history the resilience, the dedication and the inherent decency of American society. The United States achievement in recent years of conducting a great social revolution, in overcoming difficulties of immense complication and obdurateness, and doing so through the democratic process, is surely a model for all nations devoted to the dignity of the human condition. Freedom-loving men and women everywhere are the beneficiaries of your example. Not the least among them are Canadians, for whom the United States has long since been the single most important external influence, the weather only excepted.

We in Canada, facing internal tensions with roots extending back to the 17th century, have much to gain from the wisdom and discipline and patience which you in this country, in this generation, have brought to bear to reduce racial tensions, to broaden legal rights, and to provide opportunity to all.

Canadians long ago determined to govern themselves by a parliamentary system that favours the flowering of basic aspirations for freedom, for justice, for individual dignity. The rule of law, sovereignty of parliament, a broad sharing of power with the provinces, and official support of the pluralistic nature of Canadian society have combined to create in Canada a community where freedom thrives to an extent not exceeded anywhere else, a community where equality of opportunity between people and between regions is a constant goal.

The success of our efforts in the first century following confederation was great, but by no means complete. We created a society of individual liberty and of respect for human rights. We produced an economic standard of living that approaches your own. We have not yet, however, created a condition in which French-speaking Canadians have felt they were fully equal or could fully develop the richness of the culture they had inherited. And therein is the source of our central problem today. This is why a small minority of the people of Quebec feel they should leave Canada and strike out in a country of their own. The newly elected government of that province asserts a policy that reflects that minority view, despite the fact that during the election campaign, it sought a mandate for good government, and not a mandate for the separation from Canada.

The accommodation of two vigorous language groups has been, in varying fashion, the policy of every Canadian government since Confederation. The reason is clear. Within Quebec, over 80 percent of the population speak French as their first or only language. In Canada as a whole, nearly one fifth of the people speak no language but French. Thus from generation to generation there has been handed down the belief that a country could be built in freedom and equality with two languages and a multitude of cultures.

I am confident it can be done. I say to you with all the certainly I can command that Canada's unity will not be fractured. Revisions will take place. Accommodations will be made. We shall succeed. There will have to be changes in some of our attitudes; there will have to be a greater comprehension of one another across the barrier of language difference. Both English-speaking and French-speaking Canadians will have to become more aware of the richness that diversity brings and less irritated by the problems it presents. We may have to revise some aspects of our constitution, so that the Canadian federation can be seen by six and half million French-speaking Canadians to be the strongest bulwark against submersion by some 220 million English-speaking North Americans. These very figures illustrate dramatically the sense of insecurity of French Canada. But separation would not alter the arithmetic; it would merely increase the exposure. Nor would the separation of Quebec contribute in any fashion to the confidence of the many cultural minorities of various origins who dwell throughout Canada. These communities have been encouraged for decades to retain their own identities and to preserve their own cultures. They have done so and flourished, nowhere more spectacularly than in the prairie provinces of Alberta, Saskatchewan and Manitoba. The sudden departure of Quebec could signify the tragic failure of our pluralist dream, the fracturing of our cultural mosaic, and would likely remove much of the determination of Canadians to protect their cultural minorities. Problems of this magnitude cannot be wished away. They can be solved, however, by the institutions we have created for our own governance. Those institutions belong to all Canadians, to me as a Quebecker as much as to my fellow citizens from the other provinces. And because those institutions are democratically structured, because their members are freely elected, they are capable of reflecting changes and of responding to the popular will.

I am confident that we in Canada are well along in the course of devising a society as free of prejudice and fear, as full of understanding and generosity, as respectful of individuality and beauty, as receptive to change and innovation, as exists anywhere.

Our nation is the very encounter of two of the most important cultures of Western civilization, to which countless other strains are being added. Most Canadians understand that the rupture of their country would be an aberrant departure from the norms they themselves have set, a crime against the history of mankind; for I am immodest enough to suggest that a failure of this always-varied, often illustrious Canadian experiment would create shock waves of disbelief among those all over the world who are committed to the proposition that among man's noblest endeavours are those communities in which persons of diverse origins live, love, work, and find mutual benefit. Canadians are conscious of the effort required of them to maintain, in healthy working order, not only their own nation, but as well the North American neighbourhood in which they flourish. A wholesome relationship with our mutual friend Mexico and a robust partnership with the United States are both, in our eyes, highly desirable. To those ends, we have contributed much energy. And you in this country have reciprocated to the point where our relationship forms a model admired by much of the world, one molded from the elements of mutual respect and supported by the vigour of disciplined cooperation.

We have built together one of the world's largest and most efficient transportation and power generating systems in the form of the St. Lawrence Seaway. We have conceived and established the world's oldest, continuously functioning, binational arbitral tribunal: the International Joint Commission. We have joined together in many parts of the world in the defense of freedom and in the relief of want. We have created oft-times original techniques of environmental management, of emergency and disaster assistance; of air and sea traffic control, of movements of people, goods and services, the latter so successfully that the value of our trade and the volume of visitors back and forth exceeds several times over that of any other two countries in the world. It is no wonder that we are each so interested in the continued social stability and economic prosperity of the other. Nor should we be surprised that the desire of the American and Canadian peoples to understand and help one another sometimes adopts unusual forms. In what other two countries in the world could be there be reproduced the scene of tens of thousand of people in a Montreal baseball park identifying totally with one team against the other, forgetting all the while that every single player on each is American, and a similar scene in the Washington hockey arena where thousand of spectators identify totally with one team against another, forgetting that virtually every player on the ice is Canadian?

Thus do the images blur, and sometimes they do lead to chafing. Yet, how civilized are the responses! How temperate the replies! We threaten to black out your television commercials? You fire volleys of antitrust proceedings! Such admirable substitutes for hostility! More important than the occasional incident of disagreement is the continuing process of management that we have successfully incorporated into our relationship. It is a process which succeeds through careful attention, through consultation, and through awareness on both sides of the border, that problems can arise which are attributable neither to intent nor neglect, but to the disproportionate size of our two populations and the resulting imbalance of our economic strength. Those differences will likely always lead us in Canada to attempt to ensure that there be maintained a climate for the expression of Canadian culture. We will surely also be sensitive to the need for the domestic control of our economic environment. As well, in a country visited annually by extreme cold over its entire land mass—I just met the representative from Florida and I hear it also happens in your country—but in our country, a country so far-flung that transportation has always posed almost insuperable problems, the wise conservation of our energy resources assumes a compelling dimension. And for a people devoted throughout their history to accommodating themselves with the harshness, as well as the beauty, of their natural surroundings, we will respond with vigour to any threat of pollution or despoliation, be it from an indigenous or from an external source.

Our continent, however, is not the world. Increasingly it is evident that the same sense of neighbourhood that has served so well our North American interests must be extended to all parts of the globe and to all member of the human race. Increasingly, the welfare and the dignity of others will be the measurement of our own condition. I share with President Carter his belief that in this activity also we will achieve success. However, even as we have moved away from the cold war era of political and military confrontation, there exists another danger; one of rigidity in our response to the current challenges of poverty, hunger, environmental degradation, and nuclear proliferation. Our ability to respond adequately to these issues will in some measure be determined by our willingness to recognize them as the new obstacles to peace. Yet, sadly, our pursuit of peace in these respects has all too often been little more imaginative that was our sometimes-blind grappling with absolutes in the international political sphere. Moreover, we have failed to mobilize adequately the full support of our electorates for the construction of a new world order. The reasons are not hard to find. In these struggles, there is no single tyrant, no simple ideological contest. We are engaged in a complex of issues of overwhelming proportions, yet with few identifiable labels. Who, after all, feels stirred to oratorical heights at the mention of commodity price stabilization, or of full fuel cycle nuclear safeguards, or of special drawing rights? Yet these are the kinds of issues that will determine the stability of tomorrow's world. They will require imaginative solutions and cooperative endeavour, for these struggles are not against human beings; they are struggles with and for human beings, in a common cause of global dimensions.

It is to the United States that the world looks for leadership in these vital activities. It has been in large measure your fervor and your direction that has inspired a quarter century of far-flung accomplishment in political organization, industrial development and international trade. Without your dedicated participation, the many constructive activities now in one stage or another in the several fields of energy, economics, trade, disarmament, development, these activities will not flourish as they must.

My message today is not a solicitous plea for continued United States involvement. It is an enthusiastic pledge of spirited Canadian support in the pursuit of those causes in which we both believe. It is, as well, an encouragement to our mutual rededication at this important moment in our histories to a global ethic of confidence in our fellow man. Mr. Speaker, Mr. President, in that same address to which I referred some minutes ago, George Washington warned against "the insidious wiles of foreign influence" and the desirability of steering "clear of permanent alliances with any portion of the foreign world." Yet here I stand, ladies and gentlemen, a foreigner, endeavouring—whether insidiously or not, you will have to judge—to urge the United States ever more permanently into new alliances. That I dare do so is a measure not only of the bond that links Canadians to you, but as well of the spirit of America. Thomas Paine's words of two centuries ago are as valid today as when he uttered them: "My country is the world, and my religion is to do good." In your continued quest of those ideals, ladies and gentlemen, all Canadians wish you Godspeed.

Chapter 36

Future President Ronald Reagan on The Canadian Seal Hunt, Radio Address
15 May 1978

It sometimes seems that we can become more emotionally involved and aroused over mistreatment of animals than we can if the victims are human ... A few weeks ago, a writer in the *Los Angeles Times*, Parker Barss Donham, did an article on the 1978 Canadian baby seal hunt. One line in his article was very thought provoking: "If seal pups were as ugly as lobsters, their harvest would go unnoticed." Accompanying his article was a photo that proved his point. It was a snow-white baby seal with its black nose and round dark eyes looking like something you'd put in the nursery for the children to cuddle. Add to this, horrifying accounts of men clubbing these cuddly creatures to death in a mass slaughter with the inference that death comes slowly and agonizingly and it's easy to understand the protests and demonstrations every year. Now for the record, I couldn't hit one of those seals with a club; I couldn't hit a hog with a club and I squirm when I think about lobsters being chucked into that boiling pot while they are still alive. Still, I enjoy eating lobster and I love a good steak but I wouldn't want to work in the packing plant.

Now, let me go on with what Mr. Dunham had to say about the annual harvest of seal pups. How many of us know how sophisticated the protesters are in the annual crusade against the Newfoundlanders who carry on the hunt? There is an international organization that stays in business year-round primarily to raise money to protect against the seal harvest. A $40,000-a-year executive rides around in the organization's helicopter. All of that would stop if they ever succeeded in halting the seal harvest. It does give you something to think about—particularly if you are one of the contributors to the organization. Time won't permit all the facts disclosed by Mr. Donham, but here are some that shed light on what has been portrayed as bloodthirsty brutality. In the first place, use of the word harvest is appropriate. The Canadian government sets the quota of how many seal pups can be taken. The harp seal is not in danger of extinction. It is one of the most abundant seal species in the world, and the herd is growing, not shrinking. Elimination of the seal pup harvest would have a disastrous effect on the already-depleted Atlantic fishing grounds. The seals consume each year one half million tons of small fish that are a vital link in the food chain for cod, sea birds and whales.

So much for that—now for the charge that the seal pups suffer a painful and lingering death. Careful research has been done by the Canadian Federation of Humane Societies, the Society for the Prevention of Cruelty to Animals, the Ontario Humane Society and the Canadian Audubon Society. They have studied best means of killing seals: use of guns, drugs, gas and others. Their final conclusion is that clubbing with a hardwood bat or the Norwegian hokapik is the most humane method and brings on instant death or deep irreversible unconsciousness. According to these researchers the seal hunt, in terms of humaneness, compares favourably with the method of dispatching domesticated animals that provide us with our daily food supply. I'm sure Mr. Donham knew he was bucking an emotional tide when he wrote his scholarly article. It took courage but he performed a useful service.

This is Ronald Reagan. Thanks for listening.

Reproduced with the permission of the Ronald Reagan Presidential Foundation.

Chapter 37

Prime Minister Brian Mulroney's
Address to the US Congress
Washington, D.C.
27 April 1988

I come here today to celebrate the historic friendship between Canada and the United States. On the border between our two countries, there are no fences and no barricades; there are no soldiers and no arms. That 5,000-mile frontier, spanning a continent between two oceans, is, of itself, a remarkable historical fact. It symbolizes neighbourliness between two free and peace-loving nations. It signifies leadership, not only in the conduct of our bilateral relations, but for the international community as a whole.

History requires us to provide for our common security on the North American continent, through NORAD and in the NATO alliance. Geography obliges us to preserve and protect our environment, to pass on intact to future generations what providence and our forbears have so generously bequeathed us. Economics and geography together present us with a unique opportunity to further enhance our prosperity through trade. We begin, Mr. Speaker, from a common heritage of democratic traditions and a common defense of liberty. Here are reminders of that, from the trenches of one war, to the beaches of the next, places inscribed in the history of valour, where Canadians and Americans have stood together, where Canadians and Americans have died together, in the defense of freedom. Canadians and Americans can and always will be proud of their commitment to democracy and freedom.

As we made common cause in two world wars and in Korea, so do our young men and women now stand the first watch of liberty in Western Europe. In peacetime, as in war, the United States and Canada have shouldered and shared heavy burdens in our common commitment to freedom. Together, we have maintained our presence in Europe for two generations, at considerable expense to both nations ... We live between the two superpowers, but we did not and we do not see them as morally equivalent in any way. The United States is a bulwark of democracy, a beacon of liberty. The United States and its NATO allies stand for freedom. They exemplify and celebrate human rights and individual dignity.

Here, as in Canada, tolerance and respect for one another's opinions are ingrained in the national character. Here, as in Canada, governments dispose, but it is the people, the people who decide; elected representatives may govern but it is, in the terms of the preamble of our constitution, "We the people" who rule.

We are two independent nations, each with its own national interests and unique character. You have one official language; we have two. Your system of governments is congressional; ours is parliamentary. Neither of our countries is without its inequities and its imperfections. But we are, each in our own way, building caring societies that give our citizens remarkable opportunities for education and employment, enabling them and our countries to make dramatic social and economic progress. We each have sovereign interests to assert, national interests to uphold. And we can have different views of the world, just as we clearly have different responsibilities in the world.

You know, it is fashionable in some circles to suggest that America is growing weary of its role, and that its influence is in decline in the world. The evidence to the contrary is all about you, in the Silicon Valley of California, in the Sun Belt of the South, in your great agricultural heartland, in the new high technology corridor of the Northeast, in the towers of Manhattan, and throughout this splendid capital. The world still looks to America not only as a model of liberty, but as a source of persuasive international leadership. The world counts as well on the strength and independence of this Congress, a legislature of unprecedented influence and capacity for good which has endured for over 200 years, and which stands proudly as a corner-stone of this impressive democracy.

Mr. Speaker, when I sought the leadership of my party five years ago, and it was then that I acquired a deep respect for everyone everywhere who has had to run in a primary, but when I sought the leadership of my own party, I said that Canada and the United States were one another's best friend and greatest ally. Nothing in my experience in government (and we have known tensions and serious disagreement) has led me to revise my views about the profound value of an exemplary relationship between two of the world's great democracies. Our common democratic values and our shared commitment to defend them are but one worthy example of neighbourliness and leadership. The protection of our environment is another. As President Reagan has said:

> Our two countries should work together on all matters of environment, because entrusted to us is the care of a very unique and a very beautiful continent, and all of us share the desire to protect this for generations of Canadians and Americans yet to come.

For more than 75 years, since the creation of the International Joint Commission, the United States and Canada have demonstrated both sensitivity and effectiveness in environmental protection and wildlife conservations. The flow of nature is rarely constrained by boundaries. The Canada goose winters in the United States (along with a few other Canadians) and the American bald eagle nest in the forests and soars in the skies of British Colombia.

Consider what we have achieved together in just one area, since the Great Lakes Waters Quality Agreement of 1972. The Great Lakes are coming back; one sure sign of this is the return in numbers of wildlife species once thought to be on the verge of extinction. In the newly updated agreement, signed by our two countries in Toledo last November, we agreed not only on the nature of toxic wastes that have polluted the Great lakes, but also on a process for action to restore them.

Together, the United States and Canada are taking the first steps to arrest the deterioration of the ozone layer that shields the earth from the most damaging effects of the sun. The Montreal Accord is but one example not only of what we can achieve together, but of leadership for the world ... This is not to say that there are not issues of great moment between us. You are aware of Canada's grave concerns on acid rain. In Canada, acid rain has already killed nearly 15,000 lakes; another 150,000 are being damaged and a further 150,000 are threatened. Many salmon-bearing rivers in Nova Scotia no longer support the species. Prime agricultural land and important sections of our majestic forests are receiving excessive amounts of acid rain.

We are doing everything we can to clean up our own act. We have concluded agreements with our provinces to reduce acid rain emissions in Eastern Canada to half their 1980 levels by the year 1994. But, you know, that is only half the solution, because the other half of our acid rain comes across the border, directly from the United States, falling upon our forests, killing our lakes, and soiling our cities.

The one thing acid rain does not do is discriminate. It is despoiling your environment as inexorably as it is ours. It is damaging your environment from Michigan to Maine, and threatens marine life on the eastern seaboard. It is a rapidly escalating ecological tragedy in this country as well as ours. Just imagine for a second the damage to your tourism and recreation; to timber stands and fishing streams; to your precious heritage, if this is not stopped. We acknowledge responsibility for some of the acid rain that falls in the United States, and by the time our program reaches projected targets, our export of acid rain to the United States will have been cut by an amount in excess of 50 percent. We ask nothing more than this from you. I recognize that congressional funding for a clean coal technology program will help to develop new methods for reducing emissions in the longer term. I welcome that. I think it is a helpful and a progressive step. But more is needed. We invite the administration, and the leadership of Congress, to conclude an accord whereby we agree on a schedule and targets for reducing acid rain that crosses our border. I will admit without hesitation that the cost of reducing acid rain is substantial, but the cost of inaction is greater still.

Canada will continue to press fully its case to rid our common environment of this blight, and we shall persevere until our skies regain their purity, and our rains recover the gentleness that gives life to our forests and streams. And we hope that the United States Congress and the American people will respond in exactly the same way. I ask you this very simple proposition: What would be said of a generation of North Americans that found a way to explore the stars, but allowed its lakes and forests to languish and die? ... And in terms of resources, Canada plays a major role in the world. With the seventh largest economy in the free world, Canada has had, since 1984, the strongest growth rate of the economic summit countries. We are the world's largest exporter of metals and lumber, the world's second largest exporter of wheat, and we supply fully one third of the world's newsprint (I am not responsible for the editorials). Canada and the United States conduct vital energy trade. Canada is the most important foreign supplier of oil, gas, and electricity.

This is just one component of the world's largest trading partnership, in which two million jobs in each country depend on exports to the other. Consider this: three quarters of our exports come to the United States; fully one quarter of your exports go to Canada. We buy, as Canadians, twice as much from you as Japan, and we buy ten times as much on a per capita basis. Canada buys more from the United States of America than the United Kingdom, France, West Germany, and Italy combined, and I tell you, that is the record of a fair and good trader. May Margaret Thatcher forgive me. But, in point of fact, as you already know, we are your best customers. We are good partners. We are fair traders.

The Free Trade Agreement presents our two countries with an historic opportunity to create new jobs and enduring prosperity. This won't surprise you, but there are those in our country who say that in these negotiations, we gave up too much. There are those in your country, perhaps even in this chamber, who contend that we conceded too little. The agreement is not everything either side would have wanted, but as Franklin Roosevelt once observed: "Nations are co-equals, and therefore any treaty must represent compromises." This is a good, balanced and fair agreement, the most important ever concluded between two trading partners. Quite apart from phasing out all tariffs, which I think you will agree is an achievement in itself, we've established a number of important firsts: for trade in services, for financial services, for bilateral investment. And we've established a unique dispute settlement mechanism.

My administration has the majority to enact this agreement, and we shall. In the congress, you will vote it up or down, as you see the interest of your fellow citizens. It is there, on the table, for both of us to ratify: a dream as old as the century, a dream that has eluded successive generations of leaders for a hundred years, a dream that is now clearly within our grasp. Now is the time to send a powerful signal to our other trading partners, to give strong impetus to the GATT, to give new hope to those poorer nations who desperately need more liberalized trade and more generous access to our markets.

We stand at the threshold of a great new opportunity for all our citizens. This is more than simply a commercial agreement between two countries. The Free Trade Agreement for you and for me is a call to excellence. It is a summons to our two peoples to respond to the challenge of comparative advantage in the 21st century. A nation's productivity may end on the assembly line, but it begins in the classroom. The imperatives of education are compelling and clear. Canadians know we have learned that the growth areas of our economy, the areas of technology and innovation and the service sector will demand, for example, higher math scores, higher reading and reasoning skills, and greater language proficiency, if we are to remain competitive.

The demands of trade have obliged us, as a smaller country with 25 million people, to learn to be lean and aggressive, but fair, and in becoming more competitive in the world, I think we have become more knowledgeable upwardly. And so, Mr. Speaker, that is the challenge of the Pacific. This is not a mystery. This is the challenge of the Pacific. That is the challenge of the European community, 320 million strong, in 1992. That is the challenge of developing nations who cannot meet their financial obligations if they cannot sell their goods. If the poorest nations cannot get that crippling burden of debt off their backs, they can't do business with either of our great countries. From the age of the Phoenicians to the age of Venice, to our own era, civilizations have always been enriched by trade. And that is my judgment, and I fought for this, and I have carried our share of responsibility, and others in this chamber have as well. That is what the Free Trade Agreement is about—a magnificent opportunity for a new decade and a new century. The challenges and the choices for both our nations are clear: to guarantee our continued security; to ensure an environment in which our children can inherit both a standard of living and a standard of life; to provide for their education and development in a manner which will assure, years from now, their well-being and their competitiveness and their prosperity. And most of all, you and I as legislators and as leaders of our respective countries, must continue to build distinctive and independent societies on the North American continent that reflect both the excitement of change and the strength of immutable values.

Mr. Speaker, and Mr. Vice President, and Members of the Congress, succeeding generations of Americans have known the wisdom of the philosopher Ralph Waldo Emerson, who wrote: "The way to have a friend is to be one." Our two peoples, our two countries, have met that test in the past. We do so today, and I know that we shall in the future. I am confident – there is not the slightest doubt in my mind – I am confident that in the relationship between Canada and the United States of America, we will know difficulties, we will know moments of strain, we will know moments of crisis and tensions, but there is not the slightest doubt in my mind that, rooted as we are in fundamental values and democratic traditions, this relationship will always be, as Winston Churchill described it more than a half a century ago, "an example to every country, and a pattern for the future of the world."

Chapter 38

President Ronald Reagan's Radio Address to the Nation on the Canadian Elections and Free Trade
26 November 1988

This week, as we prepared for Thanksgiving, Canada held an important election, and I'm pleased to again send my congratulations to Prime Minister Mulroney. One of the important issues in the Canadian election was trade. And like our own citizens earlier this month, our neighbours have sent a strong message, rejecting protectionism and reaffirming that more trade, not less, is the wave of the future. Here in America, as we reflect on the many things we have to be grateful for, we should take a moment to recognize that one of the key factors behind our nation's great prosperity is the open trade policy that allows the American people to freely exchange goods and services with free people around the world. The freedom to trade is not a new issue for America. In 1776, our Founding Fathers signed the Declaration of Independence, charging the British with a number of offenses, among them, and I quote, "cutting off our trade with all parts of the world," end quote. And that same year, a Scottish economist named Adam Smith launched another revolution with a book entitled "The Wealth of Nations," which exposed for all time the folly of protectionism. Over the past 200 years, not only has the argument against tariffs and trade barriers won nearly universal agreement among economists, but it has also proven itself in the real world, where we have seen free-trading nations prosper while protectionist countries fall behind.

America's most recent experiment with protectionism was a disaster for the working men and women of this country. When Congress passed the Smoot-Hawley tariff in 1930, we were told that it would protect America from foreign competition and save jobs in this country, the same line we hear today. The actual result was the Great Depression, the worst economic catastrophe in our history; one out of four Americans were thrown out of work. Two years later, when I cast my first ballot for President, I voted for Franklin Delano Roosevelt, who opposed protectionism and called for the repeal of that disastrous tariff.

Ever since that time, the American people have stayed true to our heritage by rejecting the siren song of protectionism. In recent years, the trade deficit led some misguided politicians to call for protectionism, warning that otherwise we would lose jobs. But they were wrong again. In fact, the United States not only didn't lose jobs; we created more jobs than all the countries of Western Europe, Canada, and Japan combined. The record is clear that when America's total trade has increased, American jobs have also increased. And when our total trade has declined, so has the number of jobs.

Part of the difficulty in accepting the good news about trade is in our words. We too often talk about trade while using the vocabulary of war. In war, for one side to win, the other must lose. But commerce is not warfare. Trade is an economic alliance that benefits both countries. There are no losers, only winners. And trade helps strengthen the free world. Yet today, protectionism is being used by some American politicians as a cheap form of nationalism, a fig leaf for those unwilling to maintain America's military strength and who lack the resolve to stand up to real enemies: countries that would use violence against us or our allies. Our peaceful trading partners are not our enemies; they are our allies. We should beware of the demigods who are ready to declare a trade war against our friends, weakening our economy, our national security, and the entire free world, all while cynically waving the American flag. The expansion of the international economy is not a foreign invasion; it is an American triumph, one we worked hard to achieve, and something central to our vision of a peaceful and prosperous world of freedom.

After the Second World War, America led the way to dismantle trade barriers and create a world trading system that set the stage for decades of unparalleled economic growth. And in one week, when important multilateral trade talks are held in Montreal, we will be in the forefront of efforts to improve this system. We want to open more markets for our products, to see to it that all nations play by the rules, and to seek improvement in such areas as dispute resolution and agriculture. We also want to bring the benefits of free trade to new areas, including services, investment, and the protection of intellectual property. Our negotiators will be working hard for all of us. Yes, back in 1776, our founding fathers believed that free trade was worth fighting for. And we can celebrate their victory because today, trade is at the core of the alliance that secures the peace and guarantees our freedom; it is the source of our prosperity and the path to an even brighter future for America.

Chapter 39

President George H.W. Bush's Address on His
Administration's Goals Before a Joint Session of Congress
Washington, D.C.
9 February 1989

If we're to protect our future, we need a new attitude about the environment. We must protect the air we breathe. I will send to you shortly legislation for a new, more effective Clean Air Act. It will include a plan to reduce, by date, certain emissions which cause acid rain, because the time for study alone has passed, and the time for action is now. We must make use of clean coal. My budget contains full funding, on schedule, for the clean coal technology agreement that we've made with Canada. We've made that agreement with Canada, and we intend to honour that agreement.

Chapter 40

**President George W. Bush's Remarks Following Discussions
With Prime Minister Jean Chrétien of Canada
The White House
24 September 2001**

President Bush: It's my honour to welcome our close friend Jean Chrétien to the White House again. Thank you for coming. You know, after this terrible incident on September 11th, one of the first phone calls I received was from the Prime Minister, offering all his support and condolences to the United States and our citizens. It was like getting a phone call from a brother, and I appreciate that so very much.

We've got a great partner in our neighbourhood who understands what I know; that we are facing a new type of war. And those of us who love freedom, like the Canadians love freedom, now understand that freedom is under attack. And we've combined together to fight against a new enemy. And the Prime Minister understands that. We had a great discussion about a variety of issues. We discussed the need for us to continue to work peacefully along a huge border. Border relations between Canada and Mexico have never been better. And there is no doubt in my mind that the Prime Minister and the Canadian people will work hard to make sure that Canada is secure from any terrorist activity that takes place, just like I can assure the Prime Minister we're doing the same. We both have a mutual responsibility in our hemisphere to find and disrupt terrorist organizations.

An amazing thing came up the other day. Somebody said to me, "Well, you know, in your speech to Congress, there were some that took affront in Canada" because I didn't mention the name. I didn't necessarily think it was important to praise a brother; after all, we're talking about family. There should be no doubt in anybody's mind about how honoured we are to have the support of the Canadians and how strong the Canadian Prime Minister has been, and not only in his condolences, but in his offer of support for the American people. I guess there's somebody playing politics with you, Mr. Prime Minister. But I suggest to those who try to play politics with my words and to drive wedges between Canada and me, understand that at this time, when nations are under attack, now is not the time for politics. Now is the time to develop a strategy to fight and win the war. And Mr. Prime Minister, I want to thank you for being here to continue those efforts with me.

Chapter 41

Former Prime Minister Brian Mulroney's Eulogy to President Ronald Reagan Washington, D.C.
11 June 2004

In the spring of 1987, President Reagan and I were driven into a large hangar at the Ottawa airport to await the arrival of Mrs. Reagan and my wife Mila, prior to departure ceremonies for their return to Washington. We were alone except for the security details. President Reagan's visit had been important, demanding and successful. Our discussions reflected the international agenda of the times: the nuclear threat posed by the Soviet Union and the missile deployment by NATO, pressures in the Warsaw Pact, challenges resulting from the Berlin Wall and the ongoing separation of Germany, and bilateral and hemispheric free trade. President Reagan had spoken to Parliament, handled complex files with skill and good humour, strongly impressing his Canadian hosts. And here we were waiting for our wives. When their car drove in a moment later, out stepped Nancy and Mila, both looking like a million bucks. And as they headed towards us, President Reagan beamed. He threw his arm around my shoulder. And he said with a grin: "You know, Brian, for two Irishmen, we sure married up."

In that visit, in that moment, one saw the quintessential Ronald Reagan: the leader we respected, the neighbour we admired, and the friend we loved, a President of the United States of America whose truly remarkable life we celebrate in this magnificent cathedral today.

Presidents and Prime Ministers everywhere, I suspect, sometimes wonder how history will deal with them. Some even evince a touch of the insecurity of Thomas Darcy McGee, an Irish immigrant to Canada who became a father of our confederation. In one of his poems, McGee, thinking of his birthplace, wrote poignantly: "Am I remembered in Erin? I charge you speak me true. Has my name a sound, a meaning in the scenes my boyhood knew?"

Ronald Reagan will not have to worry about Erin because they remember him well and affectionately there. Indeed they do. From Erin to Estonia, from Maryland to Madagascar, from Montreal to Monterey, Ronald Reagan does not enter history tentatively. He does so with certainty and panache. At home and on the world stage, his were not the pallid etchings of a timorous politician. They were the bold strokes of a confident and accomplished leader.

Some in the West, during the early 1980s, believed Communism and Democracy were equally valid and viable. This was the school of moral equivalence. In contrast, Ronald Reagan saw Soviet Communism as a menace to be confronted in the genuine belief that its squalid underpinnings would fall swiftly to the gathering winds of freedom, provided, as he said, that NATO and the industrialized democracies stood firm and united. They did. And we know now who was right.

Ronald Reagan was a President who inspired his nation and transformed the world. He possessed a rare and prized gift called leadership, that ineffable and magical quality that sets some men and women apart so that millions will follow them as they conjure up grand visions and invite their countrymen to dream big and exciting dreams. I always thought that President Reagan's understanding of the nobility of the presidency coincided with that American dream.

One day, in Brussels, President Mitterrand, in referring to President Reagan, said: "*Il a vraiment la notion de l'etat.*" Rough translation: "He really has a sense of the state about him." The translation does not fully capture the profundity of the observation. What President Mitterrand meant is that there is a vast difference between the *job* of President and the *role* of President.

Ronald Reagan fulfilled both with elegance and ease, embodying himself that unusual alchemy of history and tradition and achievement and inspirational conduct and national pride that defined the special role the President of the United States of America must assume, at all times, at home and around the world. *La notion de l'état*—no one understood it better than Ronald Reagan. And no one could more eloquently summon his nation to high purpose, or bring forth the majesty of the presidency and make it glow better than the man who referred to his own nation as a city on the hill.

May our common future and that of our great nations be guided by wise men and women who will remember always the golden achievements of the Reagan era, and the success that can be theirs if the values of freedom and democracy are preserved, unsullied and undiminished until the unfolding decades can remember little else.

I have been truly blessed to have been a friend of Ronald Reagan's. I am grateful that our paths crossed and that our lives touched. I shall always remember him with the deepest admiration and affection. And I will always feel honoured by the journey that we traveled together in search of better and more peaceful tomorrows for all God's children everywhere. And so, in the presence of his beloved and indispensable Nancy, his children, his family, his friends and all of the American people he so deeply revered, I say *au revoir* today to a gifted leader and historic President and a gracious human being. And I do so with a line from Yeats, who wrote: "Think where man's glory most begins and ends and say my glory was that I had such friends."

Endnotes

1 Anthony Eden, *The Memoirs of Sir Anthony Eden Full Circle* (London: Cassell & Company, 1960),340.

2 Lawrence Martin, *The Presidents and the Prime Ministers: Washington and Ottawa Face to Face: The Myth of Bilateral Bliss 1867-1982* [Toronto: Doubleday Press, 1982], 69.

3 Paul Martin, *Hell or High Water: My Life in and Out of Politics* [Toronto: Douglas Gibson Books, 2008], 388.

4 Brian Mulroney, *Memoirs* [Toronto: Douglas Gibson Books, 2007], 600.

Queen's Policy Studies
Recent Publications

The Queen's Policy Studies Series is dedicated to the exploration of major public policy issues that confront governments and society in Canada and other nations.

Our books are available from good bookstores everywhere, including the Queen's University bookstore (http://www.campusbookstore.com/). McGill-Queen's University Press is the exclusive world representative and distributor of books in the series. A full catalogue and ordering information may be found on their web site (http://mqup.mcgill.ca/).

School of Policy Studies

Measuring What Matters in Peace Operations and Crisis Management, Sarah Jane Meharg, 2009. Paper 978-1-55339-228-6 Cloth ISBN 978-1-55339-229-3

International Migration and the Governance of Religious Diversity, Paul Bramadat and Matthias Koenig (eds.), 2009. Paper 978-1-55339-266-8 Cloth ISBN 978-1-55339-267-5

Who Goes? Who Stays? What Matters? Accessing and Persisting in Post-Secondary Education in Canada, Ross Finnie, Richard E. Mueller, Arthur Sweetman, and Alex Usher (eds.), 2008. Paper 978-1-55339-221-7 Cloth ISBN 978-1-55339-222-4

Economic Transitions with Chinese Characteristics: Thirty Years of Reform and Opening Up, Arthur Sweetman and Jun Zhang (eds.), 2009
Paper 978-1-55339-225-5 Cloth ISBN 978-1-55339-226-2

Economic Transitions with Chinese Characteristics: Social Change During Thirty Years of Reform, Arthur Sweetman and Jun Zhang (eds.), 2009
Paper 978-1-55339-234-7 Cloth ISBN 978-1-55339-235-4

Dear Gladys: Letters from Over There, Gladys Osmond (Gilbert Penney ed.), 2009
Paper ISBN 978-1-55339-223-1

Immigration and Integration in Canada in the Twenty-first Century, John Biles, Meyer Burstein, and James Frideres (eds.), 2008
Paper ISBN 978-1-55339-216-3 Cloth ISBN 978-1-55339-217-0

Robert Stanfield's Canada, Richard Clippingdale, 2008   ISBN 978-1-55339-218-7

Exploring Social Insurance: Can a Dose of Europe Cure Canadian Health Care Finance? Colleen Flood, Mark Stabile, and Carolyn Tuohy (eds.), 2008
Paper ISBN 978-1-55339-136-4 Cloth ISBN 978-1-55339-213-2

Canada in NORAD, 1957–2007: A History, Joseph T. Jockel, 2007
Paper ISBN 978-1-55339-134-0 Cloth ISBN 978-1-55339-135-7

Canadian Public-Sector Financial Management, Andrew Graham, 2007
Paper ISBN 978-1-55339-120-3 Cloth ISBN 978-1-55339-121-0

Emerging Approaches to Chronic Disease Management in Primary Health Care, John Dorland and Mary Ann McColl (eds.), 2007
Paper ISBN 978-1-55339-130-2   Cloth ISBN 978-1-55339-131-9

Fulfilling Potential, Creating Success: Perspectives on Human Capital Development, Garnett Picot, Ron Saunders and Arthur Sweetman (eds.), 2007
Paper ISBN 978-1-55339-127-2   Cloth ISBN 978-1-55339-128-9

Reinventing Canadian Defence Procurement: A View from the Inside, Alan S. Williams, 2006 Paper ISBN 0-9781693-0-1 (Published in association with Breakout Educational Network)

SARS in Context: Memory, History, Policy, Jacalyn Duffin and Arthur Sweetman (eds.), 2006 Paper ISBN 978-0-7735-3194-9   Cloth ISBN 978-0-7735-3193-2 (Published in association with McGill-Queen's University Press)

Dreamland: How Canada's Pretend Foreign Policy has Undermined Sovereignty, Roy Rempel, 2006 Paper ISBN 1-55339-118-7   Cloth ISBN 1-55339-119-5 (Published in association with Breakout Educational Network)

Canadian and Mexican Security in the New North America: Challenges and Prospects, Jordi Díez (ed.), 2006
Paper ISBN 978-1-55339-123-4   Cloth ISBN 978-1-55339-122-7

Global Networks and Local Linkages: The Paradox of Cluster Development in an Open Economy, David A. Wolfe and Matthew Lucas (eds.), 2005
Paper ISBN 1-55339-047-4   Cloth ISBN 1-55339-048-2

Choice of Force: Special Operations for Canada, David Last and Bernd Horn (eds.), 2005 Paper ISBN 1-55339-044-X   Cloth ISBN 1-55339-045-8

Force of Choice: Perspectives on Special Operations, Bernd Horn, J. Paul de B. Taillon, and David Last (eds.), 2004   Paper ISBN 1-55339-042-3   Cloth 1-55339-043-1

New Missions, Old Problems, Douglas L. Bland, David Last, Franklin Pinch, and Alan Okros (eds.), 2004   Paper ISBN 1-55339-034-2   Cloth 1-55339-035-0

The North American Democratic Peace: Absence of War and Security Institution-Building in Canada-US Relations, 1867-1958, Stéphane Roussel, 2004
Paper ISBN 0-88911-937-6   Cloth 0-88911-932-2

Implementing Primary Care Reform: Barriers and Facilitators, Ruth Wilson, S.E.D. Shortt and John Dorland (eds.), 2004
Paper ISBN 1-55339-040-7   Cloth 1-55339-041-5

Social and Cultural Change, David Last, Franklin Pinch, Douglas L. Bland, and Alan Okros (eds.), 2004   Paper ISBN 1-55339-032-6   Cloth 1-55339-033-4

Clusters in a Cold Climate: Innovation Dynamics in a Diverse Economy, David A. Wolfe and Matthew Lucas (eds.), 2004
Paper ISBN 1-55339-038-5   Cloth 1-55339-039-3

Canada Without Armed Forces? Douglas L. Bland (ed.), 2004
Paper ISBN 1-55339-036-9   Cloth 1-55339-037-7

Campaigns for International Security: Canada's Defence Policy at the Turn of the Century, Douglas L. Bland and Sean M. Maloney, 2004
Paper ISBN 0-88911-962-7   Cloth 0-88911-964-3

Understanding Innovation in Canadian Industry, Fred Gault (ed.), 2003
Paper ISBN 1-55339-030-X Cloth 1-55339-031-8

Delicate Dances: Public Policy and the Nonprofit Sector, Kathy L. Brock (ed.), 2003
Paper ISBN 0-88911-953-8 Cloth 0-88911-955-4

Beyond the National Divide: Regional Dimensions of Industrial Relations, Mark Thompson, Joseph B. Rose and Anthony E. Smith (eds.), 2003
Paper ISBN 0-88911-963-5 Cloth 0-88911-965-1

The Nonprofit Sector in Interesting Times: Case Studies in a Changing Sector, Kathy L. Brock and Keith G. Banting (eds.), 2003
Paper ISBN 0-88911-941-4 Cloth 0-88911-943-0

Clusters Old and New: The Transition to a Knowledge Economy in Canada's Regions, David A. Wolfe (ed.), 2003   Paper ISBN 0-88911-959-7 Cloth 0-88911-961-9

The e-Connected World: Risks and Opportunities, Stephen Coleman (ed.), 2003
Paper ISBN 0-88911-945-7 Cloth 0-88911-947-3

Knowledge Clusters and Regional Innovation: Economic Development in Canada, J. Adam Holbrook and David A. Wolfe (eds.), 2002
Paper ISBN 0-88911-919-8 Cloth 0-88911-917-1

Lessons of Everyday Law/Le droit du quotidien, Roderick Alexander Macdonald, 2002
Paper ISBN 0-88911-915-5 Cloth 0-88911-913-9

Improving Connections Between Governments and Nonprofit and Voluntary Organizations: Public Policy and the Third Sector, Kathy L. Brock (ed.), 2002
Paper ISBN 0-88911-899-X Cloth 0-88911-907-4

Centre for the Study of Democracy

Politics of Purpose, 40th Anniversary Edition, The Right Honourable John N. Turner 17th Prime Minister of Canada, Elizabeth McIninch and Arthur Milnes (eds.), 2009   Paper ISBN 978-1-55339-227-9 Cloth ISBN 978-1-55339-224-8

Bridging the Divide: Religious Dialogue and Universal Ethics, Papers for The InterAction Council, Thomas S. Axworthy (ed.), 2008
Paper ISBN 978-1-55339-219-4 Cloth ISBN 978-1-55339-220-0

Institute of Intergovernmental Relations

Canada: The State of the Federation 2006/07: Transitions – Fiscal and Political Federalism in an Era of Change, vol. 20, John R. Allan, Thomas J. Courchene, and Christian Leuprecht (eds.), 2009
Paper ISBN 978-1-55339-189-0 Cloth ISBN 978-1-55339-191-3

Comparing Federal Systems, Third Edition, Ronald L. Watts, 2008
Paper ISBN 978-1-55339-188-3

Canada: The State of the Federation 2005: Quebec and Canada in the New Century – New Dynamics, New Opportunities, vol. 19, Michael Murphy (ed.), 2007
Paper ISBN 978-1-55339-018-3 Cloth ISBN 978-1-55339-017-6

Spheres of Governance: Comparative Studies of Cities in Multilevel Governance Systems, Harvey Lazar and Christian Leuprecht (eds.), 2007
Paper ISBN 978-1-55339-019-0 Cloth ISBN 978-1-55339-129-6

Canada: The State of the Federation 2004, vol. 18, Municipal-Federal-Provincial Relations in Canada, Robert Young and Christian Leuprecht (eds.), 2006
Paper ISBN 1-55339-015-6 Cloth ISBN 1-55339-016-4

Canadian Fiscal Arrangements: What Works, What Might Work Better, Harvey Lazar (ed.), 2005 Paper ISBN 1-55339-012-1 Cloth ISBN 1-55339-013-X

Canada: The State of the Federation 2003, vol. 17, Reconfiguring Aboriginal-State Relations, Michael Murphy (ed.), 2005
Paper ISBN 1-55339-010-5 Cloth ISBN 1-55339-011-3

Canada: The State of the Federation 2002, vol. 16, Reconsidering the Institutions of Canadian Federalism, J. Peter Meekison, Hamish Telford and Harvey Lazar (eds.), 2004 Paper ISBN 1-55339-009-1 Cloth ISBN 1-55339-008-3

Federalism and Labour Market Policy: Comparing Different Governance and Employment Strategies, Alain Noël (ed.), 2004
Paper ISBN 1-55339-006-7 Cloth ISBN 1-55339-007-5

The Impact of Global and Regional Integration on Federal Systems: A Comparative Analysis, Harvey Lazar, Hamish Telford and Ronald L. Watts (eds.), 2003
Paper ISBN 1-55339-002-4 Cloth ISBN 1-55339-003-2

Canada: The State of the Federation 2001, vol. 15, Canadian Political Culture(s) in Transition, Hamish Telford and Harvey Lazar (eds.), 2002
Paper ISBN 0-88911-863-9 Cloth ISBN 0-88911-851-5

Federalism, Democracy and Disability Policy in Canada, Alan Puttee (ed.), 2002
Paper ISBN 0-88911-855-8 Cloth ISBN 1-55339-001-6, ISBN 0-88911-845-0 (set)

Comparaison des régimes fédéraux, 2ᵉ éd., Ronald L. Watts, 2002
Paper ISBN 1-55339-005-9

John Deutsch Institute for the Study of Economic Policy

The 2006 Federal Budget: Rethinking Fiscal Priorities, Charles M. Beach, Michael Smart and Thomas A. Wilson (eds.), 2007
Paper ISBN 978-1-55339-125-8 Cloth ISBN 978-1-55339-126-6

Health Services Restructuring in Canada: New Evidence and New Directions, Charles M. Beach, Richard P. Chaykowksi, Sam Shortt, France St-Hilaire and Arthur Sweetman (eds.), 2006
Paper ISBN 978-1-55339-076-3 Cloth ISBN 978-1-55339-075-6

A Challenge for Higher Education in Ontario, Charles M. Beach (ed.), 2005
Paper ISBN 1-55339-074-1 Cloth ISBN 1-55339-073-3

Current Directions in Financial Regulation, Frank Milne and Edwin H. Neave (eds.), Policy Forum Series no. 40, 2005
Paper ISBN 1-55339-072-5 Cloth ISBN 1-55339-071-7

Higher Education in Canada, Charles M. Beach, Robin W. Boadway and R. Marvin McInnis (eds.), 2005 Paper ISBN 1-55339-070-9 Cloth ISBN 1-55339-069-5

Financial Services and Public Policy, Christopher Waddell (ed.), 2004
Paper ISBN 1-55339-068-7 Cloth ISBN 1-55339-067-9

The 2003 Federal Budget: Conflicting Tensions, Charles M. Beach and Thomas A. Wilson (eds.), Policy Forum Series no. 39, 2004
Paper ISBN 0-88911-958-9 Cloth ISBN 0-88911-956-2

Canadian Immigration Policy for the 21st Century, Charles M. Beach, Alan G. Green and Jeffrey G. Reitz (eds.), 2003
Paper ISBN 0-88911-954-6 Cloth ISBN 0-88911-952-X

Framing Financial Structure in an Information Environment, Thomas J. Courchene and Edwin H. Neave (eds.), Policy Forum Series no. 38, 2003
Paper ISBN 0-88911-950-3 Cloth ISBN 0-88911-948-1

Towards Evidence-Based Policy for Canadian Education/Vers des politiques canadiennes d'éducation fondées sur la recherche, Patrice de Broucker and/et Arthur Sweetman (eds./dirs.), 2002 Paper ISBN 0-88911-946-5 Cloth ISBN 0-88911-944-9

Money, Markets and Mobility: Celebrating the Ideas of Robert A. Mundell, Nobel Laureate in Economic Sciences, Thomas J. Courchene (ed.), 2002
Paper ISBN 0-88911-820-5 Cloth ISBN 0-88911-818-3

Our publications may be purchased at leading bookstores, including the Queen's University Bookstore (http://www.campusbookstore.com/) or can be ordered online from: McGill-Queen's University Press, at **http://mqup.mcgill.ca/ordering.php**

For more information about new and backlist titles from Queen's Policy Studies, visit **http://www.queensu.ca/sps/books** or visit the McGill-Queen's University Press web site at: **http://mqup.mcgill.ca/**